LAST CASTS &
STOLEN HUNTS

LAST CASTS &
STOLEN HUNTS

EDITED BY
JIM CASADA & CHUCK WECHSLER

ILLUSTRATIONS BY
DAN METZ

COUNTRYSPORT PRESS
TRAVERSE CITY, MICHIGAN

CO-PUBLISHED BY
LIVEOAK PRESS, INC., CAMDEN, SOUTH CAROLINA
AND
COUNTRYSPORT, INC., TRAVERSE CITY, MICHIGAN
Copyright© 1993. All Rights Reserved.
Printed in USA.

ISBN 0-924357-33-9

Many thoughts,
like flying grouse,
leave no trace
of their passing,
but some leave clues
that outlast the
decades.

ALDO LEOPOLD
A SAND COUNTY ALMANAC

F ine sporting stories, especially those in magazines, are like a rainbow. They momentarily captivate us, then their transitory beauty is gone in the twinkling of an eye. I am certain that each of you has read stories that should be preserved for posterity. After reading one of these poignant pieces, one that tugged at the heartstrings or challenged the intellect, you said to yourself: "This is too fine a literary effort to be read and enjoyed, then promptly forgotten."

Such is the case with the stories offered here. Each is, in its own way, a timeless tale, a literary gem to be read and re-read. Many are fiction, because somehow efforts of this sort have more enduring appeal than those based on fact. But you will find plenty of factual narratives as well. The subject matter ranges widely. For those intrigued by danger, at least in a vicarious sense, there are hunts for man-eating leopards and huge brown bears along with a harrowing encounter with a deadly shark. The simple, yet deeply meaningful pleasures of oneness with nature are included, as is the delicate ballet of man, fly rod and fish. We are given gladness and sadness, moments of magic, times that are tragic.

The list of authors represented in this anthology constitutes a solid start towards a "Who's Who" of 20th-century outdoor writing. There are instantly recognizable names such as Jack O'Connor and Zane Grey, Aldo Leopold and John Taintor Foote. Selections from Jim Corbett and Rudyard Kipling give the collection an international flavor. And you will almost certainly make the welcome acquaintance of a few "unknowns," along with some of the finest contemporary outdoor writers in America. Yet throughout this selection of 21 stories, the reader will find one constant. The pieces, carefully chosen by a group of individuals who are dedicated to the wild world and who cherish fine writing about it, all represent sporting literature at its best.

The result is a book ideally suited for fireside reading, one which will transport you to fields and streams of dreams. At times you will be enchanted, at others left emotionally drained or breathless with laughter. Always though, you will be entertained. Enjoy!

— *Jim Casada, Rock Hill, SC*

LAST CASTS &
STOLEN HUNTS

WHEN

All The World

I S   Y O U N G

BY HOWARD T. WALDEN II

Howard Walden II (1897-1981) was an executive
in the grain industry by profession, but fishing and
writing about the sport were his twin passions. He
wrote two enduring angling books, *Upstream & Down*
and *Big Stony*, both published by Derrydale Press. Here
we have what is probably Walden's most inspired piece,
taken from *Big Stony*. It is chock full of all the
uncertainties of youth, the delights of angling, and
precisely the *joie de vivre* which typified both the
author and his literary output.

The road to school took him past the things he loved to the
things he hated. It took him, first, past the white house
that had been the home of Lank Starbuck who had taught
Chris how to fish for trout. Chris had been glad when old Lank's
son, Thad, had left, and he hadn't wanted anyone else to move
into the place. If it was empty he could go by it and think of old
Lank, but if someone else moved in it wouldn't mean old Lank to

1

him any more. A house wasn't just a house, it was who lived in it. If the man who lived in it was your friend the house was your friend, too. But when a stranger moved in, the house became a stranger and you had to get to know the house all over again, by another name. He hadn't liked it when Dr. Martin had moved in there, last summer. Dr. Martin, they had said, was needed here. There wasn't a really good doctor in Forks Township and the nearest help folks could get for a sick person was fifteen miles away. Maybe so, but he hadn't liked it.

But, thinking now about how he hadn't liked it at the time, he could see how foolish he had been. That was a kid thing – standing pat on what you have and seeing no good at all in something different. When he had begun to change was the day Dr. Martin had called on his Dad, early last fall, just after Dr. Martin had moved in. Chris had been scared, that time. He hadn't known what was the matter, but any time his Dad went to bed in the middle of the day it was scary. But after Dr. Martin had seen his Dad and had come downstairs and talked to him, he wasn't scared any more. He didn't remember what the Doctor had said. But he knew his Dad was going to get well and that everything, the whole world, was all right again.

After that he felt like looking again at the old Lank Starbuck house when he went by.

And he had even got to thinking of it, now, as the Martin house, thinking easily of it that way, not with homesickness, being glad to hook up the name Martin with it. The first day of school last September a yellow-haired girl had run out of the Martin door as he had gone by. "I'm Rosemary," she had said. "I'm going to your school. Can I go with you?"

The road took him, second, past the bridge over the Big Stony, the bridge just upstream from the March Brown Club water and just downstream from the junction of the Little Stony. He wasn't allowed to fish the water below the bridge, though his Dad owned it. That was a hard thing for Chris to understand – it was a grown-up thing – but he was beginning to get it, now. He had met two of the March Brown members and he liked them, and that made it easier for him to understand the rule and to respect it, which he had, now, for nearly a year. Those people paid a lot of money to fish his Dad's water. The idea of paying to fish was something he hadn't thought of until lately. You didn't pay to play ball or fly a kite though you paid for the ball and the kite cord. You bought a fishing rod but not the use of it. He had no money to pay for that and he knew he wouldn't pay for it if he had because he could fish the entire Little Stony for nothing. The fishing wasn't as good up there, but it was good enough, if you knew how to go after 'em. Trout were in there. So far this year he had taken twenty-eight, in ten tries, counting only keepers of course. And that, he knew darn well, was double the number Sticks Hooker had caught in twice as many tries. Sticks lived up the Little Stony, on a back road, in one of the several houses Chris's father owned in Forks Township. Living right on the stream, Sticks had all the chance in the world to fish. Sticks didn't pay for his rod, even – he cut it in the woods. And he thought Chris a kind of a stuck-up dude for fishing with a bought rod. . . . Sticks was all right, though. Chris liked him in a way, but Sticks was just enough older and bigger to try to bully him a little – and he liked Rosemary a little too well. Chris wanted to be friends with Sticks, but something – he didn't know what – got between them like a wall. Maybe it was his fault, maybe Sticks would like to be friends with him, too.

It took him, finally, to school, to books with dreary words in them, and to windows with dingy red-brown shades under which his eyes would stray to the outside world of blossom and bird song and wind-filled trees, and, over there, beyond that hump of a pasture, the little valley where the dark stream ran. It took him to the smell of chalk dust and old paper and of children who do not get enough baths, the school smell, the smell of the Hooker kids. It took him to Miss Spencer, standing in her straight black dress at the blackboard with a long pointer hovering over long rows of figures and suddenly lighting on one like a fish hawk spotting a chub, or tap-tapping over States on a down-rolled map and coming to rest on a yellow one near the middle – Miss Spencer who would say much less than she thought but make you think she meant a lot more. "To what capital of what state am I pointing, Christopher, and what is its chief industry?" And he would answer, "Topeka, Illinois, and they make glassware there," and she would lay down her pointer slowly on the eraser shelf, as if giving up the whole thing in disgust, and say, *"Christopher Wintermute."* That's all she'd say. But she'd mean, "You, the son of

3

the richest man in Forks Township, do not know that Topeka is the capital of Kansas and that they never heard of glassware in Topeka." And all the class would know that was what she meant.

He gave the whistle, that May morning, to Rosemary, as he went by. Their private signal had been decided on, sometime ago, after a good deal of deliberation. Rosemary knew the bobwhite call of the quail and had wanted to make it that. But Chris had overruled her – there were too many real bobwhites whistling in these fields in the spring and summer, and he didn't want any false alarms bringing Rosemary to her door. The whistle of the greater yellowlegs, the *whew-whew – whew-whew* – a one-note, two-syllable, once-repeated call, would be better. That was a sound heard from natural sources only in April and September around here, and not often then. It was easy and it carried, but it wasn't loud. It wouldn't stir up grown people or bring dogs running when you didn't want 'em. And besides, it was uncommon: it gave him a chance to explain to Rosemary what the greater and lesser yellowlegs were. . . . Bet Miss Spencer never heard of 'em and wouldn't know one if she saw it. Schoolteachers, who were supposed to know everything, didn't know important things like this at all.

The front door of the Martin house opened as if his whistle had made some secret contact with its lock. Rosemary took the porch steps in two strides and ran down the walk, her bright hair flying. She had on the white dress he liked, a high-waisted thing with ruffles and a sash the color of her hair.

"Want to run?" she said. "Look, I'll race you to the bridge."

"Aw, no. You couldn't keep up with me. No, I want to talk to you. Let's walk."

"You're 'fraid I can beat."

"All right, then. Give me your books so you can run free. On your mark – set – go!"

He let her draw away from him in the first fifty feet, then he spurted a little and kept an even distance between himself and the flying heels and the white dress and the streaming hair. She made the left turn onto the bridge road and gained a little on the down slope to the stream. For a girl, she could run. He hadn't expected her to hold the pace and now he had a momentary real fear that she would reach the bridge ahead of him. The heavy schoolbooks, a strapped bundle in each arm, handicapped him. But he put all he had into a final sprint and beat her to the log rail by a stride.

They sat on the lower rail, on the upstream side of the bridge. Rosemary flushed and panting, Chris trying to keep his breath even.

"You can run," he said.

"But boys always beat. I wish I was a boy."

"If you were – who'd you want to be?"

"Oh-h-h. How do I know?" She tried to make a circle in the roadside dust with the toe of her shoe. But her legs still had the running in them, they were trembling and unsure. "If I was Sticks Hooker I'd be tall and strong – the best ballplayer in school. If I was you I'd have a rich Dad, an' I could get things, nice clothes."

"Listen, my Dad isn't rich. He's got a lot of land so people think he's rich but he's land-poor. He's worried about taxes an' rents he can't collect – I heard him say so. But don't tell that – that's a secret, like our whistle."

"I won't."

"Anyway – "

"What?"

"Is that all you'd have?"

"Is *what* all I'd have?"

"If you were me. A rich Dad – if he *was* rich?"

"Oh." Rosemary erased the circle in the dust with her shoe. "You're nice, Chris. I like you."

"Better'n you like Sticks?"

"Maybe. . . . I like Sticks, too. He brought me a trout yesterday."

"One?"

"Um-h-m-m. That's all he promised."

"How big?"

"Eight inches. We measured him on my ruler. Gosh, he was good. Had him for breakfast this morning."

Chris got up from the lower rail and turned around and leaned against the upper one, up to his armpits, and looked for a long minute at the water flowing under the bridge, and his eyes followed it slowly upstream, as if studying each foot of its dark fast surface, to the point where the Little Stony comes in from the north. Rosemary stood up, too, and looked from Chris's face to the water and back to Chris's face, and kept silent, respecting

5

something she felt to be going on in his mind.

"Look, Rosemary," he said, finally, "I'll get you five trout, none under eight inches, maybe some bigger." He looked straight at her blue eyes. "Five. Maybe one will be twelve inches."

"Five? Altogether – at once? From Little Stony?"

"Sure, from Little Stony. Why?"

"Sticks said you fished the Club water sometimes because your Dad owns it – an' that's why you catch more than he does."

Chris pondered that for a moment. It was why, maybe, Sticks didn't like him. Then he looked squarely at Rosemary again. "I *have* fished down there – two or three times – last year. But each time I had to sneak it, past the guard. I'm not allowed to fish there. When I fish there I'm poaching, and Sticks can do the same thing any time he wants to try it. An' I'll tell him so. . . . Today," he added, "I'll fish Little Stony only. Word of honor. . . . Believe me?"

"Yes," she said.

"The water's right, Rosemary. I can get 'em from Little Stony."

"How do you know? Is that what you were looking at, so long – to see if the water's right?"

"Yes."

"How does it tell you?"

"I don't know. Right pitch, right color. An' the day's right – cloudy but it won't rain an' it'll stay warm. . . . It all smiles at me when it's right – it looks friendly, like you look when you smile at me." He had heard old Lank Starbuck say that, years ago, and he had never forgotten it.

"But maybe, by the time school's out, it won't be right any more."

"It's an all-day job, Rosemary. I won't go to school."

"Oh-h-h. But you can't do that. That's hooky."

"Sure, hooky." He said it casually, with an offhand assurance that puzzled her, made her think he had done it before.

"But you can't," she persisted, to draw him out. "Where's your fish pole – and what do you do with your schoolbooks? An' if you go home to get your pole, now, an' your Dad sees you, what'll he do?"

"He'd do plenty. He'd look sad an' he'd *be* sad. No one else could see he was sad but I can. An' he'd be calm. He wouldn't rant at me – he'd talk easy. An' then he'd whale me. Gosh, you don't know how he can hurt. . . . But he won't see me. 'Cause I won't go home. . . . You know what a cache is – I told you."

6

"Um-h-m-m. I remember – the time you left the muskrat skin for my fur collar by our back fence."

"That's right. Miss Spencer wouldn't tell you, 'cause she wouldn't know. Well, my rod – don't call it a pole, it's a rod – my rod is cached up along Little Stony. I leave the books there, pick up the rod, leave the rod there when I get through fishing and pick up the books an' take 'em home."

Rosemary looked at him, admiringly. There was enough deviltry in that technique to appeal to her. She wanted a part of it – but she was only a girl.

"I won't tell," she said, finally, with satisfaction. That gave her a definite role, however small, in the plot. She elaborated it: "Look. If Miss Spencer asks me where you are I'll tell her you started out with me but you got all out of breath at the bridge and decided you didn't feel like coming to school today. Is that some kind of a lie – a white lie?"

"Nope. It's true – except I didn't get *all* out of breath. I can run farther than that. I ran all the way to school once. . . . But that's good – you tell her that, before class, hear? Then maybe I won't need an excuse from Dad."

"All right. . . . But hooky. That's wrong."

"Why?"

"I don't know. It just is – like stealing."

"No it isn't. I'll tell you sometime. . . . 'By, Rose."

He headed into the woods along the north bank of the stream. When he was up to the confluence of the Little Stony he stopped and looked back to the bridge. She had gone. The road north of the bridge was not visible through the trees except for one short stretch where it topped a rise two hundred yards away. He laid his sight on this spot like a barrage, and presently the white dress and the yellow sash and the yellow hair crossed it, walking fast.

He wondered, now, why he hadn't kissed her good-bye. He had wanted to. It had been the moment, when he had left her – she had been "right" then, like the stream was right for fishing. No good, now, to call to her to stop and to run to her. The moment was past; he had lost it. . . . He could take the stream for fishing, always, when it offered itself, as he was taking it now, even at a good deal of risk – for he knew the chances to be better than even that his truancy would be found out and punished. But he couldn't take her who presented no risk at all. If his conscience had called it wrong he could understand. His conscience called plenty of things he did wrong and kept him awake at night thinking of them. But his conscience approved this and still he was afraid of it. It bothered him, like a buzzing fly that he couldn't swat.

Well, he'd swat it tonight, once and for all, and clear the air of the thing. When the time came for him to leave her this evening, after giving her the trout, he'd claim his reward. It would be another right moment, on her front porch, with the dusk drawing in, and this time he would grab it.

There was a narrow path that led him along the northeast bank of the Little Stony, upstream. A fisherman's path, it was never far from the water in its gradual climb up the valley. About a quarter-mile above the bridge Chris turned off it to the right and entered a little swale grown thick with birches and witch hazel. A woodcock whistled up out of it, a native bird, fat with the spring worms. An ancient oak stood in the middle of this small area. Chris stooped and reached into an opening at the base of the great hollow trunk and drew out a cloth-cased steel rod and a willow creel. He opened the lid of the creel to see that all his gear was intact – his double-action reel with the enameled line on it, the packet of leaders, the cork full of eyed hooks and the tobacco can for worms.

A flat brown Geography, a blunt green Practical English Grammar, a stout red Elements of United States History and a thin black Graded City Speller, well strapped with a double loop of webbing, took up the occupancy of the old trunk where the rod and creel left off.

A good trade, he thought.

Occasional hooky was not against his conscience either, anymore. It had been, once. His father had talked to him of the duties and responsibilities of men and of what men owed to their society and to the world at large. A duty was something that was unpleasant now, but that paid you some sort of reward later on. You got an actual reward – money, perhaps, or maybe only a better character – at some future time by doing something unpleasant now. God paid you, in some way, for the duties that got it for you. It had sounded right, even brave, the way his father had put it. But thinking about it later, in the dark of his room, when the ring of his father's words had died out of his ears, he thought he could see something selfish in the pursuit of duty. If you were after a reward anyway perhaps you could take your reward now – have fun now instead of later. It all came to the same thing in the end, God paid it anyway, now or afterward. That hadn't decided him, though. That wasn't strong enough – it was only his little kid idea against the ancient wisdom of his father which had proved itself too many times to be doubted. That had been one of the times he had wanted a mother's opinion, too. He had felt that a mother's judgment would have some nameless tenderness, be less severe and easier to live with. But he didn't even remember his mother, who had died when he was two years old. His father had to do.

But one day last summer when he was poaching on the Club water, sneaking around a big rock at the head of the Pasture Pool, he had met face to face, head on, a princess. His first instinct had been to run, for anyone met on the private water was probably his enemy. But he had looked into her face, met her eyes, and known at once that there was no need to run from her. She was grown up but not old, and not a real princess of course, but she looked like the princess in the fairy-tale book he had at home. She had asked him his name and given him hers, Priscilla, and told him to call her that. He had thought of "Princess Priscilla" and the words had seemed to fit, to swim together. She was the daughter, she had said, of a real Army Colonel who had fought in the war and who was a member of the March Browns. She had asked him to sit down on the rock and talk with her a while. The Pasture Pool was an open spot where the guard could see him easily if he went by, but that would be all right, she had said, she'd take care of that. The talk had turned to poaching and had gotten around, as he had known it would, to the question of whether it was his duty not to poach. "What do you think?" she had asked. And you had to answer her straight, you couldn't just answer the way a nice boy was supposed to. That was the way you answered Miss Spencer at school, but not her. She had a face and a voice you couldn't lie to. So he had turned the thing over in his mind for a couple of minutes before replying, trying to line it all up with what his father had told him of duty.

"In a way," he had said, finally, "it's my duty to poach."

"How?" she had asked.

"Well, it takes a little nerve to poach here – I have to be a little brave about trying it. That's hard. And being careful not to get caught – sneaking – that's hard, too, if you do it all day. But sometimes God pays me with a big trout, bigger'n I'd get upstream."

She had seemed to think about that for a long while. Then she had said: "I like that, Chris. I like you for saying it."

They had talked for an hour or more, there on the rock. She hadn't advised him to keep off the stream nor to go on it again, but had left that for him to decide. "Another duty is having fun," she had said, and it had sounded like his father's words in reverse, "so long as it doesn't spoil other people's fun." She had told him to have all the fun he could while he was a boy and to keep on having it when he was grown, fun in his mind when his body got too old for it. "The great men are simple men," she had said. "They never quite get over being kids."

Since that day he had never again fished the Club water.

But playing hooky was his own affair. That didn't spoil the fun of a single soul on earth.

He took the steel rod out of its cloth case and stowed the case in the hollow oak with the schoolbooks. He collected enough worms by kicking over some grass hummocks on the far side of the swale, put them in the tobacco can and headed upstream again.

The Hooker house was three hundred yards above here, well back from the other bank and partly visible through the trees. Just opposite the Hooker house his path would come out high above the stream overlooking one of the best runs of trout water on the whole of the Little Stony, a place where he had taken more than one good fish. If this were a Saturday he would give it a look but on a school day the smart thing was to leave the path before he came in sight of the house, make a wide detour through the woods and return to the path at a point well above. For if one of the younger Hooker kids saw him he would tell Sticks afterward, and Sticks might tell the teacher.

He heard their voices, across stream, as he worked his way past through the woods. Regaining the path above, he proceeded almost a mile before he stopped and assembled his gear. This was his favorite place to start. A little riffle spilled into deep fast water between two boulders below which a dark pool arched down to a flat undercut rock at its lower end. With luck he could take two fish here, one in the fast run and one from under the rock below.

Crouching well back from the bank and well above the head of the run Chris let the worm go into the dark water, deep, with a little slack to keep it down. For a second he could see its course in the riffle, then he lost it. The current straightened his slack – the worm should be between the rocks now. He held his breath for the strike and it came. He hit back, felt the strong resistance of the trout, guided the fish up through the fast water, lifted him clear and swung him to the bank. A deep ten-inch native and a good start on his day. He bent back the trout's head, gathered some ferns and laid the fat fish on them in the creel.

Another try in the same water was part of the technique he had inherited from Lank Starbuck. He went through with it, gave it plenty of time, but nothing happened. The slow center of the pool, sometimes good for a fish, yielded nothing either. He crossed the stream, wading nearly to his knees, for it was necessary to fish the undercut rock at the pool's tail from the other side. He backed away from the bank, crouched low, waited a minute, two minutes, up to the limit of his patience. Then he put on a fresh worm and swung it gently into the slow current upstream from the rock. It was out of his sight below the rock's edge, drifting deep in the black water, just the way he had wanted it to go. In a moment the drift of his line halted though the current all around it kept on. He knew what it was: there was nothing to snag him on that smooth bottom. His line, the part of it he could see, started upstream then, gaining speed. He struck and felt at once that he was into a bigger fish than he had dreamed of hooking up here. The trout raced for the head of the pool, taking line from the reel, then turned and bored downstream. The lip of the pool was a shallow curving wash over a flat rock bottom, only inches deep. The trout thrashed into it, exposing its great proportions, seemed to roll once or twice and slid back into deep water again as Chris's line went suddenly slack.

A curious and empty quiet was all through the woods and over the water. If any birds had been singing they were still now. The little pool had lapsed to its former expressionless calm. It might never have held a trout, and this one, just lost, might have been only imagined or dreamed. That vacant sense of stillness was

11

inside Chris, too, in the region of his heart. He had known it before, many times. It was pure loss. No word nor act could, at the moment, answer its thrust. Only time could put it behind – an hour's fishing, with its new problems, new hopes and perhaps new success.

He reeled in. His hook and half his leader were gone. He cut the frayed end of the leader cleanly off and tied on a new length of gut and a new hook. By noon he had regained complete control of his day and he could look back, now, on the loss of the big one and see it as a definite part of the sport of fishing. Three trout were now on the ferns in his creel, an eight-inch native and a nine-inch brown added to the first one. He needed two more to keep his promise to Rosemary.

And he'd get 'em. He'd get one extra, six in all, so he could keep one for himself. They were coming, and when they were coming he could take six if he was very careful. This was the day, perhaps the best he'd see this year. The high tide – it came once in every season, and he had spotted it. It was worth the risk he was taking, worth being caught and all that that would entail.

A wood thrush sang into the noon stillness. A gray squirrel sat on a windfall ahead of him, jerked its tail twice like a mechanical toy and raced down the log at his approach. In a wide backwater which he had to cross on his way downstream a muskrat ploughed straight as a tugboat, towing a leafed branch. He was happy in the way a trout fisherman can be happy when all the world is young and the day is right and confidence is with him. He had that rare fishing happiness which can forget for a while mere keenness for the chase and indulge itself with the quiet asides of angling. He sat down on an old stump and spent half an hour watching the river and the woods on the far bank, and thought about the little unseen lives that lived and died there, year by year, while boys went to school and men worried over taxes and their duty to a society which worried as much as they.

Then he went back to it, fishing carefully, approaching with great caution each likely run and pool on his way downstream. Another native and another brown, ten inches each, were in his creel before three o'clock. His promise of five trout to Rosemary was kept. . . . Wait till Sticks hears about this.

But he needed another one and he wanted it to be big. He had mentioned a twelve-incher to Rosemary. The one he had lost had been well over that but he couldn't say much about the "big one that got away." Even Rosemary, who knew nothing about fishing, had heard that tale too many times to be impressed. She would laugh at it and the effect of the five good trout would be lost in her scorn.

The big one, if he got it, would be for Rosemary, and that would free one of his ten-inchers for his own dinner tonight. Bringing home a trout would need no explaining: it could have been caught after school as some of his others had been this year. . . . His stomach, without food since breakfast, was beginning to talk to him, to nag at him, interrupting his fishing now and then with its assertions. He began to think too much of the dinner that he would have. Trout or no trout, it would be a good one, as it always was. Old Sarah, his Dad's cook, could turn it out. There would be a fat ham and baked potatoes and peas – or maybe a great smoking stew, with dumplings – and a huge tumbler of milk, filled twice, and all the fresh bread and butter he could eat, and an apple pie. And he could feel how sleepy he would be after it and how good his bed would feel as he would lie in the cool sheets just before sleep caught him, looking up at the ceiling at the angular shadow cast from the dim hall light by his half-open bedroom door, and feeling the spring night fanning his cheek . . .

The Hooker house was just below him now, on the opposite bank. He had come up to the point at which he had rejoined the trail this morning, after his detour around the danger zone, and if he were to retrace his steps he should leave the trail here. He stood still in the path, to ponder the question a moment and to listen. The vicinity of the Hooker house was still a no-man's-land, so far as he was concerned. It was not yet time for school to be out and his presence here on the stream would give him away now as surely as it would have this morning. Sticks wouldn't be home for half an hour at least. The other Hooker kids were making no sound. They were in the house or far off in the woods, for when they were nearby you could always hear them. He might – he might just possibly – get away with trying that good run of water directly opposite the house. It was a desperate chance – it made him feel as poaching on the Big Stony used to make him feel – but today his reward might be there.

The path from here on climbed gradually above the stream bed; just opposite the Hooker house it emerged from the trees into an open slashing, a badly exposed position for anyone sneaking it as he was. But it held an advantage: its altitude above the water gave him a penetrating view, when the sun was high, of that sand-bottomed run. There was something about that run which he never had been able to understand. Its straight fifty-foot stretch was totally devoid of windfalls, rocks or overhanging banks. It had no trout cover worthy of the name, and certainly it could offer little in the shape of underwater food. Yet it was a place where large trout loved to live. The small fish, he knew, were afraid of its bright exposure. . . . If a fish was in sight he would maneuver down to it; if not, he would leave the trail at once and go home.

He studied the house – as much as he could see of it from the shelter of the woods – before he dared the open trail ahead. A blue column of wood smoke stood up straight out of the chimney. But no sound came from it and no one was in sight. If the Hooker kids would stay indoors while he did what he wanted to do, he might yet get by with it.

Once beyond the cover of the trees there was no need to crouch for if someone looked toward him out here he would be seen, crouching or standing, and crouching would make him look more suspicious. So he walked erect along the high open trail to the vantage point where he could scan the bright water below.

He had to look sharp: there were a few vague shadows on the bottom, and a waterlogged stick or two. For a minute he saw no sign of a fish; then, as if his straining eyesight had created it, a large trout was there, directly below him, its tail fanning almost imperceptibly in the gentle current. He wondered that he hadn't seen it before, it was so distinct now. A rainbow – all of sixteen inches long. He could see its pink stripe and its myriad tiny spots. A great trout, strayed up from the Club water, probably – the biggest trout he had ever seen in the Little Stony.

He faded back up the path to the woods, walking backward, his eyes on the fish. Then he sneaked rapidly down the wooded bank to the stream and baited his hook with the worm he had been saving for just this chance.

Well upstream from his fish, Chris put the worm in with a short gentle flick and let the easy current take it down, drawing out the slack between his reel and first guide. Though he would do his best to keep the worm drifting as long as possible he knew it would sink and come to rest on the bottom fifteen or twenty feet above the trout. It would be better to work it a little nearer but he dared neither a long cast nor a closer approach. Alternately feeding slack to the current and raising his rod tip to keep the worm up, Chris could feel it along the line when at last the worm settled into the sand. His line, soaked with the day's fishing, submerged itself gradually upstream until only a few inches of it were visible between his rod tip and the surface.

There was nothing to do now but crouch and wait – and control himself, if he could. He was a little ashamed of his agony of expectation and the way his heart and his hands were affected by it. Even this fish – the biggest trout he had ever deliberately angled for – shouldn't make his heart pound like that or cause his hands to tremble so that he couldn't hold his rod steady. He tried to be cool and thoughtful, to figure the chances of that rainbow seeing his worm, and coming upstream to take it if he did, and the possibility of his leader escaping notice. To lose his terrific excitement he tried to discourage himself. But it was no good; despite all his reasoning there was still an outside chance of that giant taking hold, and it was his nearness to such success as he had never known that might prove too much for him to bear.

His rod had caught the trembling infection from his hands. That little length of visible line between his rod tip and the water jerked back and forth in the slow current. He watched it steadily as if trying by the very intensity of his gaze to make it still, and as he watched he discerned a movement in it which even his trembling hands could not have caused. The visible short stretch lengthened a little, downstream, and came five or six clear inches out of the water, straightening itself in a widening angle from the rod. It lapsed back, almost to its former position, then straightened again swiftly, six feet of dripping line knifing out of the surface below his rod. Chris Wintermute stood up and struck . . .

He tried to recall that battle afterward; once, when she was in a mood to be still and listen, he tried to give Rosemary the details out of the long view which retrospect should have made clear. But he could never quite track it down. His memory of it remained a

15

confused picture of a surface shattered like glass, a surface erupting all over at once with a great trout bursting from each eruption, a memory of spray and the noise of breaking water, a memory of a frenzied dream, of something that couldn't happen in real life, and a slow awakening from it as the fish tired, a gradual return, after an incredible time, to the familiar world on which he could plant his feet and feel safe. . . And of his happiness at the end, when he eased that huge exhausted trout up the slope of a little sand beach at the lower end of the run – but there were no words for that and he had never even tried to give that part to Rosemary or to anyone else. That was for himself, only to know – for himself only, that happiness, to think about sometimes when he was alone . . .

Just then, at that moment when the fish came up on the sand, he didn't believe it. He had known that there were rainbow trout in the world as big as this one, but that one so big should be his own, caught by himself, he didn't believe.

Neither did the two Hooker kids who had materialized from nowhere, on the opposite bank, in time to see Chris beach his fish.

"Sucker, ain't it, Chris?" one called across. "Big sucker – I seen one in here."

"Sucker, my eye." Chris was looking around for a short stout club, for this fish was too large to kill by the usual method. "He's a trout – a rainbow."

The arrival of the Hooker kids on the scene annoyed him. Up to that moment his adventure had been a complete success. To have taken this trout quickly and gotten away unseen would have made his day perfect. But now he was discovered. The Hooker kids had broken in on his secret. They didn't know what playing hooky was but they would tell Sticks they had seen him, and Sticks would know. And tomorrow it would be all over school, and tomorrow night his father would have it.

"Aw, trout ain't that big. Sticks said they ain't."

"Because he can't get 'em that big." Chris was beginning to get mad.

"He could so – if they grew that big." The youngest Hooker boy was loyal to his big brother. The other one, the next younger to Sticks, seemed to hold certain doubts. "Shut up," he said quietly. "Maybe Sticks can't. Sticks ain't so good at fishin'. . . . Let's go see it."

Chris found the right club and killed the trout with two blows on top of its head. The Hooker kids, barefooted, rolled up their faded blue overalls to their thin thighs and waded in. They had legs like those which had given Sticks his nickname. All the Hooker kids could be called "Sticks," he was thinking.

"You ought to have sneakers on, or somethin'," Chris said. "Some o' those rocks are sharp."

"Aw, we ain't got shoes," the larger one replied, thrashing across, heedless of where he put his feet. "None of th' kids in our house got shoes but Sticks. Sticks needs 'em 'cause he goes t' school."

Chris looked at them, coming across. The thought of their being without shoes, having nothing at all to wear on their feet, hurt him deeply like an insult, as if someone had called him a darned fool for ever thinking the world was beautiful. The thought, he knew, was never going to be far from it. It would come back to him again and again; in the nights, in the alone moments when he got out the thoughts he had loved, this thing would come breaking in on them and leering at them and chasing them away.

He held up the big fish before their devouring eyes. "Is it a trout?" he said.

They stood looking in silence, trying to make their minds believe the story their eyes had to tell.

"Right in our own front yard, too," the smaller one said, finally. "Betcha Sticks would have got 'im if you hadn't come by."

"Like ta have 'im for my supper t'night," said the other one. "Boy, would he taste good!"

"Um-m-m. Better'n ol' corn mush."

"I like corn meal mush all right," Chris said. "I have that for breakfast, sometimes. You don't have it for supper, do you?"

"Sure. Supper – breakfast too. All meals."

"Gosh. You must like it better'n anything."

The two Hooker kids looked at each other and smiled in a little superior way, a mutual acknowledgment of a bit of information not known to Chris.

"We hate it," the larger one said. "Wouldn't be so bad 'f you could have a lotta milk on it. 'Thout milk it's dry – gets in your teeth."

"But – if you don't like it – why, why do you eat it so much?"

They exchanged the same look a second time and the larger one spoke again: "'Cause there ain't much else in our house t' eat.

17

Mom planted some beans an' pertaters but they ain't up yet. She gets dandylions an' wood herbs. But they don't fill ya – ya can't eat much of 'em. Fried dough fills ya – we have that, some."

"Once in a while Sticks get a fish," the smaller one put in. "We try to but we don't get none. Been tryin' all mornin' to snare some suckers. No luck. . . . Fried dough fills ya too much," he added, quietly, as if talking to himself. "Made me puke, las' night."

"You make too much noise," said Chris. "That's why you don't get any fish. I heard you this morning, on the way up." He uttered those words but he wasn't thinking them. It was as if someone else, over whom he had no control, had put them in his mouth merely to keep up the talk while he thought about something else – about corn meal mush, day after day – and about why Sticks's legs and his brothers' legs were so thin – and about having no shoes –

"Get any others, Chris?"

– and about fried dough and dandelions, and Mom who had planted beans and potatoes but they weren't up yet – Mom, whom he had never seen but whom, he thought oddly, he could love.

"What does your Dad do?" he asked suddenly, seizing on a forlorn shape that had come up out of the gloom in his brain.

"Pop? He ain't home," the small one said.

"I mean – doesn't he work? Doesn't he make any money to buy food?"

"He was workin'," the older one said. "He worked in Post's garage, over at th' Forks. But he don't, now. He lost his job. Get any other fish, Chris?"

A faint complaining cry drifted down to them from the house across the stream.

"What's that?" Chris asked.

"The baby. She's sick."

The forlorn shape receded back into the murk of the corn meal mush, the fried dough and the shoeless feet, like something that slowly heaves up and goes down again in roiled water.

"Did you – did you get any others?"

"Five others," he said.

"O-o-o-h. Can we see 'em?"

Chris opened his creel and they crowded up to it, and their eyes seemed to crowd into the trout- and fern-filled cavity, staring and eager and hungry. The smaller one touched some of the trout with

18

his finger tips, daintily, as if to be sure they were real. "Gosh," he muttered, after a minute, "you're a good fisherman."

"You roll 'em in corn meal or flour," Chris said. "An' fry 'em – till they're brown on both sides. Put salt an' pepper on while they're fryin' – "

A visible trickle drooled out of the mouth of the smaller Hooker.

"Tell your Mom that," Chris added. "She might not know."

"Aw – she can cook a trout. But we don't have any. Did you think we had any?"

"You've got these," he said. "I'm giving 'em to you." . . . It was out, now; and no more thinking about his promise to Rosemary would put the words back in his mouth nor keep the trout in his creel.

Their eyes wrenched away from the trout and up to Chris's face, unbelieving, then sought each other's for some confirmation, some assurance that it was true.

"All of 'em?"

"Sure. Look, I've got to get home, fast. Can I see your Mom a minute, right away?"

"Sure. . . . Gee – six trout for supper. Come on, we'll give 'em to her. She can cook 'em. Yay! Boy – oh – boy!"

They went into the stream again, shouting, "Mom! Mom! We got six trout. Mom! Chris Wintermute gave us six trout!"

Chris followed, picking his way carefully through the knee-deep water of the lower run.

The uproar from the kids had brought Mrs. Hooker to the door. While the noise attending the display of the trout was going on Chris stood a little apart, looking closely, for the first time in his life, at this house which he had always avoided on his trips upstream. It was going to collapse. Its roof sagged in the middle and a lot of shingles were gone from the roof. Those places had been patched with scraps of tar paper and pieces of tin fashioned out of flattened oil cans. If its old boards had ever had any paint they had long since lost it; they were gray and naked to the weather. In the four front windows several panes of glass were out, replaced by squares of cardboard or brown paper. The entire structure seemed to lean as if tottering with its own creaking weight. There was not a straight line nor a right angle: the vertical and horizontal planes all slanted in ways that looked dangerous . . .

19

Sticks, living in this place, came into his mind and suddenly he found himself admiring Sticks in a way that was new and strange to him. Sticks had been able to come every day from this house, which was dying, to school and go back to this house at night and come to school again and play the best baseball of any kid there, and get good marks, and fish with a pole he had cut in the woods and give a trout to Rosemary when he was starving for it himself. Sticks had guts.

But when the kids had gone inside with the trout and quiet had come again over the little square of clean-swept dirt which was the front yard, and Mrs. Hooker stood there in the leaning doorway, in a little area of sunlight, as if framed by the old house behind and above her – Chris knew that the house was not going to collapse, after all. Mrs. Hooker held it up and always would hold it up. Mom . . . Mom was where Sticks got his guts. He didn't go to school from a dying house – he went from Mom and he took something of Mom with him to make him good at baseball and to get him good marks.

No one could call *her* "Sticks." She was tall and broad in her blue gingham apron and her hair was a gold-gray, neatly drawn back from her high proud forehead. She stood straight and clean, a brave and kind figure, looking at him. Her mouth was straight across, as if set in a fighting position against something that battled her from inside, but her blue eyes had sunlight in them and they were smiling at him.

And suddenly he knew that he could not say what he had come to say. She was too proud, too strong, to take it from a kid. No. . . . He would have to tell his father, later. And that would mean confessing that he had been fishing up here today. And tomorrow, when Miss Spencer asked his father for an excuse for his absence, the two things would hook up, fit together. . . . But he couldn't tell Mom. She would talk him out of it and he didn't want to be – he couldn't be – talked out of it. If he were talked out of *that* he'd want to take his trout back. It would be the end, the complete and final ruin of a day that had suddenly cracked up on him anyway.

He returned her smile and tipped his cap to her. She took a step toward him but as she did so the baby cried again from somewhere in the old house. Chris saw her step halt and retrace itself. He saw a little wincing look, as if from a sharp pain, cloud

20

the sun and the smile that had been in her eyes. She turned from him, and her fine straight back disappeared into the gloom of the leaning and rotten doorway.

He walked away, down the path. He crossed the stream again, hurried back to his hollow oak trunk, stowed his rod and creel, took up his books and started home.

There was no fishing left in his mind, now – none of the high hope of the morning. That moment, only six or seven hours ago, when he had left Rosemary at the bridge, seemed to him now an age away, back in his early childhood. Something bigger than fishing had taken up all the space in his brain and his heart, a thing he had gotten hold of and couldn't drop, a tremendous thing that was heavy, perhaps too heavy for him to handle. A man's thing. It didn't make him sad except in a small way, in its revelation of a certain loss to himself. He could not define that loss, but he knew what it was. It was the loss of his pure kid's joy in fishing and in life. For it *was* lost now, beyond recall. He would fish again, and do other things again, and get fun out of them, but behind them always would be this thing he had seen today, which was poverty and famine, something he had thought of vaguely and heard of from his father, but had never really believed until this afternoon. It was not particularly the Hookers on the Little Stony but the Hookers who – he knew now – were all over the world, the Hooker way of life multiplied a million times.

That thing had made him older. It was perhaps that boundary line in his life about which he had so often wondered. There was a line somewhere, he had told himself, that a kid came up to and stepped over, and when he stepped over it he was a man. This was it, then, and he had stepped over it.

The day had done that for him, at least. In all other ways it had licked him. His promise to Rosemary was broken. His truancy was going to be found out and surely punished. And Rosemary was involved in that, too, since she had given an excuse for him to the teacher. He was going to be in bad with Rosemary, his father, the school, everyone. But along with all that mess of failure, the day had given him – suddenly and when he least expected it – a man's job to do. And he had begun on that job and would finish it when he got home. . . . And maybe those ways he had been licked were kid ways, and the way he had won was a

21

man's. He didn't know. . . . He wondered, as he walked up the long drive to his house, how his father now, and Rosemary later, would take his separate confessions, and whether he could bear up, proud, in the way that Sticks was proud, in the way that took guts, if they should condemn him for what he had done.

His father was nowhere around, outside. Perhaps he was in his little office off the sitting room, at his ledgers, as he often was at this time of day. Chris opened the door, tossed his cap on the rack in the long hall and looked into the adjoining sitting room and his father's office beyond it. Both were empty. He called upstairs, "Dad."

Sarah labored heavily in, on her flat pads, from the kitchen, and the early nebulous fragrance of a dinner's beginnings followed her through the opened door.

"Yo' Dad ain' home, Christ'pher. He an' Harry Stack taken ol' Korn over t' Long Holler t' wait on some cow."

"Oh. Did he say when he'd be back?"

"Dinnah tahm, reckon. He said not much befo' then."

Chris went upstairs to his room, took off his wet shoes and stockings and lay down on his bed looking up at the pattern of the ceiling paper. He wanted his father to be home, right now, while his mind was made up to tell him what he had to tell. Time was against him. It was almost four o'clock and if he had to wait until dinner time to see his father he might find reasons, in those long hours, to go back on his plan. For if he didn't tell his father he might still get away with it, so far as his playing hooky was concerned. The chances were pretty good. The excuse he had told Rosemary to give Miss Spencer wasn't so bad, after all. It might hold, and if it should then Rosemary was not mixed up either. . . . Perhaps it were better, that way. Let the other thing wait a week, until his absence from school should be well forgotten. But that would give Mom Hooker a week longer to worry. She looked as if she could stand it, but because she looked that way he didn't want her to have to . . .

No. As soon as his Dad came in he'd tell him.

He got up after a while, put on dry stockings and shoes, unstrapped his schoolbooks and tried for half an hour to master the six pages of his *Practical English Grammar* which, he guessed, would be the lesson for tomorrow. He liked it – alone among all his studies at school – and ordinarily he would have had it cold in fifteen minutes. . . . He left it at last and went to his window and looked out on the fading unpeopled afternoon. And as he stood there his father's big truck purred up the road, turned in between the gate posts and crunched up the gravel drive. Harry Stack was driving and the big Holstein bull, Sir Piebe Korndyke Segis Colantha – affectionately known to the household as "Old Korn" – rode with majestic dignity in the rear, home from another seeding in a far country.

Chris heard the truck stop and then go on again as Harry Stack drove it back to the barn. He heard his father come in at the front door and walk through the sitting room to his office. He stood there at the window a few seconds more, looking out, then turned and went downstairs.

As Chris entered the office his father looked up from an entry he was making in a little ledger marked "Bull Services." He turned his craggy, inflexible countenance up to his son. It was a large face of promontories and furrowed cliffs, with eyes of a color hard to define, so deeply shadowed were they under the great eaves of its brows.

"Well Chris," he said, "how'd it go at school?"

"I wasn't at school today, Dad."

"Eh?" That rigid and chiseled face showed little if any change: the emotions worked deep underneath it but only a terrific upheaval could disturb its surface rock.

Chris sat down in the odd chair at the side of his father's big roll-top desk. "I played hooky, Dad."

Christopher Wintermute, Sr., looked at his son studiously for a moment and returned to his entry on the ruled page. "I'm sorry, Chris," he said. "I've felt good today and I don't like it to end up like this. You know what my stand is on hooky."

"I know. I felt good this morning, too. The stream looked right – it was a peach of a day – and I knew I could take 'em. I promised Rosemary five and I got six."

"Of course." His father blotted the entry, closed the book and regarded his son keenly. "That was the temptation. This afternoon I could have charged old Amos Kinsey thirty dollars for a service and he'd have paid me. That might have been a temptation, too. But I charged him twenty. . . . We have been all over that, before. It seems that a father's words have no weight in this day. . . . Well."

23

He sighed and got up from his chair, closed the door and the single window. From a corner of the little room which the door had concealed while it stood open he procured a short thin cane. There was no woodshed formality about the elder Wintermute's administrations of justice. "My stand on hooky is the same as it was last time," he said. "Hooky is hooky, even when you confess it like a man. . . . Loosen your belt, Chris, and take 'em down."

His father had never shown him anger. He could call him Chris, the affectionate nickname, even when he was about to flog him. The whippings were as impersonal as a lightning bolt except for the expressions of wounded and betrayed trust which always preceded them and the deep forgiveness which came afterward, in the dark. That would follow, tonight, after Chris had gone to bed. His father would come upstairs, enter Chris's room, take Chris in his arms and kiss him. He would speak but a few words and they would be shaky, and the dim hall gas jet would make a blended pattern of light and shadow on the uplands and valleys of the great face, like moonlight over a landscape.

Chris stood before his father, small and white and naked from his waist to his knees, his embarrassment gone in the deeper tide of his apprehension of pain. He had steeled himself for the sting of that lash, the increasing agony as the repeated blows would seem to cut into flesh made tender and raw from the first one. The last time he had not cried out until the ninth, with only one more to go. There were always ten, never more or less.

"I'm ready,"he said. "But before you start can I tell you something – something awful important that I found out today?" He felt a little ashamed of himself, as if he were begging for mercy, as his father stood looking at him in a faint surprise.

"Well?"

"Dad, you own that old house on Little Stony, the one the Hookers live in?"

"I do. Why?" The elder Wintermute was impatient as if he, too, had steeled his will to the task his conscience had imposed and dreaded, now, lest time take the fine edge from his decision. "Make it quick," he said, "and let's get this over with."

"How much rent do you charge 'em – if you don't mind telling me?"

"Ten dollars a month. . . . What is this, Chris?"

24

He felt the warm nudge of confidence, sensing that his first sally had scored.

He followed it up: "Do they pay it?"

"Every cent – promptly when due. What is your interest in the Hooker house?"

"Would you – do you need that ten dollars a month?"

"It is business. I have a right to it and they need the house. But – "

"They need a decent house. That thing – you wouldn't keep your cows in it. Listen, it's – "

"The lease stipulates no repairs, at that rental. And anyway, what – "

"Have you seen it lately?"

"No."

"Well I did, today, when I was up there fishing. Dad, it's falling down. It's rotten – the paint's gone — the shingles are off – windows busted and patched up with cardboard."

His father took this in silence. . . . What had been faint and far off was with him, now, and full grown, the knowledge that he was going to win. Beating or no beating, he had his man on the run. . . .

"It's falling in on 'em, I tell you. Four kids in there – and the littlest one sick. An' the old man – Mr. Hooker – lost his job. They haven't any money. I mean no money – not a cent – 'cept what they might be givin' toward your rent. The kids have no shoes to wear – only Sticks has shoes, the big one, 'cause he has to go to school. An' not a thing to eat but corn meal mush an' fried dough an' dandylions an' wood herbs that Mom – Mrs. Hooker – picks. She's got potatoes an' beans planted, but they're not up yet – "

"Before you go any further, Chris – pull your pants up. A man can't talk with his pants down, and I can't talk to him." Wintermute's expression hadn't changed in the slightest except that under his great brows the shadow was perhaps deeper. "It's stuffy in here," he said. He moved to the window and opened it. He sat down in his desk chair again, facing the gathering twilight beyond the window. "I didn't know it was that bad up at the Hooker place," he mused. "I've been meaning to get up there, but I've been busy." Then he wheeled suddenly toward his son. "Well, what are you leading up to?"

"Your taxes are heavy, you told me – "

"Well?"

"An' you said it's a hard job making a living at farming."

25

"It is."

"But we're so much better off than they are. . . . Dad – would you – would you fix that house up for Mom – Mrs. Hooker – an' the kids – an' maybe let 'em have it rent free, at least for a while? I thought you would an' I was going to tell Mrs. Hooker – but when I saw her I couldn't. She's proud, Dad. She wouldn't take that from a kid. . . . But she would from you. Look, I'll chip in my allowance."

Wintermute looked for a long moment into the eyes of his son. They met his own steadily and all he could see there was a flaming eagerness.

"God," he said, at length. "I didn't know they were that poor." His eyes turned from Chris to some papers on the desk before him. "Yes," he said, wearily. "Yes, of course. What else can a Christian do? . . . I'll go up there tomorrow. Listen," he turned again to Chris and his great face was coming alive as the beginnings of a smile trickled into all its furrows like a spring rain on parched ground, "suppose we put up a dinner for them tonight? Sarah's got a big ham on – "

"Don't have to – tonight. I gave 'em my six trout – and one of 'em was – well, that long."

"Eh? You gave 'em the fish you promised to your girl?"

"Would *you* have?"

His father didn't answer. He got up from his chair again, stepped to the door and opened it. He put the cane back in its old place in the corner behind the door; then he took it up again suddenly, broke it in half across his knee, tossed the two pieces into the waste basket beside his desk and sat down again.

"You have grown, Chris," he said. "Hooky is a kid's game and a licking is a kid's punishment. Still, hooky is hooky. . . . I'll take your rod and tackle for the rest of the season. . . . No. That's a kid's punishment, too. You may have them – and fish when your conscience, as a man, tells you it's all right. . . . I think we can swing this Hooker matter, financially, without the aid of your allowance. And perhaps new shoes for the kids." His voice trailed off until it was scarcely audible, but Chris heard him say: "and perhaps a job for the father. We'll see."

The big knocker on the front door banged three times.

"Go see who it is, Chris, while I – liquidate this matter of the hooky." Wintermute took out his pen and drew a letterhead from the dark recesses of his desk. "There is still your excuse to write to your teacher."

At the door stood Rosemary Martin, looking worried. Beyond her, at the end of the stone walk, stood Dr. Martin's black coupe, with Dr. Martin in it.

"I brought my Dad to plead for you – if it's not too late." Rosemary spoke nervously, in a half whisper. "He said your Dad would do anything for him."

"You told him I played hooky?"

"Yes." She looked at him sharply, as if annoyed that he should question her. "Is it too late?"

"Yes – no – I mean, I told Dad myself. An' it's all right."

"Oh. . .. Wait." She ran down the walk and said something to Dr. Martin. He nodded and backed out of the drive and drove off down the road. Rosemary ran back to Chris and he could see that the anxiousness was out of her face. But she asked him, immediately and in a stern whisper, "Where are my trout?"

"If I had kept 'em I'd have brought 'em to you."

"If you'd kept them! Do you mean to say you caught them, and – well, where are they?"

"I caught six – one that big. I was going to bring five an' keep one for myself." He didn't feel that he could explain everything to her now. Tomorrow he could, but just now he was tired explaining to others all that was so clear to himself. But he began, weakly: "Did you ever see the Hooker house – how they live? – "

The solemn and slightly hurt look left her face. She stepped to his side and surprisingly took his hand in hers. "Never saw it till this afternoon," she said.

"This afternoon?"

"Yes. I went up there – with Sticks. He knows you played hooky an' he's goin' to tell it all over. . . . Look, let's go out to your summer-house. It's nice there – we can talk." She led him down the steps and back toward the little rustic and morning-gloryed structure.

When they were seated on the old gray boards of the bench she said: "I'm being mean to you, Chris. I know all about the trout. I went up there with Sticks and Dad. Sticks came down to our house this afternoon – he ran all the way – to get Dad. His baby sister is sick. Poor kid."

27

"I heard her cry. She sounded awful sick."

"She won't die, Dad said. Listen, I saw that house – I even went inside. It makes me cry to think of it – of Sticks living there – "

"Dad said he'd fix it up. He owns it. An' get 'em some shoes, maybe."

"Oh, I'm awfully glad." Then she added, "I saw your trout, too."

"What did Sticks think of those fish?"

"He said you were the best fisherman and best feller he knew in the world – an' he wished you liked him. Honest."

"Aw – did Sticks say that, honest?"

"Honest an' truly. And he's not the only one who thinks so."

"Who else?"

"*I* do – there."

They were silent, pondering the import of that confession. The dusk in the summer house deepened. The broad lawn spread away, and beyond it the maples stood breathless in the quiet evening.

"You gave up something you wanted, and that's brave. And you told your Dad you'd played hooky. That was the best way. That was brave, too."

"Look, did you give Miss Spencer that excuse, this morning?"

"No. It takes nerve to do something you know is wrong. An' I'm not brave – like you. But afterwards I wished I had. That's why I brought Dad along, soon's I could, to help you. But this morning it seemed too much like a lie. . . . And besides, I was mad at you then."

"Why?"

"Because you left me so quick – at the bridge – after I'd promised to help you. You didn't kiss me good-bye, even."

He thought, vaguely, that he would never, ever know anything about girls, as long as he lived.

"Can I make that up to you, now?" he asked, after a moment.

"If you don't, I might still be mad."

Reprinted by permission of Elizabeth Walden Hyde, Shelburne, Nova Scotia.

THE
Bronze Goose

BY KENNETH H. OTTERSON

For the true sportsmen, each success is a bittersweet
one, with the consummate moment of triumph always
being tinged by a touch of tragedy. In this striking piece
of fiction, Kenneth Otterson (1922-1972) writes, "it is
the hunter who loves the birds most and who grieves at
their passing." Here we are reminded that such
thoughts matter, and the insightful reader will be left
pondering the future of sport even as he enjoys a story
which quietly instructs while it entertains.

Carl Oberg saw the bronze goose when he was a boy of ten.
His father, who farmed a quarter section a mile east of the
Missouri River bluffs in South Dakota, had shot the
Canada honker one wintry afternoon just before Christmas.
When Carl came home from school that day, his father was
standing in the doorway of the kitchen shed, waiting. He
summoned Carl preemptorily, which was unlike him, and led the

29

boy to the kitchen table, whereon lay the bird.

The goose was a large one, as Canadas go, scaling perhaps 11 pounds even though it was not in full flesh. But the remarkable feature was its coloration. The breast was a peculiar yellow-brown, rather than the usual gray. Everything about the bird indicated a worn oldness. The black of its head and neck was shot through with odd rusty streakings, and the cheek patch, ordinarily white, was the dull yellow of a wet chamois cloth. Its bill had the seams one notices in the faces of old men who have endured much weather. The scaly feet and legs were scarred deeply, and the claw of one toe was missing.

In her practical way, Carl's mother recognized the age of the bird. "No use to cook that one," she said. "He'll be too tough to eat."

But his father paid her no heed. He sat down and talked to Carl about the goose, describing the hunt and how he had killed the bird. Then he took the goose and hung it on a nail high on the shed wall. Next day he carried it into Preecely and showed it around and left it at Pete Larson's cafe for further display. Pete carelessly put it in his woodshed overnight, and neighborhood dogs left only remnants of skin and feathers strewn about the alley. But men had seen it and wondered.

Around Preecely the "bronze goose" became a legend. The bird gained its title from Carl's father's description of the moment of glory when the sun gleamed on the feathers as the great form winged past him, almost at eye level, up the ravine between two knobs. It was a loner, a bird that left the river, fed and returned to it always alone. There were a few such geese each year, invariably old birds who had lost their mates.

The taking of the bronze goose had set his father apart, and men up and down the river came to hear the story firsthand. Those who had seen it declared the bird was of great age – seventy-five, and perhaps a hundred years old. His father had been a market hunter and was renowned for his big kills, but the bronze goose set him even farther above ordinary men.

Carl was thinking of those long-gone days as he sat in his grocery store office on a December day thirty-five years later. His eyes were on the frosted windowpane, and his ears heard the fierce gusts of the morning wind.

This wintry day marked the closing of the waterfowl season,

and Carl had not hunted geese all fall. He and Dick Johnson, his longtime friend and hunting companion, had gone out for sharp-tailed grouse west of the river, enjoyed several duck shoots on their favorite slough, and taken a few cock pheasants. But a vast uneasiness worked in him concerning his beloved Canada honkers.

Paul, his son, coming up twelve years old, was involved in his refusal to hunt geese that fall. The boy was like the young Carl of the old days – same wiry, tough build, same shock of light hair, same alert blue eyes.

Come February, Paul would be twelve. Then his father would present him with his first shotgun, a single-barrel .410. So Carl had promised and so it would be, but now he was troubled by the unquiet feeling that fathers have when they wonder if they are doing the right thing. It did not involve Paul's safety; Carl believed boys should grow up with guns, under proper supervision. It went far deeper than that.

Carl stepped close to the window and scraped away a little of the frost. Winter whirled outside. Fine, hard granules of snow fled down the alley and spilled from the roof in quick smoky bursts.

Carl turned away again, weary with his problem, despairing of its solution. Again the question racked his mind: "How can I be selfish enough to give him a love of wildness and wild things when soon none will be left for him to love?"

For years the waves of migratory waterfowl that swept from the Canadian breeding grounds each autumn had been diminishing. Unthinking men might not have noticed it, for this region had always been a stopping-off place for mallards and Canadas. But everywhere the sloughs were being drained. It was like a fever among farmers in the state, this eagerness to ditch and tile. Where once the glistening, reed-bordered sloughs had been common, now a man could drive for miles and see no water.

In the old days, goose hunting had been a matter of talking with friends who farmed beside the river bluffs, then waiting along the fence rows of the stubble fields and cornfields, or up on the hills, for the flight. But then gunners began to multiply, and farmers got the notion of selling hunting rights on their property. Some would even guarantee a goose, and to make good they built elaborate decoy setups and pits. They let the corn stand, picking ten or fifteen rows twice a week to keep the geese coming to the fresh gleanings. Baiting was illegal, but this was not. Hunting became a commercial thing, an ugliness where once was joy.

It was a pitiful remnant he was leaving to his son, he and all the other men who had shot strongly and well – perhaps too well – from their youth on. The legions of wildfowl funneled down from the Saskatchewan breeding grounds through the Mississippi Flyway, thousands remaining in the Preecely vicinity until the blizzards in their white fury buried the forage fields. Even so, incredibly, a few thousand wintered in the flats, honkers and mallards, gorging themselves when the wind or a thaw removed the snow from knolls. Carl had even seen them alighting in feedlots, flatly treading beneath the cattle in their hunger. Before a blizzard they sensed the change, and in the old days when winter shooting was allowed he had killed mallards so stuffed with corn that their breast skin split open when they struck frozen ground. The old days. . .

Yes, a small heritage to leave a son. Then he thought: Maybe I'm all twisted around. Does my son – does any son – want what I've loved so well? Today's kids were different. They had so much more, and so much less. Were mothers changing too? In his day the outdoors had been a boy's natural home, a gun or fishing rod his companion. Mothers wished it so. Anna, his wife, took a cool view of hunting. "Paul and the other children have television," she had said one day. "Let them watch it. They learn things; they'll be smarter than we ever were. I always know where they are when they're home. Let things be. Don't go putting ideas in his head."

Carl was shaken and angry. "Hunting's better than television, at least. It's better than staring at that screen all the time."

"Television's civilized – it's not like lying out all day in the mud like a savage, waiting for a bird to shoot at." She stared at Carl. "It would suit me fine if you'd stop talking about hunting to him – stirring him up."

Maybe that was it. Maybe he was building up a love in Paul for something the boy could never attain. Maybe that was cruel, though he did it in all kindness.

This torment was too much, too much. Suddenly Carl felt he must get into the storm, face it, buckle into the raging wind, and shout his lungs out in fury at time and men – who take and do not give back. With a gesture of decision he strode into the outer store.

32

"Mary," he said to his niece (and only clerk), "call Dick and tell him I'll pick him up in half an hour. No goose in his right mind will fly higher than a telephone wire today."

Mary's eyes widened in surprise. She had been well aware of his inner turmoil, though she couldn't quite fathom the reason for it. Now she smiled warmly, her ear at the phone, as he put on his coat and walked to the door.

She's glad for me, thought Carl. Then it's been showing! His mouth twisted wryly. As if a man could shoot geese almost all his life and then abruptly refuse to hunt them, and the strain, the turmoil, not show!

He hunched into the wind and the stinging grains of snow. Winter had come early, more bitter to the cheek than February would be when a man was used to it. He shivered, excitement beginning to tingle in him. A wind like this and a hunt impending – would it ever be otherwise, this lifting of the head, this sniffing the raw wind, this feeling of elation like that of a small boy hurrying to the fair?

Give it up? Carl shook his head, thinking, not today. Let this be the last of it, if it must be, but for today, live it, live it! Maybe, when he was on the bluffs of the Missouri, lying on the snow waiting for the honkers to come off the sandbars, watching the black mass of them far below, something would tell him what he must do.

His wife met him at the door, a worried look in her eyes. "What's the matter, Carl? Did you forget something?"

He shook the snow from his stormcoat and hung it carefully on the hallway hook. "No. Dick and I are going after geese."

Her mouth went flat. "I knew you'd give in. I'll bet he bothered you all morning."

"Haven't seen him," said Carl. "I had Mary call him for me."

"Carl, I thought –" His wife paused. "Never mind. I'll fix you a lunch."

"Make the coffee good and strong."

He loaded the car, carefully checking each item: heavy flight pants, sheepskin coat, wool-lined helmet and mittens, the box of magnums 2's. It felt good to handle the maggie loads again. The heavy sheepskin coat, pants and helmet he would not put on until they reached the hunting ground.

33

In the kitchen Anna was packing lunch in his rucksack. Without forethought he said, "Too bad Paul's in school. He could go along."

Anna tucked the vacuum bottle in the rucksack, paused a long moment, then turned and fitted the strap on his shoulder. She shook her head slightly, but her eyes held a fond, humorous tenderness. "You're hopeless. And Paul is just as bad. When I tell him you went for geese, he'll have a fit. But tonight you tell him there's always next year. Go on. Dick's waiting."

Carl stooped and kissed her cheek roughly, embarrassed, and patted her shoulder. He nodded. "Next year. We'll see."

When he pulled to a stop at the curb, Dick rushed down the walk, laden with gear. He flung the armload in the back seat and leaped in beside Carl. "You old devil! It's a good thing Mary called when she did, or I'd have been long since gone. I gave you up for lost two months ago."

Carl grinned. "I figured somebody had to show you how to hunt geese." Swiftly he meshed the gears and drove down the wintry street.

In some places the blowing snow almost obscured the road. It was a ground blizzard; faintly overhead the sun shone. The fields lay barren to the eye without a dab of brightness anywhere, as if gaudiness had no place on the winter plains.

Wind beat against the car, and streamers of fine snow raced across the gravel. Strong winds, snow-laden, made geese restless. On the sandbars small groups would be rising out of the main body winging heavily into the wind a few feet above the sand, alighting a short distance away. A continual lifting and settling would go on, without purpose.

Carl turned south off the gravel onto the section-line wheel ruts. The unused road was drifted shut. Blowing snow obscured the outlines of the bluffs a mile away. Dick grunted. "I figured she'd be blocked. Is it worth the hike or shall we take our chances on the public shooting grounds? The road might be open into them."

"Let's try here," said Carl. "Looks like we'll have it all to ourselves."

They pulled on the heavy outer clothing and slipped the guns from their cases.

"Leave your lunch and binoculars in the car," said Dick. "I'll carry mine and you can carry the geese."

The northwest wind lashed them as they crossed the fence and

34

plunged through a knee-high drift. The fury of driven snow was blinding. They headed south, following the fence row. The flat haylands gave no indication of the river's nearness, but seemed only an endless prairie land. The road ended at the final fence line. Gasping, they floundered through a drift in a slight depression and attained bare ground beyond. The wind pushed them up a gradual incline, and abruptly they were on the brink of the valley. The suddenness of its appearance never ceased to affect Carl.

Across the huge sweep of the bottoms swarmed the loose dry snow, almost obscuring the opposite ridges, whose summits were four miles away. The river here followed a southeast tangent for three miles, the curve southward beginning two miles downstream from where they stood. The wind roared and it seemed impossible that any living creature could long endure it in the open.

A hundred yards to the east the stubble of a cornfield was containing the bulk of the driven snow. Carl silently jerked his head in that direction and they moved toward the field. Behind them the little arcs of drifts which their feet had formed vanished instantly. At the edge of the cornfield the blizzard ended as though a solid wall had been upthrust, and the wind howled much less furiously.

"They're there, all right," Dick shouted. "They've kept a pothole open just this side of the trees." He unstrapped the glasses from about his neck and handed them to Carl.

In the lenses the geese were a black mass the size of a saucer. Two or three thousand birds, guessed Carl, and he sighed aloud.

"How shall we work it?" asked Dick.

Carl lowered the glasses and peered at the place where the geese were gathered. Now he could see nothing of the black saucer. But knowing the location, he had to figure where the geese would come out across the bluffs – and that might be at any point in the five miles of heights. Then, too, the utmost range at which Carl would shoot was around fifty yards. Many factors had to be weighed before they picked their blinds.

Carl knew that once the leader of a flock became used to certain ravines, it preferred to take its flock out through one of them. But wind direction was important. The geese always chose to buck the wind, as all birds do, being then in absolute control, their feathers lying tightly against their bodies. Against a storm of too great velocity, though, they could not make sure headway; so they'd quarter, flying at an angle into the blast until they cleared the bluffs, then turning upwind. In a gale they often flew downriver with the howler on their tails, then gradually turned and raised the bluffs with the force still behind them – "hindquartering," Carl called it. This last offered the most difficult of shots for the hunter, since the birds hurtled past and were usually at the extreme limit of range.

Carl squinted into the haze, gauging the wind's strength, its exact direction. Within him his "goose feeling" was working, a thing he could not explain. But it was a true indicator, composed of the experience of other days – wind velocities, blown snow, biting cold and flights materializing out of the wintry scape. So now he let the thing work in him.

Dick always chided him about it but had respect for it all the same. He was grinning now. "Stomach rumbled yet?"

Carl pointed a mittened hand across the slopes. "They'll come out across that section. Some of them, not all. They'll be broken up today. Only a few bunches. The rest will go out with the wind down below."

"Where shall we dig in?"

"You take the head of that long ravine. I'll stay this side of you about a block."

Dick lifted his fist, pulled it down twice in their old salute – a gesture of hoped-for success or of success attained – and plunged away through a drift. Carl watched him go, smiling. Then he peeled his sheepskin sleeve back to get at his watch. Eleven o'clock. It wouldn't be long, if the geese were coming out this way.

He followed Dick's tracks until he came to the nearer edge of the long ravine. His partner was busily kicking snow ten yards below the summit on the farther side. Carl slid down the hill and found a gouge four feet deep, cut by a spring freshet. He cleared the snow from it, alternately scraping and packing till he had a level stand for his feet. Then he placed a tumbleweed in front of him, leaned his gun against it, lifted his earflaps and listened intently. He heard nothing but the wind.

The air was not so thick with flying snow down the long ravine. He could make out dimly the shadow of the trees on the river bottom, and see quite clearly the network of the years below him. He had a quick, warm feeling that only yesterday he had stood on these same bluffs with his father, when the wind keened a song of hot-blooded youth, not of age and disillusion mournful with loss past recovery.

He heard a faint shout. Instinctively he crouched behind his tumbleweed, seizing his gun. His heart pounded. He peered through the twiggy mass, slipped off his right mitten and thumbed the safety, letting his eyes rove the sky, seeing no movement.

Dick shouted again, unintelligibly. At the same moment he heard it – faint, far and shrill, the sound like no other in earth or heaven, the crying of geese in flight. The great, crushing weight of regret dropped away from him. Then he glimpsed the powerful, sustained rhythm of beating wings.

A bunch of five had begun the feeding flight. They were already across the first low ridges and but a mile away, quartering the wind toward the blinds. Which ravine would they follow? A trembling began in Carl. He slid the safety forward on his gun.

The flight began to lift slightly for the slow-rising mounds. On it came, the cries clamoring through the valley. Peering at the geese through the tumbleweed made them seem within range, so hugely they loomed. But Carl remained crouched as if frozen. Wait, wait, scarcely breathing, bare hand stiffening in the cold, praying for them to come over, the ancient hunter's prayer with eyes fixed on the quarry, "Come, come, keep coming, come, come."

Then, when it seemed certain they must pass within range, they shifted gradually upward and followed the ravine to his right, momentarily disappearing from view behind the hill, reappearing to struggle over the height a scant ten yards above the ground. Their cries diminished until he could hear them no more.

Carl shivered and stood erect, his knee joints aching. More would be coming, he knew. He had selected their positions well; he and Dick should get shooting. But the thought was in him, What if that flock were the last of all the honkers on the continent, vanishing over the bluff into nothingness forever? The wind sound was the more desolate now for their having given it life. How irreplaceable were the creatures of the air and earth!

Cries began again down the valley; more flights were on the wing. For an hour the flocks continued to come. Several times

Carl was tempted to shoot, but the birds were wide. His magnum would bring them down at that distance, but he did not want to take a chance of crippling.

Dick was shooting. Carl looked in time to see one of a flock of nine falling heavily. As Dick leaped from his blind Carl shouted, lifted his arm and gave the salute. Dick waved. My turn now, thought Carl.

A flock of four, which he had believed would pass as wide of him as the others, heavily attempted the bluff which raised on his right, but could not gain headway. Four straining bodies gave ground, swinging over Carl's ravine, lowering to twenty yards above the twisting bed. They came directly at him.

Carl let them come until the brim of his helmet hid them from view. He waited five more seconds till their cries were a torrent overhead, then rose. Instantly they flared, shrill alarm in their throats. He picked the last bird and laid the ribbed barrel just ahead of its bill. It collapsed at his shot. Instinctively he swung on the next bird, had it full fair above the barrel – but did not press the trigger. The three remaining geese crossed the ridge.

Carl stepped out of his blind. His bird lay motionless at the bottom of the slope. But before he could move to retrieve it he heard Dick's yell. A warning note was in the shout, and instantly he leaped into his blind. A flock was working in front of him a mile away but too far to the west; they would break over at least three ravines away. What was the matter with Dick anyway?

He almost rose, but the single plaintive utterance which could only be that of a loner caught him in time. The bird was close, very close, but where? Frantically he searched the sky before him. It was maddeningly difficult to place the position of a loner by its cry. He was afraid to move his head, knowing the bird must be almost within range.

Then, from almost directly above him, the single note came again. Carl came up in one smooth motion, bringing the gun to his shoulder. The loner was above him, slightly wide, hanging in the wind high enough above the snow gusts, perhaps fifty yards, for the sunlight to strike the feathers. The glow on the burnished breast was unmistakable – a dull yellow like no other, the color of bronze.

Carl brought the tube in front of the almost stationary head. A squeeze of his finger would have tumbled the bird in a stone-dead

38

fall, but the goose emerged before the barrel slowly and hung beating there. Then, unable to make headway, it flared with the wind under its wings and fell away down the slope into the ravine, where lesser air currents enabled it to turn and throb slowly up over the summit to disappear in the blowing snow.

Dick arose from his blind, picked up his goose and half ran in excitement to Carl. He dropped on his knees, panting, eyes alight, a broad grin on his face. "Wasn't that a sight! You sure folded your bird. What happened, your gun jam on that lone bird?"

"Yeah," said Carl slowly. "Yeah. Could you see him very well from where you were?"

"Not too well. Looked like a big one, though. What's wrong with you? You look like you saw a ghost."

Carl attempted a smile. "Just half froze is all. You've got a nice young one there."

"Hey, I'll get yours." Dick plunged down the slope.

Carl gazed up at the bluff over which the loner had gone. It could not be – yet he had seen it. He had a sense of unreality, as though he were his father on these hills. But his father had taken his bronze goose – and he had not.

Dick returned, hefting the goose critically. "Same as mine, I'd judge. About eight pounds. A pair of table birds."

Carl took the birds. He thrust his fingers through the gray breast feathers, stroked the black sheen of the head and neck, thinking, So I could be holding the bronze goose this moment.

"Let's eat and coffee-up," said Dick. "Looks like the flight's about over, but we ought to stick it out. The wind will go down this afternoon. Won't have to buck it back. We might pick up the other two birds we're allowed."

"Okay," said Carl. He felt a little sick.

The wind began dying at 4 o'clock, and at sundown the air was still. Only one more flock had left the river, and it had passed far to the east of them. The river valley was visible as far as the eye could see. The ancient folds lay frozen in the trance of winter. Not a solitary living creature was visible. They emptied their guns and stiffly climbed the bluff. At its summit they paused.

"Listen," said Dick.

Faintly, then Carl heard them. Swiftly he searched the sky.

"Look at them come." Dick pointed.

Against the bright, luminous sky one sees just after sunset on clear, cold days the geese were etched, flock upon following flock. Those farthest away bore on with steadily beating pinions, the nearer birds beginning their glide, great wings cupped. It was beautiful beyond speech, almost heart-aching to behold, and suddenly Carl was aware of the gun slanted back across his curved arm, and without reason (but with a certain knowing) he saw that the gun gave the sight a greater beauty, for it was his hunter's soul that transfixed him at the sight of the living splendor overhead.

"I pray to God," said Carl, "this never leaves us, or we shall be poor men."

"Amen," said Dick.

Carl thought, if men always love it, they will never lose it. But how can men – youths now – like Paul love it if they never get to know it?

Then he knew what he must do. Banish despair, for despair was lack of faith in his son, other sons – a generation of them. His father had been a market hunter, and Carl himself had killed beyond need in his own youth. Why could he not teach his son moderation, instead of letting him learn it with pain, as he had, so late?

Strangely, it is the hunter who loves the birds most, who grieves at their passing – not because there will be no targets aloft for his gun but because he knows best, by being closest, the glory he has inherited, along with the struggle, on the bleak plains.

The words he had read of the New Englander, the hermit who was so fiercely engaged in man's well-being, the man Thoreau, came to him now. "We cannot but pity the boy who has never fired a gun; he is no more humane, though his education has been sadly neglected." And Carl thought, How shall I be close to my son save in these things? And with a fierce gladness he realized he had left Paul a bronze goose too – even if the boy never saw it.

"I hate to go," said Dick, "but maybe we'd better. Here, I'll carry your goose."

"No," Carl said. "He's not so heavy as that, nor I so old."

"Too bad you didn't get that loner, Carl. He looked as big as a barn over your head."

"One's plenty, anyway."

Dick lifted his bird and hoisted it over his shoulder. "Guess

40

you're right. One's plenty. Got to leave a few for seed, don't we?"

Carl looked his friend in the eyes. "Then you knew all the time?"

Dick grinned. "Your gun never jammed yet, and never will, the way you baby it."

Carl paused for a final look at the valley. Far out over the river, the last flocks were spiraling swiftly in corkscrew fashion to join the others on the sandbars. As they always would.

Reprinted by permission of Mrs. Kenneth Otterson, Sioux Falls, South Dakata.

Last Cast

O N   T H E   D O G W A T E R

BY BEN SCHLEY

There is something about trout fishing which lends
itself to the telling of grand tales, and fine
fictional works loom large in the sport's literature.
Here is an overlooked story, one not normally included
in the many fly-fishing anthologies. In it, Ben Schley
finds gladness from the depths of sadness, reminding us
of the manner in which clean waters and wild trout
can be a commentary on life.

I used to see old Artemis Hovle now and then as he slowly
tapped his way along East Water Street, his white cane
exploring the uneven surface of the brick pavement between
the Post Office and Frenchy Coiner's barbershop at the corner.

I would always speak to him and, now and then, he would
return my greeting with a feeble wave of his free hand. But more
often he would pass slowly on, seemingly lost in thought as he

followed his cane on to O'Rourke's store on the village square.

But one morning, as he stumbled on an overturned brick and seemed to be somewhat confused, I took hold of his arm and eased him into safer going. He was a slender, stooped little man with a pale and deeply-lined face. "There, that's better, Mr. Hovle," I said. "Seems to me the town should be doing some repair work, don't you think?"

"Yes, yes, thank you so much. Oh," he said in a high-pitched voice, "It's Mr. Greenacre, isn't it? You work for Josh Saulter up at the trout hatchery on the North Branch of Barkers Brook, don't you? How is old Josh? Kin to my long-dead wife, you know. Haven't seen him for years. Haven't been to the hatchery either, not since I lost my eyesight. The branch used to be full of fat little brookies but I suppose they are all caught out now. Nothing there now but rainbows you fellows dump in. You're not a fisherman so I suppose it doesn't matter to you. What a pity; hatchery workers seldom go fishing, fly fishing, that is."

"Oh, but you couldn't be more wrong," I said. "I fish every chance I get. I tie all my own flies and own more fly rods than I should. One of the reasons I work at a hatchery is so I can be near good trout water."

It took the old man a few seconds to digest this. Then he nodded his head and suggested we sit somewhere and talk fishing for a while.

It was a bright, warm morning, and I was in no hurry so I took his hand and steered him across the square to the village green. I found an empty bench. "Here we are. We can sit right here," I said.

He eased himself down on the slatted wooden bench and patted the seat beside him. "Here," he said, "sit on my right. I don't hear so good on the left."

I sat down, and he took off his shapeless gray hat and ran his fingers through his sparse white hair. I could see several snelled wet flies stuck in the heavy felt.

The old man leaned back and seemed to relax. "Sun always feels so good this time of the year. There's bound to be a good fly hatch later on, don't you think? Hendricksons probably, though it is a mite early."

A thin smile crossed his face. "Now, Mr. Greenacre, let me tell you something interesting. Your voice sounds very much like Ed

Hewitt's. You know who I mean, Edward R. Hewitt. Used to live over on the Neversink River in New York, you know. He was the fellow who wrote so much about trout and salmon fishing and was always experimenting, always trying something new. Well, your voice has the same nasal quality. I'd know it anywhere. Ed had a big nose, big and red as the belly of a brook trout. Used to blow it all the time. Sounded like a damn fog horn it did. Hell, it would even put feeding trout down if they was close by. Here, let me have a look at you."

The old man leaned toward me and his pale, spidery hands touched my face. His fingers were slender and cold. He ran his hands along the bridge of my nose, into the sockets of my eyes, around my mouth and along my chin. "I knew it, I knew it!" he cackled. "You and Ed could be brothers, though it seems to me you're a mite better looking. Died way up in his 90s, he did, just a few years after I lost my eyesight. Tell me one thing, Mr. Greenacre, is your nose red? It felt kinda red, you know.

"Ed used to come over and fish every year, usually about this time or a bit later. He was usually by himself, but one time he brought Mr. LaBranche along. They really didn't fish very much – just sat around and argued about fly patterns and such.

"Barkers Brook was full of browns in those days and some of them was pretty good size too. And we had some great fly hatches ... March Browns, Hendricksons, Cahills, Green Drakes. You name it, we had it.

"Now Hewitt, he was a real brain, that man. Why he would be out there from sunup til dark experimenting and blowing his big red nose. Oh, but he took lots of fish too. He always called Barkers Brook the Dogwater. And the name sorta stuck. All the old timers call it that. Dogwater, yes, just Dogwater.

"You know, it makes me want to cry when I think about those great days we used to have on the Dogwater. All the fish then was streambred, just brownies and a few natives. Oh, I suppose there are a few of them left, but mostly what I catch are your little hatchery rainbows and they don't take a fly very good."

"How in the world do you manage to fish with a fly?" I asked.

"Well," the old man replied, "I have had to give up a lot of things since I lost my eyesight, but fly fishing isn't one of them. By dammit, I fish some most every day or night; makes no difference, middle of the day or midnight, if I feel like fishing I just get up and go. Don't catch much but, hell, it's better than blowing my brains out. Only time I can't fish is when the wind's blowing. Tangles my leader and line."

I glanced at the frail, stooped figure beside me ... at the pale, drawn face and marveled that this relic of a once vital person could continue to maintain his enthusiasm for fly fishing.

"Well sir," he said as if sensing my disbelief, "it's not easy, not easy at all. My home is almost on the banks of the Dogwater. It's the old Haversaw place on Spartus Road right where the stream comes out of the gorge and falls over that big limestone ledge and comes into what we call the Ironstone Pool. You know where I mean don't you?"

Forgetting his sightless eyes, I nodded an affirmative, then said, "Yes, it's a lovely spot and the run at the tail of the pool looks great. But I've never fished it. Can't. It's posted, isn't it?"

The old man tapped his cane sharply on the ground and his voice became shrill. "Well, I had to do it!" he said defensively. "It's the only place I have to fish. Otherwise those bastards from town would be in there with bait and clean it out. I own half a mile up along the Dogwater, clean up to the Clover Mountain Road. All that is open. You can fish it any time.

"Oh, Ephie and I have it fixed up pretty good. I can put a fly most anywhere I want in the pool except up at the top where there's a big rock overhang. I figure there must be a big old brown holding up there, and I aim to get him someday if he ever moves down.

"Ephie's my daughter. Only child. She never married and I doubt she ever will. Old Ed Hewitt was here the day she was born. Born right in the middle of the damndest Green Drake hatch you ever saw. Ed said the flies was so thick he couldn't hardly fish. Caught only a couple little browns. I couldn't fish that day on account of Ephie being born and her poor mother passing away only a few hours later. I was right busy for a day or so, I tell you. But I did catch the spinner fall a couple days later and, boy, did I take some nice fish!

"It was old Hewitt who suggested I name her after the Green Drake. He said the scientific name of the drake was *Ephemera guttulata*. So I named her Ephemera. But I call her Ephie. Pity she never took to fly fishing herself. But she's been a big help anyway,

45

particularly after my affliction took me."

I knew Miss Hovel slightly and thought her a pleasant woman but no beauty. No wonder she was single. With a name like Ephemera, it would take a pretty desirable woman to find a husband.

Mr. Hovle chuckled. "I know what you're thinking. No, her middle name is not Guttulata. It's Haversaw, after her mother's family.

"Ephie's the one who started me fly fishing after I lost my sight. I would have given up without her. But she kept after me, and one day she rigged up my 9-foot Orvis Battenkill with a double taper line and a short leader with a loop on the end. Then she marked off ten-foot intervals on the line with dabs of cement so I could tell how far I was casting. I use snelled flies so I can change them easy. They're simple patterns and I keep them at different places on my hat.

"Then Ephie strung a cord on posts all the way from the back door to the water and then on around the west side of the pool. She put some boards on the edge of the water for markers so I can stand on them and know where I am. I have the whole place layed out in my mind just like a map. When I feel like it I just step out the kitchen door, grab the rod and head for the Dogwater. Night or day, it doesn't make any difference to me."

In my mind's eye I could see the old boy out there casting away in the middle of the night and asked if he ever caught many trout.

"No, not many. But I keep on trying. There isn't much else for me to do and maybe sometime I'll hook that big old brown I know must be up there in the head of the pool. Let's see," he mused, "I've caught six fish so far this year, but two of them was chubs so they don't hardly count. All the rest was rainbows about nine inches long. Hatchery fish, all of them. Their fins was kinda wore down. They must have drifted down from upstream."

The old man made a couple of imaginary false casts with his cane. "I miss a lot of fish because I have to strike by feel or sound. Sometimes, when it's quiet, I can almost tell when a fish is gonna take. It's like it comes up and sorta breathes on the fly."

"How did you know the fish you caught were rainbows?" I asked.

"Rainbows? Well, they feel kinda brittle and hard. Now brookies are like velvet, wet velvet. Smooth. Soft. And browns? Well they just feel brown, sort of brassy maybe. And they smell different, not bad, just different. But I haven't caught a brown this year or a brookie either. Only rainbows. All with bad fins."

A few days later I drove along Spartus Road, past the Hovels' small brown house and up the hill. I parked in a clearing and walked through low brush until I could see the Ironstone Pool. Shreds of mist lay over the water and a thin, cold drizzle had set in. Artemis Hovle was standing at the edge of the water about thirty yards from his house. He was casting methodically, then retrieving his line slowly. He was wearing a long raincoat.

After a few minutes he reeled in his line and took hold of the cord that was stretched along the edge of the pool. Then he crept slowly along to another position, paused for a few seconds, stripped line off his reel and began casting.

As I walked slowly back to my pickup an idea began to take shape in my mind. Why not, I thought, give the old boy some real trout to fish for, put a little excitement into his fishing efforts?

At that time we were phasing out our seven-year-old brown trout brood fish and had some large males to get rid of. They were beautiful fish, perfect in every respect except for missing right pelvic fins, clipped off when they were fingerlings in order to identify them as breeding stock. There was no reason why I couldn't slip a few of them into Ironstone Pool. No one would know, least of all the boss, who lived six miles away and wasn't likely to notice the fish were gone anyway.

I waited for the right time. Several days later the weather turned cold and a strong wind keened in from the north. Around midnight I slid a tank on the bed of my pickup and filled it with water. Then I netted four big struggling male brown trout out of a pond and dumped them into the tank.

It was only a twenty-minute drive to the hill overlooking Ironstone Pool. I cut my lights and drove slowly through the sparse undergrowth until I was about fifty yards from the water. The moon was low. The Hovles' house was dark. Except for the wind in the trees and the muted roar of the brook, all was quiet. I carefully dipped the browns out of the tank and carried them to the edge of the pool. I slipped them into the dark water. They swam quickly away.

The following morning I left the hatchery with a load of fingerling rainbows for a stream in the northern part of the state. The truck broke down on the return trip and I didn't get back until the next day.

So it was Thursday before I got to the Post Office. I was coming out of the building reading a letter from my sister when I saw Ephie Hovle getting out of her faded Buick. Anxious for word of her father, I walked toward her. She was dressed in black. Her graying hair was plaited and wound tightly around her head. "How is your father?" I asked.

She put her hand on my arm. Tears, like raindrops, welled up in her deep-set eyes. "Then you haven't heard? Father's gone. Passed away night before last."

What could I say? I fumbled for words and finally managed to say something about the passing of a great angler and that Artemis Hovle would be missed by his fishermen friends. Meaningless words.

Ephie turned away for a moment, then dried her eyes with the back of her hand. "If Father had to go, I suppose he went the way any fisherman would want to go. The poor man died with his pole in his hand, and a great big fish on the end of his line."

Big fish, big fish on the end of his line! Oh Christ, what had I done?

Ephie continued as I stood half in shock. "You see, I got up in the night and looked in on Father. It was maybe two or three o'clock. He wasn't there. But I didn't think nothing of it because it wasn't all that unusual. He would fish any old time, just whenever the notion took him. So I went on back to bed and didn't get up until it was good light. I peeked into Father's room then and he still wasn't there.

"Well, I began to fret. So I called out and when he didn't answer, I looked out the back door. His pole was gone and so was his boots. So I pulled on a coat and ran out in the rain. I found him laying there on the bank with his head clean under the water."

Ephie suppressed a sob and continued. "Well, I waded into the water and grabbed him by the hair and tried to lift him but he was stiff and I couldn't budge him. So I got out of the water and took ahold of his legs and pulled him up on shore. His eyeglasses was gone and his old blind eyes was rolled back and as white as milk.

"Even after he was up on the shore he still had ahold of his pole and the line was wrapped around his wrist. I pried it loose when I realized there was something on the end of the line. Well then, I just pulled it in. On the end of the line was the biggest brown trout I ever seen. So I threw it back up on the bank. It thrashed around in the bushes for a bit then went quiet.

"I called Dr. Bedvold and he came out and had a look. Then he called the funeral home and they took Father away. Later on the doctor called and said his heart had just given out – couldn't stand the excitement, he said.

"Well, that's all there is to it. We will bury him tomorrow up at Memory Gardens on Connerys Mountain. That's where Mama is buried, you know. Services will be at one at St. George's Chapel."

I didn't say a word. Couldn't. I turned and walked slowly away. For a while I sat on the bench where Artemis Hovle and I had talked of trout fishing and the Dogwater and Ed Hewitt. It seemed a long time ago.

Only a few people braved the driving rain when they lowered all that was left of Artemis Hovle into the earth. I stood back and took shelter under a leaning spruce, while Josh Saulter stayed beside Ephie under a wind-whipped awning. Later, as I turned to go, Ephie spotted me.

"Come to the house," she said. "Come on up. There'll be a bite to eat, and we can talk about trout fishing and about Father."

I approached the Hovels' house with a heavy heart and a deep sense of guilt. The rain had stopped. Mist, like a shroud, hung over Ironstone Pool.

Ephie let me into the tiny living room. A dozen or so people were gathered around a scarred oak table on which lay the remains of a gigantic male brown trout, its head and tail extending far beyond the confines of a china platter. It was obvious that the fish had been poached. Its skin had been peeled off and folks were picking meat off the ribs and popping it into their mouths. The sight almost made me ill, and I turned away, only to find Ephie at my side.

"Help me turn the fish over, Mr. Greenacre," she said. "There'll be plenty more meat on the other side." She put two large wooden forks in my hands. "Here, you roll it over, I'll hold the platter."

Reluctantly, I slid the forks under the fish, managed to raise it a few inches, then heaved it over on the platter. It was the first time I had had a good look at the entire fish. Every fin was intact! None was missing! This was no hatchery trout. This was a wild, Dogwater-bred brown trout. Old Artemis Hovle was right when he said that there was a big old brown trout holding up at the head of Ironstone Pool. Thank God. Oh, thank God!

I dropped the forks and with my fingers, pried off a big chunk of firm flesh. I put it in my mouth. It was the best damn trout I ever tasted.

Green Eyes

BY MICHAEL McINTOSH

Michael McIntosh is one of today's most prolific and popular gun writers. Those familiar with his books, or who read his column on shotguns in *Sporting Classics*, will know that McIntosh is a man who is not only intimate with his subject, but who writes about it with conviction and verve. This is a whimsical tale of the sort of bird hunting (and I'll leave the interpretation of what that means to you) which most of us, if we had but the guts to admit as much, would find simply wonderful.

G oodbye, Miss October," Scotty said and laid the calendar page reverently on the fire.

Mac laughed. "A one-track mind," he said. "Pitiful." But he, too, watched solemnly as the paper flared and blackened, leaving a momentary cameo at the center, where a stylish setter watched two woodcock rise against a screen of slender aspens. "You're also three days early," Mac said, "Unless I've

51

managed to lose track of time altogether."

"So I'm fickle," Scotty said. "Miss November's no slouch, either." He hung the calendar back on its nail by the kitchen door. "Never could resist brown eyes."

The eyes in question gazed soulfully over a dead mallard.

Tom came in through the kitchen with an armload of firewood and glanced at the calendar. "Handsome Labrador," he said. "Is it November already?"

"Only to the fickle," Mac said.

Tom dumped the logs in the woodbox, chunked a fresh bolt of oak onto the fire, kicked off his unlaced boots, and slid a chair close to the hearth. "Scotty, you're the only man I know whose favorite pinups all have wet noses and like to drink out of puddles."

"Funny, Sarah says the same thing," Scotty mused. "I suppose I'd change my mind if your average pinup type knew the difference between a vent rib and a nailfile."

"Meeting a woman who hunts can be more of a shock than you might imagine," Tom said. "I met one once, and I've never been the same since.

"It was one of those days that makes every trite, goofy thing ever written about October seem like the grandest poetry. It had poured rain for about three days and then turned clear. The English brew a special run of ale in October – delightful stuff, winey as an overripe apple. Well, the air was like that. What leaves were left had all gone gold, and the tamaracks were bright, blazing yellow. It was the sort of day you can't even think about without getting as sappy as a kid on a first date.

"I was basically a kid myself, barely two years out of the University, the ink hardly dry on my diploma. I'd moved back here after a few miserable months in a big law firm in Minneapolis – which was long enough to find out that big-city life wasn't for me. I was working hard to put together a practice in Tamarack, hunting when I could, which wasn't very often.

"But I got one whiff of the air that morning and decided it was no day for wills and land titles or any such dusty stuff. So I packed up my gun, put Jericho in the car, and took off.

"We poked through a couple of coverts and flew a few grouse. I got a good shot at one that Jericho pointed beside an old log road, and by late morning I was feeling about as good as any young fellow has a right to feel.

"We had our lunch under a big oak by a pasture, lazing in the grass and watching a hawk. I had a mind to spend the afternoon in a covert about a mile to the west, one I hadn't been in since I was a kid, and decided to walk cross-country instead of driving around to it. I'd never been in the center of that section, didn't have a clue if there was any cover in it, but it seemed like a good day to find out.

"We crossed a couple of hills and came down to a little stream. I could see some gray dogwood on the other side, figured there might be a grouse or two close by, so it didn't surprise me when Jericho went on point in the tag alders. When I got up closer, though, I could see he wasn't pointing. He looked like he was honoring, which struck me as odd, since I was by myself and had only the one dog.

"But that's exactly what he was doing – backing a little setter that was dead serious about something at the base of an alder clump.

"I looked around, didn't see anybody, and stood there not quite sure what to do next. The little setter was wearing a collar and bell and looked well cared-for. I'd just about decided to flush whatever she was pointing and see if she had a tag, when a voice out of nowhere said, 'That's a picture to put on a calendar.'

"I almost jumped out of my boots, it startled me so. I turned around and there she stood, next to a popple tree, smiling.

"Lads, I will take that picture to my grave. I can't begin to tell you all the things that whirled through my mind in those few moments. I'm not even sure it was a few moments. Time simply stopped moving. I was looking into a pair of eyes the most brilliant, astonishing green I ever saw, looking at a face framed in dark, curling hair, all lit by a smile I couldn't describe if I tried for the rest of my life. And I have.

"For one completely irrational instant I imagined her on horseback, galloping over the moors of Scotland, all tumbled hair and flashing eyes, some wild, fey spirit whose name would be Dierdre. . .don't even ask where all that came from.

"Actually, I just stood there gawping. How long, I don't know, though she was still smiling when I gathered up enough of my wits to notice that she was carrying a gun.

" 'Uh. . .I. . .uh. . .your, uh, dog.' I said, or something equally inane. She kept smiling at me as if I hadn't said anything, which was basically the case. She was looking at the dogs. The little setter was still on point, and Jericho was still honoring, waving his tail slowly from side to side. 'Bird,' I said, with what I imagine was a grin you don't often see outside an asylum.

"She turned those green eyes on me again and I thought my legs would give out. You know, we have a pair of ligaments behind our knees that respond to emotion – fear, panic, relief, any really powerful feeling. Right then, mine were twanging and jittering like guitar strings. She said, 'I hate to break up such a lovely picture, but she's just a youngster and probably won't hold that point much longer.'

"She might as well have spoken in some ancient tongue for all I could do to reply anything but 'Awp.'

"She walked past Jericho and up to the little setter. A woodcock twittered up from behind the alders, and she took one step to the side, swung her gun, and dropped it neatly.

" 'Fetch, Nellie,' she said. Nellie darted out and started nosing after the bird. Jericho trotted along behind her, and I sat down on a log to see if I could get my knee-joints reconnected to my brain.

"By the time Nellie fetched the woodcock and her mistress had it stowed in her vest, I was more or less in control of most of my senses – at least enough to have a look at the rest of this enchanting woman. In those benighted days, every female younger than your grandmother was universally referred to as a 'girl.' This one was young, but she was no girl. She was tall and slender, and neither the fawn-colored shirt nor the brush pants nor the canvas vest obscured the fact of a decidedly womanly body underneath. She was carrying a 20-gauge Fox gun, wearing Bean boots and a tweed hat, and I was losing my mind.

"She walked over to me, peeling off her glove, held out her hand and said, 'I'm Caroline Fitzgerald.' So much for Dierdre. I took her hand and said what I thought was my name, adding, 'We've never met.' I'd been away a few years, but I'd never forget a stunner like her.

"If she was impressed by my grasp of the obvious, she didn't say so. Instead, she laughed, a musical sound that made my blood hiss and tingle. 'I live in St. Paul,' she said. 'We're here for the fall.'

"I had no idea whether 'we' meant a husband, a family, or the Marine Corps Band, and she was still wearing a glove on her left hand. So, with all the subtlety I could muster, I gave her another of my now-patentable stupid grins and said, 'We?'

" 'My parents and I. My father bought this land a few years ago, as a summer place.' She breathed another throaty laugh 'He thinks it's only a mite less remote than the Arctic Circle. I think it's lovely.'

"I stopped myself from saying something irretrievably dopey and said something only moderately dopey instead. What, I don't remember. I do remember stammering an apology for trespassing and received a charming assurance that I wasn't likely to be jailed for it. Jericho, who was old enough to stick around when I wasn't moving, had lain down to wait. Nellie, from the sound of her bell, was somewhere upstream, no doubt searching for more woodcock. Caroline asked if I'd care to join her.

"In those days, woodcock were not my favorite sport. I was a grouse hunter, dyed-in-the-wool. But if Caroline Fitzgerald had invited me to shoot grasshoppers or aspen leaves, I'd have accepted happily.

"Much of that afternoon is a blur to me now. It was a blur to me then, actually, except for Caroline. I couldn't take my eyes off her – which made the hunting sort of a rough go. It's a wonder I didn't break my fool neck. At least she had the good grace not to laugh out loud.

"That alder run was stiff with woodcock, and before long I began to see that Caroline Fitzgerald was remarkable for more than just her incredible eyes. It's rare enough to come across a woman who hunts and rarer still to find one who hunts as if it's the most natural thing in the world. Most of them either act as if they'd really rather be doing something else, or they go about it with a kind of bloodthirsty aggressiveness that isn't becoming even to a man.

"But not Caroline. She was neither clumsy nor hesitant nor one of the guys. She was just a woman who clearly enjoyed what she was doing.

"She had a sure, gentle touch with her dog, which, she told me, technically was her father's, though she and Nellie had sort of

55

adopted one another as favorite companions. She was a good shot, not spectacular, but good, and she handled her little Fox with the same natural grace that she did everything else.

"Once, I flushed a 'cock that flew straight toward her and dropped down right at her feet. When it flushed again a few moments later, she let it go without firing, though I knew she had an open shot. She told me later that when it realized she was standing there almost at arm's length, it fanned its tail and strutted like a little turkey cock before quitting the scene. 'Any bird with that kind of audacity deserves a break,' she said.

"It's the sort of thing that only another bird hunter understands, and it raised Caroline Fitzgerald another notch or two in my estimation – if that was possible.

"She filled her limit about three o'clock. I had two or three, and I was so befuddled by her that I wasn't shooting well at all, so I didn't mind quitting. We found a sunny log and sat talking while the dogs dozed. We told each other the sort of life-history things that people exchange at such times, though I'm afraid I did most of the talking. She had a fine way of putting you at ease .

"Finally, she thanked me for a pleasant afternoon and said that perhaps we'd meet again. I was prepared to do almost anything to make sure that happened, so I asked if she'd care to join me in a couple of coverts I knew. She said yes, and after arranging to meet at her father's house the following day, she gave me one last smile, whistled for Nellie, and struck off into the woods.

"Jericho and I turned back the way we'd come. Before we got to the car, we moved at least four more grouse, two of which were such wide-open shots that Jericho got miffed with me when I blew them both. Actually, I don't even remember pulling the triggers, and I wouldn't have bet a brass nickel on being able to hit the ground with my hat. All I could see were Caroline Fitzgerald's eyes.

"Next morning, I found the house where the elder Fitzgerald evidently intended to spend his golden years – a newly built log edifice only a bit smaller than the Minnesota Supreme Court building. Caroline's father was a railroad man with a taste for sport and more than enough ready cash to satisfy any urges he might have. He was tending to some business in Duluth that day, but I met Caroline's mother, a charming lady who owned somewhat less intense versions of Caroline's green eyes, and spent a few minutes marveling at the gymnasium-sized living room, all built of native timber and stone. The place still stands, by the way, though it's a resort now.

"I'd spent much of the previous night trying to collect myself into a state that might be a bit more poised than the uproar I'd felt the day before. Naturally, I got things off to a fine start by trying to drive off in high gear instead of low, but if she saw anything unusual about lurching and chugging down the lane, she didn't mention it. I finally got the transmission and my blood pressure under control, and we set out in earnest, Jericho and Nellie perched in the back seat like a couple of shaggy chaperones, Caroline relaxed and chatty beside me.

"She was wearing a plaid shirt that was mostly green and dark red, and the colors made her eyes fairly glow. She'd gathered her hair into a braid and pinned it up at the back; uncovered by her hat, it showed auburn highlights in the sun. It's a good thing there isn't much traffic on the back roads hereabouts, because it was all I could do to keep the car between the ditches. She seemed to have no notion at all of how extraordinarily beautiful she was. But then, I was aware of that enough for both of us.

"In the first covert, Jericho nailed a grouse not ten minutes from the car. I offered Caroline the flush, but she declined, saying that such a good omen deserved a better shot than she. Considering my track record since meeting her, I was not inclined to consider myself a candidate. Jericho probably would have laughed out loud if he hadn't been busy at the moment. Still, the red gods are not without a sense of pity, it seemed. I killed the bird stone dead with the first barrel.

"And that seemed to break the jinx. I didn't lose any appreciation for the way Caroline looked or sounded or moved, but I suddenly found myself able to function like a relatively normal adult.

"I don't think I've ever enjoyed hunting more. Once we got into the alder bottoms, we found woodcock everywhere. Something magical seemed to happen. I never was the sort of crash-ahead type who hunts as if he's going for a record in the obstacle course, but I've always liked to get right into the thick of things for grouse – still do, as you know. It's still the most satisfying way to hunt grouse, but that day I truly discovered woodcock. I discovered a degree of finesse and elegance and grace that simply isn't available from any other bird. I'd always thought of woodcock as rather bumbling, hapless little things that never seemed quite connected with a hunter. Go after a smart old grouse and you immediately strike up a relationship with it – the two of you start acting and reacting to one another as if you're the only living things on earth.

"The same thing happens with woodcock but in different ways, more subtle. Woodcock touch a gentler emotion, one that runs just as deep as any other but vibrates with a softer resonance. A grouse can be anything from a saxophone to a bugle. A woodcock is always a cello.

"Next time you're dressing birds in a mixed bag, notice that a woodcock's heart is almost as big as a grouse's, even though its body is far smaller. That ought to tell you something. I didn't think of all these lofty metaphors that morning, of course, but I certainly felt them. As I said, it was magical.

"Even the dogs seemed to feel it. Some of Nellie's sweet nature rubbed off on Jericho, and he comported himself in a more gentlemanly way than usual. At one point, Caroline asked me to help refine Nellie's back-pointing work, which already was better than you'd expect of a dog her age. She'd had some early training from a professional, but Caroline told me she wanted to do the finishing herself.

" 'Did you train Jericho?' she asked. 'He's a fine hunter.'

" 'I did, but most of what he knows has come from experience. I've always liked working with dogs but I'm no professional .'

" 'Experience has its lessons,' She said. 'And we learn them if we're lucky.' She looked at me with suddenly serious eyes. 'You're a lucky man, Tom, to be here where you really want to be and to do what pleases you. That may be worth more than you imagine.'

"There was a strangely hard edge to her voice, and it set me back. Before I could say anything, she turned away and started off after the sound of the dog bells.

"What she'd said kept running through my mind. I'd never thought of myself as lucky or unlucky, certainly not in coming back to Tamarack. That was a decision that had nothing to do with luck, so far as I could see. It was simply a choice between being a big-city attorney or a country lawyer. It seemed perfectly clear-cut to me, but my word, there's nothing like the certainty of youth. Only later did I realize she was right.

"Caroline seemed quieter, more thoughtful. We hunted on, circling back to the car, not saying much. She'd made a lunch for us, and I'd already picked the place where I wanted to go. The old Petersen place was my favorite even then, and I wanted Caroline to see it.

"You know how the Petersen looks on a fine October day. It didn't look much different then. The old house hadn't been deserted as long and naturally wasn't as weathered as it is now, and the timber on the far hill was younger and thicker. But the meadow and the stream and the beaver pond and the pine grove by the house were all there. It seemed fitting to take the most beautiful woman I'd ever met to the most beautiful place I knew.

"We unpacked the lunch basket under a big Norway pine at the end of the grove and sat where we could look down the meadow toward the stream and the woods beyond. The meadow was rank with grass still summer-green, rippling in the breeze. I don't recall what we ate – pine cones and thornapple twigs, for all I knew, or cared. To be there was as complete a measure of contentment as I could imagine. She was still subdued, but that's what the Petersen place does to you anyway. I figured she'd say what was on her mind when she felt like it.

"I turned back from looking to see where the dogs were and found her staring at me, solemn as a judge.

" 'Tom,' she said, 'there's something I want you to know about me. We don't know each other, really, but I think you'll understand what I have to say. I've never said it to anyone. It's only now, in fact, that I'm able to explain it to myself. I'm engaged to be married.'

"Well. There it was. No great surprise, I suppose, but I felt as if I'd swallowed a chunk of ice the size of my fist. At that moment, I couldn't have said a word if you'd held a gun to my head.

" 'I am betrothed to a pleasant young man with a good future,' she went on after a moment. 'The right pedigree, old St. Paul family – well-connected, I believe the phrase is. We've known each other for years, the same social circles, you know.' She enunciated the words carefully, ironically. She looked out over the meadow and turned her eyes back to me.

" 'He's a decent fellow and I do care for him. Which will make it all the more difficult to tell him that I'm not going to marry him.'

59

"I realized I was holding my breath and let it out.

" 'You have no idea what it's like to be a woman.' She had me there. I shook my head. 'In some ways, it's not much different from being a dog, except a dog doesn't know it's a piece of property to be bought, bartered, or given away. Most women don't, either, or aren't willing to admit it.' She smiled a sweet, sad smile. 'This doesn't make much sense, does it?' I shook my head again.

" 'Tom, I'm engaged to be married because that's what I'm supposed to do. At a certain point, everyone assumed Charles – that's his name – would ask me to marry him: our friends, his parents, my parents, Charles, even I. And of course if he asked, I'd accept. Well, he did, and I did, and everyone was pleased, and there were engagement parties and announcements and everything that's part of the process of transferring ownership of a woman from one man to another. I don't suppose you studied that sort of thing in law school, but it's all quite a standard process. That was ten months ago. The wedding is to be three days after Christmas. But it isn't going to be.'

"She picked up an apple and turned it over and over in her hands. 'Why not?' I asked.

" 'I don't remember exactly when I realized that I'd made all sorts of decisions without making any choices. Perhaps it was when I really began to see what was in store for me. I began to see that I was about to take up my mother's life and her mother's life and the lives of all the married women I know. My father, obviously, is quite wealthy; so are all his friends, and so are all my friends. The men spend their lives getting richer. The women are sedate and cultured, managing households and the upbringing of children, taking a genteel interest in the arts and in such worthy causes as don't threaten the world they live in.'

"She stopped for a moment, her eyes glistening. 'The more I thought about it, the worse it made me feel – unhappy and frightened and angry. I don't want to be some pampered pet on a velvet rope, living a serene and useless life.

" 'Spending the fall here was my idea. I could've stayed in St. Paul. But I insisted on coming, to get away and think. A week after we got here I took off the ring Charles gave me. I told my mother it was because I didn't want to lose it outdoors. Tonight, I'll tell her the real reason. They'll both be quite upset, partly because they truly want me to be happy, but partly, too, because it's going to be very awkward for them to have a daughter who'd do such a scandalous thing as break an engagement. It's going to ruin their round of holiday parties this year. But that will have to be as it will be.'

"She shot me a suddenly mischievous look and said, 'Part of this is your doing, you know.' I started to apologize, but she stopped me. 'Not what you think. Don't you see, Tom? You did what I want so much to do. You set your life on a course of your own choosing. You followed your heart instead of surrendering to a life that would, in time, give you everything you wanted except happiness. And your heart led you back here. And you know, you were right.'

"I said, 'Caroline, everything you say is true. I can't pretend that I really know how you feel about. . . all this. You said so yourself: I have no idea what it's like to be a woman. In fact, I never even *thought* of it until now. But I do know what it is to give up the certainty of comfort for the hope of being truly happy. It was the right choice for me, and I wish no less for you.'

"She leaned over and kissed me on the cheek, said 'Thank you,' and started gathering up the remains of our lunch. 'Show me the rest of this beautiful place. I need to stretch my legs.'

"At the moment, I felt a need to stretch my head. My mind was fairly tumbling with all she'd said, things as alien to my experience as the far side of China, yet things so clearly real that it was impossible not to recognize them.

"Guessing that she'd like some time to herself, I suggested we split up to hunt the stream coverts. I'd cross over above the beaver pond and take the far side, and she could go through the alders below the house. We'd meet below the beaver dam where it's easy to cross the stream and then go back through the woods together. She agreed. We put the lunch basket in the car and set off.

"The rain had sent the creek running full, and I had to go way upstream to find a crossing. Once over, I ambled along, not really hunting, my mind too full of Caroline to pay much attention. I walked right up on Jericho on point and flushed the bird before I even knew he was there. He gave me a disgusted look and went on downstream. I heard one shot from Caroline's direction and figured she'd found a bird.

"I was about a hundred yards above the beaver dam when I heard a dog start shrieking. It was coming from about where Caroline should have been by then, and the first thing I thought was that Nellie had run into a porcupine. I beat through the brush as fast as I could, thinking to wade the stream below the dam, cursing porcupines and bad luck in general. When I got free of the brush at the end of the dam, what I saw stopped me cold.

"It wasn't Nellie screaming. It was Jericho. And there wasn't any porky. The damn fool had run out onto the beaver dam; I guess he'd decided to go with somebody who was really hunting. In those days, the dam wasn't quite as big as it is now, but it was big enough to stop a lot of water. The rain had raised the pond to spill-over, and the center of the dam was starting to wash out. Water was pouring through a three- or four-foot gap, and Jericho had tried to jump across or swim around it or something. In any case, he got his leg fast in the sticks, and he was caught. It was all he could do to keep his head out of the water, and every time he slacked off, the current pulled him under. He was a big dog, strong as a moose, but he couldn't hold out forever.

"Then I saw Caroline.

"She was on the dam, heading toward Jericho and having a hard time keeping her feet. You know what trying to walk on a beaver dam is like, even when you're going slow. I was afraid she'd get her own foot caught. I had no notion whether she could swim. I had visions of her disappearing under the water and never coming up, and I felt such a stab of fear that I could scarcely catch my breath. I shouted to her, but she didn't seem to hear, so I started shucking off my vest.

"Just as I started out on the dam myself, she got to the middle, grabbed hold of a branch, and leaned out to Jericho. He was about done in. She caught his collar and gave a heave that would've taxed the strength of any man. And she pulled him free.

"Then everything changed to slow-motion. She lost her grip and hit the water, and the two of them tumbled through the gap and out of sight.

"For about three seconds, I'm sure my heart stopped dead still. The downstream side was mostly marsh, but there was a fair-sized pool in the main channel, and the water spilling through had turned it into a cauldron. I was sure I'd find them both dead.

"I scrambled down the back side of the dam and started floundering through the mud and rushes, sinking in to my knees. It was like trying to swim through honey. I couldn't see or hear anything except rushing water and my own slogging around. My lungs felt like I was breathing fire. It seemed forever before I got to a hummock, climbed onto it, and stood up.

"I saw nothing but rushes and marsh grass and cattails. If I'd had the breath, I'd have screamed in sheer anguish. Then I caught a flash of white through the grass and saw Jericho about twenty yards away, hauling himself up onto a hummock of his own. I shouted Caroline's name, and then again. When I heard her shout back, 'Over here,' my knees went so watery that I almost went head-first into the mud.

"I got to her just in time to give her a hand out of the stream. She was bedraggled as a drowned cat, her hat gone, hair undone and plastered to her face. But she was smiling, her green eyes flashing. I felt some vital connection in me break and reform. I hugged her until she gasped for breath.

" 'I didn't know if you could swim,' I said after a moment.

"She pushed back her wet hair and grinned. 'Even children of the idle rich manage to learn a few useful skills, you know. Where's Jericho?'

"I whistled and heard his bell, whistled again to give him the direction, and presently we could see the rushes waving as he made his way to us, limping and as wet as Caroline but otherwise undamaged. The three of us slogged our way out of the marsh, gathered up Caroline's gun and vest, and walked to the meadow. Nellie, who had watched it all from the edge of the woods, lay down next to Caroline, and for a long time no one said anything.

"She lay in the grass, eyes closed, breast rising and falling as her body absorbed its adrenaline. I wanted to hold her and say things that probably would have embarrassed us both a day later. Instead, I told her to wait there and waded back through the marsh – I wasn't likely to get any wetter or muddier no matter what I did – and collected my own gun and vest.

"When I got back, she was kneeling beside Jericho, gently flexing his leg and making soft sounds to him.

" 'Nothing's broken, as far as I can see,' she said, 'but he's probably going to be gimpy for a few days.'

" 'He'll have plenty of company,' I said. 'Let's get you home to dry out.'

" 'Tom, wait. Sit down here a minute.' I did, 'This has been quite a day, all in all, and in an odd sort of way, I think I owe you my life.' She held up her hand. 'No, don't say anything. I didn't come anywhere near drowning, though I could have. But that's not what I mean. Just being with you and being able to tell you all the things I've told you has been like a reprieve, a freedom I'd almost given up hoping for. You're a sweet man, Tom, and I'm very fond of you.

" 'If this were a fine romantic story instead of real life, we'd probably have sworn undying love right there in the mud when you pulled me out. We were both frightened enough. But we've also lived enough to know that's not how it happens– not that the feelings wouldn't have been real; they just wouldn't have been the feelings we thought they were. I've already made one nearly awful mistake, and I'd be foolish not to learn from it.'

" 'This all sounds like good-bye,' I said.

"She smiled. 'No, Tom, it isn't good-bye at all. It's only to say that whatever happens from now on will be for the right reasons – or at least the best reasons I can find. I'll have to go back to the Cities for a while, to face some unfinished business, but I won't be gone long. And then I'm coming back here. I think there's a lot of lovely territory to explore here. I'd like to know it all better.' "

The fire was only a mound of glowing embers where a few flickers of flame licked up. Mac and Scotty were sunk deep into their chairs. The dogs sprawled snoring on the hearth rug. A faint night wind muttered in the pines beyond the windows.

Tom drained his glass.

"Lord, lads, you should've muzzled me an hour ago. I must get myself home, though Caroline will be long asleep. Let's meet in the village for breakfast. I think tomorrow might be a good day to see if there are any woodcock at the Petersen place ."

THE LORD OF
Lackawaxen Creek

BY ZANE GREY

Zane Grey (1872-1939) needs no introduction to
American readers. His *Riders of the Purple Sage* is one of
the most popular books ever written. Grey's best-selling
novels, however, were but one part of this dentist-turned-
angler; in essence, they were only a means to an end.
Fishing was his true obsession. Here, Grey gives us a firm
grip on both his powers of description and what the
angler's quest meant to his life.

Winding among the Blue Hills of Pennsylvania there is a
swift amber stream that the Indians named Lack-a-wax-en.
The literal translation no one seems to know, but it must
mean, in mystical and imaginative Delaware, "the brown water
that turns and whispers and tumbles." It is a little river hidden
away under gray cliffs and hills black with ragged pines. It is full
of mossy stones and rapid ripples.

All its tributaries, dashing white-sheeted over ferny cliffs, wine-brown where the whirling pools suck the stain from the hemlock root, harbor the speckled trout. Wise in their generation, the black and red-spotted little beauties keep to their brooks; for, farther down, below the rush and fall, a newcomer is lord of the stream. He is an archenemy, a scorner of beauty and blood, the wolf-jawed, red-eyed, bronze-backed black bass.

A mile or more from its mouth the Lackawaxen leaves the shelter of the hills and seeks the open sunlight and slows down to widen into long lanes that glide reluctantly over the few last restraining barriers to the Delaware. In a curve between two of these level lanes, there is a place where barefoot boys wade and fish for chubs and bask on the big boulders like turtles. It is a famous hole of chubs and bright-sided shiners and sunfish. And, perhaps because it is so known, and so shallow, so open to the sky, few fishermen ever learned that in its secret stony caverns hid a great golden-bronze treasure of a bass.

In vain had many a flimsy feathered hook been flung over his lair by fly casters and whisked gracefully across the gliding surface of his pool. In vain had many a shiny spoon and pearly minnow reflected sun glints through the watery windows of his home. In vain had many a hellgrammite and frog and grasshopper been dropped in front of his broad nose.

Chance plays the star part in a fisherman's luck. One still, cloudy day, when the pool glanced dark under a leaden sky, I saw a wave that reminded me of the wake of a rolling tarpon; then followed an angry swirl, the skitter of a frantically leaping chub, and a splash that ended with a sound like the deep chung of water sharply turned by an oar.

Big bass choose strange hiding places. They should be looked for in just such holes and rifts and shallows as will cover their backs. But to corral a six-pounder in the boys' swimming hole was a circumstance to temper a fisherman's vanity with experience.

Thrillingly conscious of the possibilities of this pool, I studied it thoughtfully. It was a wide, shallow bend in the stream, with dark channels between submerged rocks, suggestive of underlying shelves. It had a current, too, not noticeable at first glance. And this pool looked at long and carefully, colored by the certainty of its guardian, took on an aspect most alluring to an angler's spirit.

66

It had changed from a pond girt by stony banks, to a foam-flecked running stream, clear, yet hiding its secrets, shallow, yet full of labyrinthine watercourses. It presented problems which, difficult as they were, faded in a breath before a fisherman's optimism.

I tested my leader, changed the small hook for a large one, and selecting a white shiner fully six inches long, I lightly hooked it through the side of the upper lip. A sensation never outgrown since boyhood, a familiar mingling of strange fear and joyous anticipation, made me stoop low and tread the slippery stones as if I were a stalking Indian. I knew that a glimpse of me or a faint jar vibrating under the water, or an unnatural ripple on its surface, would be fatal to my enterprise.

I swung the lively minnow and instinctively dropped it with a splash over a dark space between two yellow sunken stones. Out of the amber depths started a broad bar of bronze, rose and flashed into gold. A little dimpling eddying circle, most fascinating of all watery forms, appeared round where the minnow had sunk. The golden moving flash went down and vanished in the greenish gloom like a tiger stealing into a jungle. The line trembled, slowly swept out and straightened. How fraught that instant with a wild yet waiting suspense, with a thrill potent and blissful!

Did the fisherman ever live who could wait in such a moment? My arms twitched involuntarily. Then I struck hard, but not half hard enough. The bass leaped out of a flying splash, shook himself in a tussle plainly audible, and slung the hook back at me like a bullet.

In such moments one never sees the fish distinctly; excitement deranges the vision, and the picture, though impressive, is dim and dreamlike. But a blind man would have known this bass to be enormous, for when he fell he cut the water as a heavy stone.

The best of fishing is that a mild philosophy attends even the greatest misfortunes. It is a delusion peculiar to fishermen, and I went on my way upstream, cheerfully, as one who minded not at all an incident of angling practice; spiritedly, as one who had seen many a big bass go by the board. I found myself thinking about my two brothers, Cedar and Reddy for short, both anglers of long standing and some reputation. It was a sore point with me and a stock subject for endless disputes that they could never appreciate

67

my superiority as a fisherman. Brothers are singularly prone to such points of view. So when I thought of them I felt the incipient stirring of a mighty plot. It occurred to me that the iron-mouthed old bass, impregnable of jaw as well as of stronghold, might be made to serve a turn. And all the afternoon the thing grew and grew in my mind.

Luck otherwise favored me, and I took home a fair string of fish. I remarked to my brothers that the conditions for fishing the stream were favorable. Thereafter morning on morning my eyes sought the heavens, appealing for a cloudy day. At last one came, and I invited Reddy to go with me. With childish pleasure that would have caused weakness in any but an unscrupulous villain, he eagerly accepted. He looked over a great assortment of tackle, and finally selected a five-ounce Leonard bait rod carrying a light reel and fine line. When I thought of what would happen if Reddy hooked that powerful bass, an unholy glee fastened upon my soul.

We never started out that way together, swinging rods and pails, but old associations were awakened. We called up the time when we had left the imprints of bare feet on the country roads; we lived over many a boyhood adventure by a running stream. And at last we wound up on the never threadbare question as to the merit and use of tackle.

"I always claimed," said Reddy, "that a fisherman should choose tackle for a day's work after the fashion of a hunter in choosing his gun. A hunter knows what kind of game he's after, and takes a small or large caliber accordingly. Of course a fisherman has more rods than there are calibers of guns, but the rule holds. Now today I have brought this light rod and thin line because I don't need weight. I don't see why you've brought that heavy rod. Even a two-pound bass would be a great surprise up this stream."

"You're right," I replied, "but I sort of lean to possibilities. Besides I'm fond of this rod. You know I've caught a half dozen bass of from five to six pounds with it. I wonder what you would do if you hooked a big one on your delicate rod."

"Do?" exclaimed my brother. "I'd have a fit! I might handle a big bass in deep water with this outfit, but here in this shallow stream with its rocks and holes I couldn't. And that is the reason so few big bass are taken from the Delaware. We know they are there, great lusty fellows! Every day in season we hear some tale of woe from some fisherman. 'Hooked a big one – broke this – broke that – got under a stone.' That's why no five- or six-pound bass are taken from shallow, swift, rock-bedded streams on light tackle."

When we reached the pool I sat down and began to fumble with my leader. How generously I let Reddy have the first cast! My iniquity carried me to the extreme of bidding him steal softly and stoop low. I saw a fat chub swinging in the air; I saw it alight to disappear in a churning commotion of the water, and I heard Reddy's startled, "Gee!"

Hard upon his exclamation followed action of striking swiftness. A shrieking reel, willow wand of a rod wavering like a buggy whip in the wind, curving splashes round a foam-lashed swell, a crack of dry wood, a sound as of a banjo string snapping, a sharp splash, then a heavy sullen souse; these, with Reddy standing voiceless, eyes glaring on the broken rod and limp trailing line, were the essentials of the tragedy.

Somehow the joke did not ring true when Reddy waded ashore calm and self-contained, with only his burning eyes to show how deeply he felt. What he said to me in a quiet voice must not, owing to family pride, go on record. It most assuredly would not be an addition to the fish literature of the day.

But he never mentioned the incident to Cedar, which omission laid the way open for my further machinations. I realized that I should have tried Cedar first. He was one of those white-duck-pants-on-a-dry-rock sort of a fisherman, anyway. And in due time I had him wading out toward the center of that pool.

I always experienced a painful sensation while watching Cedar cast. One moment he resembled Ajax defying the lightning and the next he looked like the fellow who stood on a monument, smiling at grief. Cedar's execution was wonderful. I have seen him cast a frog a mile—but the frog had left the hook. It was remarkable to see him catch his hat, and terrifying to hear the language he used at such an ordinary angling event. It was not safe to be in his vicinity, but if this was unavoidable, the better course was to face him; because if you turned your back an instant, his flying hook would have a fiendish affinity for your trousers, and it was not beyond his powers to swing you kicking out over the stream. All of which, considering the frailties of human nature and of fishermen, could be forgiven; he had, however, one great fault impossible to overlook, and it was that he made more noise than a playful hippopotamus.

I hoped, despite all these things, that the big bass would rise to the occasion. He did rise. He must have recognized the situation of his life. He spread the waters of his shallow pool and accommodatingly hooked himself.

Cedar's next graceful move was to fall off the slippery stone on which he had been standing and to go out of sight. His hat floated downstream; the arched tip of his rod came up, then his arm, and his dripping shoulders and body. He yelled like a savage and pulled on the fish hard enough to turn a tuna in the air. The big bass leaped three times, made a long shoot with his black dorsal fin showing, and then, with a lunge, headed for some place remote from there. Cedar plowed after him, sending the water in sheets, and then he slipped, wildly swung his arms, and fell again.

I was sinking to the ground, owing to unutterable and overpowering sensations of joy, when a yell and a commotion in the bushes heralded the appearance of Reddy.

"Hang on, Cedar! Hang on!" he cried, and began an Indian war dance.

The few succeeding moments were somewhat blurred because of my excess of emotion. When I returned to consciousness, Cedar was wading out with a hookless leader, a bloody shin, and a disposition utterly and irretrievably ruined.

"Put a job on me!" he roared.

Thereafter during the summer each of us made solitary and sneaking expeditions, bent on the capture of the lord of the Lackawaxen. And somehow each would return to find the other two derisively speculative as to what caused his clouded brow. Leader on leader went to grace the rocks of the old bronze warrior's home. At length Cedar and Reddy gave up, leaving the pool to me. I fed more than one choice shiner to the bass and more than once he sprang into the air to return my hook.

Summer and autumn passed; winter came to lock the Lackawaxen in icy fetters; I fished under Southern skies where lagoons and moss-shaded waters teemed with great and gamy fish, but I never forgot him. I knew that when the season rolled around, when a June sun warmed the cold spring-fed Lackawaxen, he would be waiting for me.

Who was it spoke of the fleeting of time? Obviously he had never waited for the opening of the fishing season. At last the tedious time, like the water, flowed by. But then I found I had another long wait. Brilliant June days without a cloud were a joy to live, but worthless for fishing. Through all that beautiful month I plodded up to the pool, only to be unrewarded. Doubt began to assail me. Might not the ice, during the spring break-up, have scared him from the shallow hole? No. I felt that not even a rolling glacier could have moved him from his subterranean home.

Often as I reached the pool I saw fishermen wading down the stream, and on these occasions I sat on the bank and lazily waited for the intruders to pass on. Once, the first time I saw them, I had an agonizing fear that one of the yellow-helmeted, khaki-coated anglers would hook my bass. The fear, of course, was groundless. The idea of that grand fish rising to a feathery imitation of a bug or a lank dead bait had nothing in my experience to warrant its consideration. Small, lively bass, full of play, fond of chasing their golden shadows, and belligerent and hungry, were ready to fight and eat whatever swam into their ken. But a six-pound bass, slow to reach such weight in swift-running water, was old and wise and full of years. He did not feed often, and when he did he wanted a live fish big enough for a good mouthful. So, with these facts to soothe me I rested my fears, and got to look humorously at the invasions of the summer-hotel fishers.

They came wading, slipping, splashing downstream, blowing like porpoises, slapping at the water with all kinds of artificial and dead bait. And they called to me in a humor inspired by my fishing garb and the rustic environment:

"Hey, Rube! Ketchin' any?"

I said the suckers were bitin' right pert.

"What'd'you call this stream?"

I replied, giving the Indian name.

"Lack-a-what? Can't you whistle it? Lack-awhacken? You mean Lack-afishin'."

"Lack-arotten," joined in another. "Do you live here?" questioned a third.

I said yes.

"Why don't you move?" Whereupon they all laughed and pursued the noisy tenor of their way downstream, pitching their baits around.

"Say, fellows," I shouted after them, "are you training for the casting tournament in Madison Square Garden or do you think you're playing lacrosse? "

The laugh that came back proved the joke on them, and that it would be remembered as part of the glorious time they were having.

July brought the misty, dark, lowering days. Not only did I find the old king at home on these days, but just as contemptuous of hooks and leaders as he had been the summer before. About the middle of the month he stopped giving me paralysis of the heart; that is to say, he quit rising to my tempting chums and shiners. So I left him alone to rest, to rust out hooks and grow less suspicious.

By the time August came, the desire to call on him again was well-nigh irresistible. But I waited, and fished the Delaware, and still waited. I would get him when the harvest moon was full. Like all the old mossbacked denizens of the shady holes, he would come out then for a last range over the feeding shoals. At length a morning broke humid and warm, almost dark as twilight, with little gusts of fine rain. Of all days this was the day! I chose a stiff rod, a heavy silk line, a stout brown leader, and a large hook. From my bait box I took two five-inch red catfish, the little "stone-rollers" of the Delaware, and several long shiners. Thus equipped, I sallied forth.

The walk up the towpath, along the canal with its rushes and sedges, across the meadows white with late-blooming daisies, lost nothing because of its familiarity. When I reached the pool I saw in the low water near shore several small bass scouting among the schools of minnows. I did not want these pugnacious fellows to kill my bait, so, procuring a hellgrammite from under a stone, I put it on my hook and promptly caught two of them, and gave the other a scare he would not soon forget.

I decided to try the bass with one of his favorite shiners. With this trailing in the water I silently waded out, making not so much as a ripple. The old familiar oppression weighed on my breast; the old throbbing boyish excitement tingled through my blood. I made a long cast and dropped the shiner lightly. He went under and then came up to swim about on the surface. This was a sign that made my heart leap. Then the water bulged, and a black bar shot across the middle of the long shiner. He went down out of sight, the last gleams of his divided brightness fading slowly. I did not need to see the little shower of silver scales floating up to know that the black bar had been the rounded nose of the old bass and that he had taken the shiner across the middle. I struck hard, and my hook came whistling at me. I had scored a clean miss.

I waded ashore very carefully, sat down on a stone by my bait pail, and meditated. Would he rise again? I had never known him to do so twice in one day. But then there had never been occasion. I thought of the "stone-rollers" and thrilled with certainty. Whatever he might resist, he could not resist one of those little red catfish. Long ago, when he was only a three- or four-pounder, roaming the deep eddies and swift rapids of the Delaware, before he had isolated himself to a peaceful old age in this quiet pool, he must have poked his nose under many a stone, with red eyes keen for one of those dainty morsels.

My excitation thrilled itself out to the calm assurance of the experienced fisherman. I firmly fastened on one of the catfish and stole out into the pool. I waded farther than ever before; I was careful but confident. Then I saw the two flat rocks dimly shining. The water was dark as it rippled by, gurgling softly; it gleamed with lengthening shadows and glints of amber.

I swung the catfish. A dull flash of sunshine seemed to come up to meet him. The water swirled and broke with a splash. The broad black head of the bass just skimmed the surface; his jaws opened wide to take in the bait; he turned and flapped a huge spread tail on the water.

Then I struck with all the power the tackle would stand. I felt the hook catch solidly as if in a sunken log. Swift as flashing light the bass leaped. The drops of water hissed and the leader whizzed. But the hook held. I let out one exultant yell. He did not leap again. He dashed to the right, then the left, in bursts of surprising speed. I had hardly warmed to the work when he settled down and made for the dark channel between the yellow rocks. My triumph was to be short-lived. Where was the beautiful spectacular surface fight I expected of him? Cunning old monarch! He laid his great weight dead on the line and lunged for his sunken throne. I held him with a grim surety of the impossibility of stopping him. How I longed for deep, open water! The rod bent, the line strained and stretched. I removed my thumb and the reel sang one short shrill song. Then the bass was as still

73

as the rock under which he had gone.

I had never dislodged a big bass from under a stone, and I saw herein further defeat; but I persevered, wading to different angles, and working all the tricks of the trade. I could not drag the fish out, nor pull the hook loose. I sat down on a stone and patiently waited for a long time, hoping he would come out on his own accord.

As a final resort I waded out. The water rose to my waist, then to my shoulders, my chin, and all but covered my raised face. When I reached the stone under which he had planted himself, I stood in water about four feet deep. I saw my leader, and tugged upon it, and kicked under the stone, all to no good.

Then I calculated I had a chance to dislodge him if I could get my arm under the shelf. So I went, hat, rod, and all. The current was just swift enough to lift my feet, making my task most difficult. At the third trial I got my hand on a sharp corner of stone and held fast. I ran my right hand along the leader, under the projecting slab of rock, till I touched the bass. I tried to get hold of him, but had to rise for air.

I dove again. The space was narrow, so narrow that I wondered how so large a fish could have gotten there. He had gone under sidewise, turned, and wedged his dorsal fin, fixing himself as solidly as the rock itself. I pulled frantically till I feared I would break the leader.

When I floundered up to breathe again, the thought occurred to me that I could rip him with my knife and, by taking the life out of him, loosen the powerful fin so he could be dragged out. Still, much as I wanted him, I could not do that. I resolved to make one more fair attempt. In a quick determined plunge I secured a more favorable hold for my left hand and reached under with my right. I felt his whole long length and I could not force a finger behind him anywhere. The gill toward me was shut tight like a trap door. But I got a thumb and forefinger fastened to his lip. I tugged till a severe cramp numbed my hand; I saw red and my head whirled; a noise roared in my ears. I stayed until one more second would have made me a drowning man, then rose gasping and choking.

I broke off the leader close to the stone and waded ashore. I looked back at the pool, faintly circled by widening ripples. What a great hole and what a grand fish! I was glad I did not get him and knew I would never again disturb his peace.

So I took my rod and pail and the two little bass, and brushed the meadow daisies, and threaded the familiar green-lined towpath toward home.

Reprinted by permission of Dr. Loren Grey, Woodland Hills, California.

The Shotgun

BY BUD TEMPLE

There is something about a fine shotgun that can lay
claim to a man's soul. The perfect blending of warm
wood and cold steel, the delicate balance of a carefully
crafted firearm; they captivate the hunter when afield
and console him during the long days when the season
is closed. Here is a poignant piece by Bud Temple that
first appeared in the pages of *Gray's Sporting Journal*
more than a decade ago. It proves that grand sporting
stories of the sort we associate with yesteryear
know no generational bounds.

M r. Thornley was a fellow member of a fraternal organiza-
tion to which I belong. He was considerably older than I,
and it was a long time before I got to know him, let
alone to realize that he was very much interested in the out-of-
doors, that he was, in fact, an excellent river fisherman, and, as I
found out later, an extremely knowledgeable and competent
grouse hunter.

Mr. Thornley was a professional gambler. I can see him now sitting night after night at what club members called "the big table." Green eyes alert as a hunting cat's while his memory catalogued each card exposed, and his mind made the computations.

Mr. Thornley was not a flamboyant character. His conservative suits had the narrow lapels. The word I'll use to describe him is reserved. Not cold, not aloof, certainly not haughty. He was simply a quietly reserved, very private person, whom everyone addressed as Mr. Thornley.

When conditions were right, he fished the Wabash River, sometimes for channel cat, but mostly for smallmouth bass. There was a pleasant path on the north bank and he knew every riffle and pool the stream held from the Wabash Street bridge east five miles to Steel's Bend.

My son and I would frequently see Mr. Thornley when I took the child for walks along the river so that he could learn to identify some of the more common trees, to watch the birds and just to wade and play.

When we met the older man, we always stopped to inquire about the fishing.

One hot day we were talking to him from a spot where the path topped a steep bank about 20 feet above the water's edge. Suddenly (acting on some childish impulse) the youngster jumped from the trail onto the face of the gravel bank and half-ran half-slid down to the river.

When he got stopped in front of the fisherman, he had torn his jeans, his curly hair was full of sand, but he was smiling a shy smile. Almost losing his nerve, he hesitated a moment, then suddenly thrust out a boyish hand offering a stick of chewing gum, which Mr. Thornley accepted with grave thanks.

In a town like Wabash a man with no church affiliations, who maintained an apartment over a store building, and (worse than that) who gambled for a living, was simply not recognized by the socially prominent element. Mr. Thornley was quite aware of the peck system. He made no attempt to buck the social structure, but I'm sure he was pleased when my wife, at my suggestion, invited him to join us for Christmas dinner.

Christmas afternoon I picked Mr. Thornley up a little early, and the two of us were in our kitchen, drinking eggnog. I noticed him glancing at the gun rack beside the fireplace, and to make conversation, I opened the door, reached in and handed him a fine over-and-under that I used for trap shooting.

He took the gun casually, broke it to check the firing chambers, glanced at the engraving and snapped to attention. Carrying the gun over to the window, he stood there staring at the artwork with disbelief on his face.

"This is absolutely amazing," he said finally. "You see I once owned a truly fine gun. My father left it to me. I can't really remember my father, but they said he always went first class. That shotgun was the only thing he left me that I didn't gamble away. It was a side-by-side double, and for the most part the engraving was almost identical to this.

"An old fox in front of a pup fox on one side, and an old-style setter pointing, same low tail, same puppy sitting back watching, on the other side. There are more of these birds on your gun, but they sure look like the ones on mine. They're not pheasants. I never knew what they were. They look alive.

"Both guns are really in a class by themselves, but I doubt if they were made by the same man. I see this over-and-under was made in Suhl, Germany. It's no doubt much older than mine. Mine was built in England.

"Over the years guns get moved around. Perhaps this gun went through England on its way to the U.S. Someone probably liked the trim and duplicated it.

"Well anyway, mine is gone now. Some thief stole it out of the trunk of my car two years ago when I was at a big skeet shoot south of Cleveland. I tried every way to get it back. I advertised, offered a sizable (no questions asked) reward, but I never heard a thing. I knew some contacts and had them get in touch with all the big fences in that part of the country. Nothing turned up.

"It probably won't do me one bit of good, but I will be looking for that gun until the day I die."

Dinner was an easy, relaxed interlude. We talked about fishing, had a couple more drinks and a country-style, help-yourself-and-pass-it meal. When it was time to go, Mr. Thornley paid the food the usual compliments and thanked us again for the invitation. He had picked up his hat to leave, but he paused at the corner of the room and looked around. "That fine little boy," he said softly, "that Christmas tree. It's like a picture."

Mr. Thornley had eaten the holiday dinner with us for two years in a row. Certainly we had become much better acquainted, yet it was not until the September following his second visit that he asked me to hunt ruffed grouse with him.

I had returned from a business trip and stopped at the club bar when he spoke to me.

"Bud, could you spare a minute or two?" he asked with that quiet dignity that was so much a part of him. I nodded, and we walked into the reading room.

"Have you ever hunted ruffed grouse?" he asked.

"No," I answered.

"I think you would enjoy it. Away back in the Twenties some boys from Detroit and I got a hold on six hundred and forty acres near Baldwin, Michigan. We were going to hunt deer. I lost interest in deer hunting. Started hunting ruffed grouse instead." (He always said "ruffed grouse," never "grouse," never "pats"). "Later we had to sell out; times were bad. We sold to a private club, but I pulled a shenanigan and simply traded my interest for a life membership in the lodge. A life estate, the attorney called it. The club owns the land but I can use the facilities and hunt there as long as I live and I can take one guest with me if I want to. I simply have to notify them when I will be on the property. I know dozens of places to hunt in Lake County. We won't just stay on club property. We won't need a guide either. If you will drive your car, I will furnish the gas and oil. If you're interested I'll notify the club when to expect us."

We set the date for October 24th.

It was fun driving north with Mr. Thornley and, except for one little incident, he seemed an entirely different, much more relaxed person than the individual I knew in Wabash.

We talked about this and that and had gotten around to the subject of dogs. Mr. Thornley made the observation that a dog that could handle ruffed grouse was worth its weight in gold, but that in his opinion no dog at all was preferable to a poor one.

"A friend of mine used to have a little spayed setter gyp," he said; "she was just something else, moved real fast, never got far away; and if you even ticked a bird, she would find it. That was a long time ago; before I left Detroit," he added.

79

"How did you ever happen to leave Detroit and come to a small town?" I asked innocently.

He turned his head in my direction. Those green eyes stared at me for a moment. He knew his conversation had provoked my question. He would not ignore it.

"Purple Gang," he said flatly.

The subject was closed.

For a young man who had built a rather solid reputation as a quail hunter, my initial efforts at grouse shooting left a lot to be desired.

We had hunted for several hours. Mr. Thornley had shot once and killed one bird. I had shot twice on three different occasions, six times in all, and had never touched a feather.

Then to add to my embarrassment, we were crossing an oak-covered flat when a bird jumped way out and Mr. Thornley scored again.

My face was a little red. After all I was the young man. I was the one everybody had commented on as being such a fast shot. I felt a twinge of jealously. My back must have been a little straight because Mr. Thornley tucked his bird in his coat and said, "Why don't we turn and work down that hill. We can go to the car, eat a sandwich and rest up a bit."

It sure seemed like a good idea to me and, as it worked out, it was a very lucky break.

Just as we reached the edge of the hill so that we could see down the steep bank we both saw a grouse hop up from the ground and perch in a small bushy tree about halfway down the slope.

Mr. Thornley looked at me intently. "You could pick him off from here," he said "be real good eating. No shot in the breast."

Thank heavens I had gotten my head screwed back on correctly. Without taking my eyes off the bird I said, "Look, if I just wanted meat I'd go to the store and buy a chicken."

His voice softened. "Shoot low," he said quickly. "I'll flush him. When he powerdives down that hill – remember – hold under him."

I followed his instructions and at the sound of the shot I was thrilled to see my first grouse fold.

We walked down the slope to pick up the trophy, and I stood there a moment holding it. Marveling at the bird. Marveling at the very miracle of anyone intercepting a flying grouse with a string of shot.

Mr. Thornley was watching me. "You'll learn to love this sport," I heard him saying.

I thought to myself, "What a pleasant disposition he has." But before our four-day shoot ended, I would see a different side of his character.

We had hunted many places in the Baldwin area. National forest, abandoned farms, private land – with and without permission – and, of course, the 640 acres to which Mr. Thornley retained legal shooting rights for himself and a guest.

On this particular afternoon, he had called the lodge to advise the caretakers we would be on his old property. Evidently some club member was not aware of his privileges. We were hunting where we had every legal right to be, moving a bird now and then, and getting an occasional shot. We had worked our way to within a couple hundred yards of the lodge property and had turned to leave when I flushed a bird and killed it.

At the sound of the shot someone shouted at us to get the hell out. Screaming obscenities and threats, the man hurried toward us.

We paused to analyze the situation and, as so frequently happens, when we stopped another bird jumped, and we both shot. The sound provoked a new outburst. "I've got you located now," he screamed and arched an empty bottle off the hill in our direction.

I started to move toward the public road but my companion took hold of my arm. "Shoot again," he said. "Toll him in."

I did as he told me, but when I turned and looked at Mr. Thornley's face, I was amazed at what I saw, at the malice, at his wicked half-smile of anticipation. The years in Detroit had left their mark. I sensed what he had in mind and knew the gun would get in his way. I reached over and took it from him.

When the club member crashed through the tag alders, my friend was standing with his back turned, watching him over his shoulder. The man grabbed Mr. Thornley by the shoulder to swing him around, but Mr. Thornley was already turning. Open handed, with head-jarring force, he slapped the man on the left side of the face. The splat of the blow was so solid it was sickening.

Then, still with merciless power, Mr. Thornley hit him across the lips with the heel of his palm.

Hand covering his bloody mouth, the fellow staggered over to a tree stump and sat down. But Mr. Thornley contemptuously placed his boot against his chest, straightened out his knee and sent him sprawling.

81

We stood there for a moment listening to him blubber. Then taking his gun from me, Mr. Thornley said, "Let's go find some birds."

These hunts became an annual event. But other than the Christmas dinners and the October interlude, I really did not see much of my friend.

Once I asked him where he had been keeping himself the last few weekends. He said he had been following the skeet shoots. "Are you doing any good?" I asked.

"I'm not shooting," he replied. "I play a little poker if they get a game started. But mostly I'm watching for that shotgun. You don't see too many side-by-sides at the skeet shoots these days, let alone one like I lost."

The two of us started spending a lot more time in Michigan, and each trip I learned to appreciate more and more what has been called "the mystique of grouse hunting," that unexplainable sweep of spirit that can possess a hunter as he walks inside those autumn tapestries, those sacred coverts where ruffed grouse dwell.

Mr. Thornley also exposed me to the practical aspects of our avocation.

"There's a lot of feed here," he would say as he pointed out winterberry, aspen, sumac and other staples in the grouse's diet. Or he might suggest we hit a certain thorn-apple patch at late evening. "This time of year birds like to fill up on those little apples just before roosting. Watch it now; if we jump any here, they'll break for that cedar swamp."

During the heat of the day he would seek out cooler places to work. "These birds enjoy comfort as much as you do," he would tell me. "They like wet places too; they walk around on those little hummocks in the swamps. It pays to work them."

He was a master at the pause-and-wait game of nerves you play to make a grouse stampede. I never knew him to hurry when working cover.

His peripheral vision, his hearing, and his shooting reflexes were superb. Taking all shots as they came, I am sure he averaged close to three out of four. If a man tells you he can consistently do better than this when hunting grouse, watch him because he will also lie about other things.

He once told me, "Bud, when you shoot ruffed grouse, do it right now, don't hesitate. When you hear a bird flush, reflex action

82

should start you throwing your gun. Lay the barrel on him. Ride it just an instant, and keep the gun moving as you touch off the shot. If you have a prayer of a chance, take it, don't wait for a better look."

When Mr. Thornley missed a bird he never seemed to get upset. I remember one incident in particular. We had driven back to an old slashing and parked beside a dim road that meandered on through the popple trees. My friend had loaded his gun and was standing by the car when a bird flushed and flew straight down the trace. You could not have asked for an easier shot. He took his time, fired twice, and missed both times. Turning to me and smiling, he said, "I always wanted a shot like that."

Later in the evening I kidded him about this episode.

"Hey, you don't know how I miss my old double barrel," he replied.

I know he thought about it a lot. Once the following spring he called me and seemed a little excited. "Do you still go to Akron, Ohio often?"

"Sure do, do you want to ride over?"

"Yes," was the answer. "I heard from a big gun dealer in Barberton. He might have something I've been looking for."

We drove over and I followed his directions to the "store." It looked like a second-rate bar to me, but I asked no questions.

In a few minutes Mr. Thornley returned to the car and shook his head. "He had a lot of guns but not mine," he said dejectedly. "I'll never find mine. Whoever stole it did not steal it to sell or to shoot skeet with. He probably hunts with it a little, but it's not going to turn up where I can locate it. I might as well kiss it good-bye."

Frankly, I felt the same way. But that fall he finally got a break. I stumbled onto his first real lead.

One Monday morning when I was headed east across northern Ohio, I dropped my trap gun off at a gunsmith's in the Toledo area to have the recoil pad replaced, and I stopped the following Friday on my way home to pick it up.

The proprietor brought out my gun, and while I was paying him, he kept looking at the engraving. "Strange thing," he said. "I had a fellow bring a side-by-side in here yesterday that had engraving almost identical to this. Same fox and pup, same old setter and pup and same kind of pigeons, or whatever they are. Of course everything was spaced different on a double."

"Let me look at it," I asked.

"It's not here. He just brought it in to be checked. He said it had been in a closet for 12 years and he wanted to make sure it was okay. Nothing wrong with it so he took it with him."

"Do you have his name?" I asked.

"No, I didn't charge him so I didn't make out a bill. I never saw him before and probably won't see him again."

"I sure would like to get his name," I continued.

"Sorry I can't help you. All I know is he said he wanted the gun checked out. He had joined some fancy gun club up in Michigan. It must be quite a layout. Huge old club house. He said the place had its own landing strip. Some members fly their private planes in and tie down right by the back door."

All the way back to Wabash I kept trying to figure out what to do with the information I had picked up. I simply could not figure out how to locate an unnamed lodge in time for Mr. Thornley to get there and check on a man he had never seen.

When I hit town I called my friend out of a card game and told him what I had learned. "It looks hopeless to me," I said. "I just don't see how you can move fast enough."

Mr. Thornley didn't seem to hear, just sat there looking at me through half-closed eyes. I ordered drinks but he didn't seem to see his. Finally he took a sip of the whiskey and started to speak. It was almost as though he was thinking out loud.

"A lodge such as the fellow described, huge club house and with its own air strip, it can't be new. They probably control three or four thousand acres. You can't pick up that kind of acreage these days. Those fancy layouts are basically supported by trout fishermen. The hunters certainly help, but they just have to control miles of good trout water."

"What are you leading up to?" I asked.

"Old Two Track Smith," he answered. "The old timber cruiser up at Baldwin. Two Track's poached every private trout stream in Michigan. If there is an outfit that's big in the lower peninsula, he's been on it. He'd sure know about the planes coming in too. Light airplanes make those woods cats jumpy. Two Track and I always hit it off real well. I'll call and see if he can give me any leads."

He couldn't get his call through that evening, but he was

knocking on my door before noon the next day.

"I think I found out what I need to know. Two Track says with that air strip it just has to be a big spread east of Torch Lake. He said the club house is mammoth. Told me how to get there.

"I'll just have to check this out. Do you suppose you could go with me?" It was the only time I remember his asking me a direct favor.

"Sure," I answered. "I'll go with you. We'll take my car, it's heavier. But I have two questions. If we find the place, how will we get in to look around? It's a private club. And if you do get in, how will you get a close look at the guns? They'll probably be in carrying cases."

"Look," he came back. "I would recognize that old leather case of my father's if I just glimpse it. If I see the case, I'll take a chance of my gun being in it.

"Getting in the place won't be any problem if you go with me. I called up there and used your name. I said you might want to do an article about the lodge. The manager liked that idea, said we would be most welcome."

That Torch Lake Lodge club house was certainly plush. It was rather late and starting to spit rain when we found it. We introduced ourselves, signed the register and settled down to wait.

It didn't take too long. The wind and the rain picked up and the hunters headed for shelter. Singly and in small groups they returned to the lodge, complaining about the heavy foliage and the dampness.

No one had a gun or gun case that looked interesting. But we did get a big break. Because of the rain, management had provided a lot of old towels and a large can of rust preventative. And one of us was always near the table when they took advantage of this.

I was getting discouraged, but finally a guide drove up in a pickup truck and a round-faced, heavy-set man got out. He looked to be around 35 years old. I didn't like the fellow's appearance. But the guide evidently didn't like him, period, for he collected his pay without so much as a smile and left.

One thing I was sure of, the man had his gun protected by a fine old heavy leather case obviously made for a side-by-side double. When he removed the gun to dry it, I was too far away to see the engraving. But Mr. Thornley was quite close and when he turned and motioned for me to follow him into the bar, his face was so serene I knew he had found his shotgun.

We sat there enjoying our drinks. Mr. Thornley was calm and relaxed, but I was full of questions. How would he actually recover his property? He had once told me the gun was not insured when he lost it. He had no numbers recorded. How could he prove, really prove, the gun was his?

Perhaps he intended to buy it back. "How much money will you offer him?" I asked. Mr. Thornley looked at me as though I had lost my reason.

"Why should I buy back something that's already mine?" he countered. "Look, there are a couple of boys in Detroit that just happen to owe me a little favor. Now that I've found out who has it, all I have to do is wait until Mr. Ohio takes it home. Ten, twelve days after I put in a call, I'll have my gun back. I've done without it for 12 years; ten or twelve days won't make much difference."

As it worked out he didn't have to wait 12 days. He didn't even have to wait 12 hours.

The rain set in in earnest. All the guests were accounted for, and dinner was served early. After the meal, someone started a poker game. Mr. Thornley sat in. Most of the rest of us stayed at the bar, telling stories and shaking with a dice box to see who bought the after-dinner drinks.

Mr. Ohio was with our group. He was getting a little drunk. I didn't think the liquor improved him any, but he was lucky with the cubes. When one of his acquaintances suggested we get some larger dice and start a crap game, he hurried to his room and returned with a pair.

There was money in that club. The whiskey was working on the boys and a little fast action seemed like a good idea. Someone remembered a plywood form about a foot high that just fit the inside edges of the billiard table and shut off the pockets. It made a good backstop for the dice, and the betting started.

Mr. Ohio was hot from the very start. His gloating cackle every time he made a point irritated me more and more. But nevertheless at the end of 30 or 40 minutes' shooting, he had a wad of tens and twenties in his left fist and was clearly the big winner.

It was about this time Mr. Thornley left the poker group, and walked past the crap table just as one of the shooters was quitting.

"How about you, old man?" Mr. Ohio asked. "Your dice if you want to play. Let's see if you've got any hair on your belly."

Mr. Thornley laid a twenty on the table and reached for the dice with a caressing motion. He stood there for just a second, rolling them between the palms of his hands. In some strange way he reminded me of a musician musing over the keys of an organ. Suddenly, with a brushing movement, he spun the dice onto the table.

"Tough point," someone said.

Once again he picked up the dice and rolled them between his palms reflectively before making another no-decision toss. Then, shaking the dice in his cupped right hand, he stepped back from the table a few feet and threw them underhanded. The dice just cleared the near edge, snapped against the opposite plywood wall and turned up his numbers.

"Shoot the forty," he said. And moved back in close to the table like a man moves up to a workbench.

Things changed; it didn't happen all at once, but gradually. The wad of bills in Mr. Ohio's hand grew smaller and smaller. The size of the bets picked up. They were now shooting fifty and a hundred at a crack, and the time came when Mr. Ohio did not have enough money in sight to fade Mr. Thornley's wager.

"Hell, I'm not broke yet," he blustered, and unbuttoning his shirt pocket, he pulled out a roll of bills that was so large he had secured them with a heavy rubber band. The game took off again.

I could not detect how, but I was positive in my mind that Mr. Thornley was manipulating the ivories. More than the mechanics of his playing, I was fascinated by the strange force that seemed to radiate from the man. Some power of mind. You felt he could exert an influence on the dice even when his opponent was rolling. Within another 30 minutes Mr. Ohio was flat broke.

"I don't suppose you'd take a check," he asked hopefully.

"No, no checks," Mr. Thornley replied, not unkindly. Then (as though he had just thought of it) he added. "Say, I like a man like you. You've got hair on your chest. Go get your shotgun, you can shoot that out for fifteen hundred."

Mr. Ohio looked startled. The price to him seemed more than fair. His luck would turn. He didn't want to lose face, not in this group.

"I'll be right back," he said. Gulped down his drink and left to get the gun.

While he was away, Mr. Thornley counted out the bills. When Mr. Ohio returned and got his money, Mr. Thornley handed me the gun and then tossed his come bet on the table.

"Shoot five hundred," he said. The younger man winced but covered the wager.

Mr. Thornley threw the dice, and although I was watching him closely, I don't think he even bothered to look at them.

"It all goes," he said. "This is your big chance, Mister. Shoot the works."

Ohio turned chalk white and, like a man in a trance, dropped his remaining $1,000 on the table. Once again Mr. Thornley threw the dice, and the game was over.

Ohio stood there staring at the table. It took a moment for him to grasp the fact that he had been hustled. If possible, he got even more pale, and then as the full impact of what happened hit home, he turned beet red.

"You old son of a bitch," he snarled. "You got the shotgun. You got me for three grand. Do I have anything else you want?"

"Yes," Mr. Thornley replied in his cold professional voice. "There on the table in front of you. Toss me that rubber band you had around your bankroll."

We left early the next morning and drove on down to Baldwin. But Mr. Thornley did not hunt much this trip. He seemed tired, in fact, he never did really hunt very much again.

"You make this turn," he would tell me, "I'll bring the car around and pick you up at the Little South Branch." Or it might be, "I have some money riding on the series. I better sit this one out and listen to the game." Plainly, his legs were giving him trouble.

Over the next year or two he gradually started to miss more and more birds; and I knew that if he could not shoot well, if he could not make clean kills, he would give up the sport entirely. I was with him the day he wrapped it up.

It was in the late evening of the last day of the last trip we took together. We had a very favorite hunting spot that consisted of two narrow oak-and-pine-covered ridges, jutting out in the form of a "V" from an old road that skirted a big cedar swamp.

These ridges both extended into an open hay marsh and at the end farthest from the road, each had a feed pocket of grouse berries and thorn-apple trees. At the point of the "V" there was an old bridge crossing a small creek, and the county had placed a trash barrel and a seldom-used picnic table here.

It was our habit to each work one of these ridges the last thing in the evening, then repair to the picnic table, dress what game we might have, fix a couple of drinks and head back to Baldwin.

On this particular evening I had worked the short ridge and, not having moved any game, I walked to the edge so I could check on how my companion was making out. It was a very windy evening and perhaps this made the bird jumpy. Whatever the cause, I heard and could plainly see a grouse that flushed about 60 yards ahead of him. Mr. Thornley heard it too, because I saw him turn and face into the wind in the direction of the sound. The bird swung away in a steep climbing arc, lifted completely above the trees, and with the wind at his tail, swung back toward the hunter. It had to have been moving at least 50 miles per hour. I knew that ridge. I knew my friend could only get intermittent glimpses of the target. I was not optimistic about his chances, although in his salad days he probably would have pulled it off. I watched his swing as the gun followed the flight line and even as far away as I was, it appeared jerky. He never caught up with the bird; in fact it looked as if he shot 30 or 40 feet behind it.

I kept watching the grouse and realized it was veering my way. I had plenty of time and swung on the bird the way you swing on a passing canvasback.

Coming in from behind I swung the gun faster and faster, the sight beads moving past its body until I felt the lead was right and continuing the swing I pulled the trigger and centered it up in a charge of number eights. The bird's head dropped and, knowing the grouse had died in the air, I watched as it crashed through the branches of a small tree and thudded to the ground near the path to the car.

Mr. Thornley came over, we picked up our trophy and walked back to the bridge. I dressed it while we got the ice, the whiskey and those two short, very sheer glasses he always packed so carefully.

I sat straddling the low cement bridge railing, taking small bites of the straight bourbon, letting it roll over my tongue. It was a good brand. Mr. Thornley sat sideways on the rail, head down, staring into the staunch little stream. Finally, he turned his face toward me and started to speak very softly, but I could hear each word.

"Bud, I never said anything, but these trips have meant a lot to me, more than you'll ever know," he said and paused, looked down into the water, then turned to me again. "Those Christmas dinners in your home, I've looked forward to them." You tell the Mrs., each year I've looked forward to them." He paused again. "Bud, you're aware there's a lot of narrow gauge in Wabash. They looked down their nose at old Thorn, but you always knew me."

I took another bite of the straight whiskey and handed his conversation right back to him. "Old Thorn," I said, "I've always been very proud to know you." I told him this because it was true and because I thought it might please him; but he never looked up, he merely leaned forward a little farther. I could not see his face.

The conversation embarrassed me and to change the subject I mentioned the grouse we had just killed. "Your shot string must have been awfully close," I said. "I think the charge caused it to swing my way."

"Horse shit," he answered absently, as though talking about something unimportant. And then in a curiously flat voice he added, "That's the last shot I'll ever take."

I did not know he meant anything except that he was getting too old to hunt. I should have known because he spoke with such finality. I should have paid more heed. This man had sat in too many games not to sense when the cards were running out.

We sat a while longer. Not talking, just watching the evening shadows gather and listening to the little stream.

I had poured my third drink but I noticed an almost imperceptible gathering of his shoulders. He might be chilled. It was time to go.

Fall gave way to winter. There was too much snow to hunt quail so I went south for a few weeks. When I returned it was late December, and I stopped at the club to tender Mr. Thornley his usual Christmas dinner invitation. I didn't see him around, so I checked with the bartender.

"Hell, Bud, didn't you know? They planted the old boy about ten days ago," he informed me.

"You mean he's dead?" I asked, stunned. "What happened?"

"Nothing happened, he just up an' died; he's gone. Ask Digger about it. He's in the other room."

"You heard it right," the mortician told me. "He walked into the office early on a Monday morning a few days ago and told me he wanted to make his arrangements. I took him back to the display room and left him alone awhile. He picked out his own casket. Paid cash. Not many people do that, you know. The price of the casket covers the complete cost of our service, you know."

Somehow an attorney had gotten into the act. I talked to this man. "No, as yet, they haven't found a single relative. Nothing left in the estate anyway. Oh, I'll be paid of course, but there was really nothing left in the estate, really nothing left at all."

I asked about my friend's shotgun. It was the most beautiful side-by-side I had ever seen. Perfectly balanced, with 26-inch barrels, bored open and open. Ideal for grouse. I thought perhaps he would want me to have it. But strangely enough, I was by-passed.

The gun was to go to my son. The little boy who gave Mr. Thornley the stick of chewing gum. That afternoon on the river. Those many years ago.

Reprinted by permission of Mrs. Julia Ann Temple, Wabash, Indiana.

THE VISITING
Fire-Eater

BY PHILIP WYLIE

Philip Wylie (1902-1971) endeared himself to a
generation of readers through his Crunch and Des
stories in the *Saturday Evening Post*. His forte was an
understanding of human nature, and here we have an
enjoyable example, typical of the Crunch and Des tales,
where in the end the good guys come out on top.

Things were fine. Too fine, Crunch found himself thinking
as he pushed out into the Bay. The weather was good; the
fishing, which provided his livelihood, was good; the
Poseidon, on which he was master, had been running like a
sewing machine; Sari, his wife, had money in the bank and three
new dresses; young Bill was learning to talk with a precocity that
amazed everyone at the Gulf Stream Dock; and now the *Trident*

was ready for her maiden voyage.

As if he disbelieved the extent of his fortune, Crunch removed the cover from the *Trident's* engine and gazed dubiously at it. Then, with a surge of his shoulder, he spun the flywheel. There was a cough and a purr. Crunch grinned, headed toward open water, and waved at the men on the dock. He pushed up the throttle and watched the rush of bubbles. Ten – maybe eleven knots. Plenty. He eased her down. The vessel moved almost without a ripple and the motor merely whispered.

"Boy!" he murmured. There was, evidently, no end to his luck.

He decided to cruise on down to the dock and let the other boatmen see what he and Desperate had created in their chartless days and free evenings. He steered toward the County Causeway. The shortest route lay between and among various cruisers and yachts lying at anchor. He headed toward them, and a fly fell into his ointment.

"Holy smokes!" The voice came clearly to his ears. "Look what's coming! Somebody's put a motor on a gangplank!"

Crunch grinned and waved. He saw a gentleman in a yachting cap hurry to the rail and stare. The gentleman's face became mirthful. "What you got there, sailor? A motorized boardwalk?"

"Prog boat," Crunch yelled back.

He notched up the gas and moved along the side of a sloop. Two young men were polishing her brightwork. They spied the *Trident* and chortled. "Hey!" one yelled. "Are you sinking? Or is it a submarine?"

Crunch was still grinning, but not quite so happily. He steered away from the sloop. It was true that the *Trident* looked funny. But not that funny, he thought. It was also true that there was no other craft like her. But a man with imagination ought to be able to guess her purpose.

She was sixteen feet long and six feet wide and she consisted principally of two wooden pontoons decked over with boards. There was a rail all around her except for the stern, where you got aboard. Forward were two stools and, between them, mounted on a universal joint above the rail, was an automobile headlight. She had a small inboard engine with a direct drive shaft that ran to a propeller between the pontoons. The pontoons were shovel-nosed and there was a covered live well between them, amidships. There were two benches aft. Outside the rails were brackets for harpoons and gigs. She carried a bucket of rope and also a sort of reel made of an old car wheel with the brake assembly re-rigged for hand operation. She had only a foot of freeboard; she drew only ten inches; a man could walk all over her; she did look something like a motorized section of dock, but anybody ought to be able to tell that she was meant for night harpooning on the flats.

Nevertheless, as he approached the stern of the *Paloma*, from Southampton, a crowd assembled there, and Crunch began to flush. He'd seen the houseboat before – coming in from cruises to the Keys. It belonged to a gaudy personage on Miami's Riviera named Terry Walm. Crunch had a great admiration for anything so beautiful, so costly, so seaworthy. It would be unpleasant to be made fun of by the *Paloma's* company.

Laughter welled across the water, so Crunch turned the *Trident*. But, as a man will discover in a long life of hardship, it takes only a trifle to precipitate humiliation. For some reason, his motor conked. Tide and inertia carried him toward the people on the houseboat. He went to his engine with a profane annoyance that looked dignified at a distance.

"What is it?" somebody yelled. "A hatch cover?"

"It's a raft," a girl said, delightedly lifting her voice. "He's playing shipwreck! Ahoy, Robinson Crusoe!"

Crunch stared at his engine.

"Storm coming!" somebody else bawled. "Never mind, Sailor! We'll save you! Hey! Captain! Man the boats!"

Crunch found the trouble and fixed it. A loose connection. He looked up. The people on the *Paloma's* stern were almost over his head. He grinned again, but their certainty that Crunch was a crackpot with some "invention" was so great that they observed neither the amiability nor the sensitiveness of his grin. Instead, a young man in white flannels who was holding a highball called, "I say Skipper! Has she been christened yet?" Before Crunch could reply, the young man poured his drink onto the *Trident* and said, "I christen thee H.M.S. *Pancake!*"

Ice and water whisky hit the deck and splashed Crunch. He did not grin any more. Quietly, he spun the flywheel. The motor started. He headed toward the causeway, under it, and across to the Gulf Stream Dock. His appearance there was a sign for another moment of hilarity, which died as soon as the skippers could clearly see the details of the *Trident*. Mr. Williams came down from the shore. "Crunch," he said, "I think you've got something there. Where you going to put it?"

"Under the dock – if you don't mind. We'll pay extra for the space...."

"Will she lie under it – at high tide?"

Desperate, who had assisted his skipper with lines, answered that. "We measured before we made her. Plenty of room!"

So the *Trident*, a distant relative of the *Poseidon*, was moored astern of that well-known ship – under the dock. When the operation had been completed, Crunch joined his mate. "I took a hell of a ribbing coming over," he said. "Especially from a lot of wise guys on the *Paloma*."

"You sound sore."

"Sure, I'm sore! What's the matter with the *Trident*? Wait till we get her in action! But to hear those rich yahoos laugh, you'd think I'd claimed the *Trident* would take the gold out of sea water – or that she worked by perpetual motion! They got my goat!"

"Well," Des replied, "skip it! I got a phone call while you were up at the shipyard. Long distance."

Crunch quickly shook off his indignation. "Yeah? Who?"

"Old Man McLaen. Remember him? The guy we took bonefishing?"

The *Poseidon's* master chuckled. "I sorta do. Is he coming down?"

"Not yet. Can't. Busy. But he's sending us a guy. Fellow named Cradbey."

"Hell of a name!"

"Important guy. A sportsman, McLaen said. Seems old Mac had some big deal about set with this guy – and the guy went cold. Then Mac got talking about Florida fishing – and this Cradbey wanted a whirl at it before goin' home. So Mac put him on a plane – and phoned us. He's going to turn Cradbey over to us to soften him up. Then – when he gets enough fresh air, sunburn and fish, Mac comes down and closes the deal. See?"

Crunch smiled. "Sure. Nice of Mac to send us the business. But I hope they keep on biting! You say he's a fisherman?"

Des frowned. "Well ... sportsman was the way Mac put it."

"And how long we got before this Cradbey goes wherever his home is?"

"About a week – and his home's England."

"England?"

"Yeah. He's flying back next Friday. I said he was English, didn't I?"

"No." Crunch's eyes were amused. "Of course, you didn't say he wasn't – "

"Sure. One of them – what-do-you-call-'ems? Viscounts."

Crunch took a cigarette from his pocket without troubling to remove the package first. He stuck the cigarette between his lips. "Viscount, eh?" He struck a match. "Does a Viscount polish a Duke's boots – or vice versa?"

"How in hell should I know!"

Crunch and Des were on hand at the airport that night to assist the Viscount in the matter of luggage, or in any other way. If old Mac wanted him taken care of, he'd be taken care of, Viscount or not. The plane came shooting down out of the moonlight and the Viscount came shooting out of the plane. He was stocky, baldheaded, and a man of many words. He had a high, imperious voice. Worn high, Crunch said afterward, from over-use.

"Steward!" he said, as his foot touched Florida soil for the first time, "Please hurry up my luggage! It's deuced late and I'm tired!"

"I'm sorry," said the man he had addressed, "I'm the pilot."

"Then – find me a steward, what?"

Des was staring. So was Crunch. "One of those," said the latter quietly. They went forward. "I'm Crunch Adams, of the *Poseidon*. You're Viscount Cradbey?"

The Englishman pivoted. There was a monocle in his eye. It flashed redly with a reflection from the field boundary lights. "I'm Cradbey," he said with vigor. "Adams? *Poseidon*? Oh. Yes – yes – yes! The boat! Splendid! I'm no seaman, you know. Never cared for the briny." To their surprise, he held out his hand. To their further surprise, it was not a lilylike palm, but firm. However, he turned back to the plane almost immediately and began crying for a steward.

He assembled his bags as if he were a collie herding sheep. In that same vociferous mood, he dispatched them to the car which had been sent for him by the Royal Carribean Hotel. Crunch and Desperate tagged along in the noisy wake of the whole proceeding, but he said nothing until he was ensconced in the car. What he did say, then, was in part too British for understanding. The gist of it was that he would see them early the next morning, that he had the address of their boat in his pocket, that travel in America was a devilish pest, that there had been ten thousand flies in the airplane, that the country reminded him of the Siberian bogs, and that he trusted they'd catch a couple of tons of fish for his pains.

Crunch told Sari about it before they went to sleep.

"You've got to put up with it!" she said urgently. "Mr. McLaen's such a sweetheart – and he loves you two boys. He didn't do this just to throw some fishing your way. He did it because fishing is his idea of the best thing on earth a man can do."

"Yeah. I know it. But this oaf squeals like the fiddle in a hoe-down."

"Mac told Des he was a sportsman. What kind?"

"Some new kind," Crunch answered grimly. "We'll find out tomorrow. Let's get some sleep. I have a hunch I'll need to be rested tomorrow. Cool and collected."

They found out about the Viscount's sporting laurels on the next day. It was no trouble at all to make the discovery. He showed up at six in a pair of disgracefully battered slacks, a mackintosh, and a felt hat that must have been handed down from father to son through many reigns. "Never fished!" he said before he was within what a normal man would consider earshot. "Strictly a game hunter! Africa! The Gobi! Hear it's exciting! Passionately fond of excitement! Set sail. Captain, what!"

"What ho," said Crunch laconically – and he turned away as he saw a suspicious gleam behind the monocle.

Des was steering. The Viscount was trolling. Crunch came up topside.

"Can you fish with one of those things in your eye?" Des asked. "I been wondering."

Crunch shrugged. "Maybe it'll drop out. Maybe it'll chum up something."

"Barracuda might snap it up. Might choke on it." Des stared at the sky. "There's going to be a squall later this A.M."

From below, after a while, came the voice of their passenger. "Damn it, men! Nothing happening! Ten fifteen! Flies out here, too! Whole deuced cockpit alive with 'em! Does Old McLaen call this excitin'?"

Crunch slid below. He picked up the insect spray gun. After a search he found the fly that had tormented his noble passenger.

He killed it. Viscount Cradbey was staring first at one bait and then at the other. There was a flash of lightning. Thunder rolled. The black tumult pushed out over the sea. Its calm was ruffled by a brief press of wind.

"It's going to rain by and by," Crunch said. "Maybe you'd better come in under cover."

The man turned. He removed his eyeglass with all the signs of dismay. "Come in? Stop fishin'?"

Crunch nodded.

"D'you mean you quit it because of a drop of rain?"

"Usually. The lightning slows down the fishing anyway. . ."

The man from England stared. "Slows it down? Get slower than this? Can't be, Captain! Nothing from nothing equals nothing! Funny, what? Why – up the Saigon – we'd sit in those damned native boats for days in a cloudburst waitin' for a shot! I won't melt, Captain! The Cradbeys have been waterproof for generations. Just pour me out a peg of Scotch, like a good fellow, and I'll give you Americans an object lesson in how to go after game!"

A contradictory character, Crunch thought. If he wanted to get wet, let him get wet. The *Poseidon* churned along on blue water that slowly turned purple. The shore disappeared in a gray sheet of rain. The intermittent puffs of wind became forceful. Des hopped below to get his sou'wester. The thunder rolled nearer. A head-splitting shaft of lightning hit the sea near by and filled the air with ozone. Presently the rain came – moving toward them in a silvery sheet on a pock-marked front that reached and enveloped the boat. The sound was a liquid roar; the sea flattened out to a floor upon which billions of glass globules danced; wind felt through the rain, shifting and rearranging it; the *Poseidon* was closed off from everything but a small opaque world of falling water. Water streamed from the Viscount, and he sat in it, muttering.

Crunch had pretty well abandoned hope for Mr. McLaen's deal.

And then his gloomy forebodings were interrupted. There came a voice – unexcited, not even very interested. "Isn't that some sort of something or other out yonder pecking at the bait?"

Crunch lifted his head. He stared. His feet hit the deck so hard they stung. "Marlin! Des!" he bellowed up into the rain. "White! On the port side!"

The marlin was there, rain or no rain, thunder or no thunder, following the bait as it slid through the bubbling calm, its rounded dorsal out of water and its bill batting. Crunch ran out in the cockpit. The rain soaked him to the skin.

"I suppose," the Viscount said calmly, "from what Old McLaen told me, the next time he hits it, I pull it loose from the bally outrig-thing?"

Crunch glanced at him, at the fish, and nodded. "Now!"

But his passenger had already seen the strike and knocked out the line. He was speaking again, thoughtfully. "Count ten, eh? One, two, three, four, five, six, seven, eight, nine, ten. Strike – am I right?"

He struck. "Three times, isn't it? One, two, three."

He put the rod in the socket. The marlin was running fast out toward the open spaces.

"You hung him!" Crunch exclaimed. "Perfect! Dandy!"

The Viscount let go of his whipping rod with one hand in order to adjust his eyeglass and stare at Crunch. "Nothing difficult about it, is there? Mac explained the thing most clearly. Jove. There he is. I keep a tight line – right?"

Crunch took a firm hold on a cleat. There are many men – old hands – who think that, pound for pound, a white marlin is the most powerful, phrenetic and elusive species of scaly dynamite into which a hook may be driven. This was a big white. Ninety pounds, maybe. He was raging around on the rain-drenched ocean like a barrel of skyrockets.

And the Viscount was merely sitting there – peering. Occasionally, when the maniacal fish drove his nine silver feet toward the boat, he quickly wound in line. "Active, aren't they?" he said.

Crunch ground his teeth. "Active," he agreed.

Up above was Desperate, wearing the half-ecstatic, half-terrified look characteristic of him when there was a big one jitterbugging in the wake of the *Poseidon*. The white marlin landed flat after its last pinwheeling leap. Its forked tail quivered in the rain spray. It sounded.

"Pump him up, now?" the passenger said inquiringly.

Crunch did not look at him. He just nodded.

The Viscount began on the fish. "Practiced up in Michigan," he said. "On a piano stool with a walking stick. Up slow and easy – eh? Down quick – and crank! We used to fish like this in grab bags at Worlemshire Castle. When we were little nippers, you know. Magnet on a bit of string. Caught all sorts of things. Sweets, mostly."

Crunch stared at the man's back. Ought to be tossed overboard, he thought. We could go in and say he attacked us. Or that he fell over while we weren't looking. I'd have to tie an anchor on him first, though. He probably learned to swim – in the castle moat. That idea revived Crunch a little. He began to pray that the marlin would throw the hook.

It didn't. After forty minutes of heartbreaking effort, it quit, and came in almost belly up. The Viscount reeled easily. He was not panting. He was not anything – so far as Crunch could see when he leaned over to boat the fish. In fact, after a blow had killed it, and it lay in the cockpit changing swiftly from delirious indigos to dull grays, the Englishman produced a dry handkerchief from underneath his mackintosh, wiped his monocle, and condescended to have a look.

"Somehow," he said, "all dead fish look more or less alike."

He walked over to the electric refrigerator and opened a can of ale. He poured it into a glass. He came back, while Crunch was putting a piece of canvas over the fish. It was too big to go in the box. "Poor old McLaen," he said almost to himself. "Calls that excitement, eh?" He chuckled. "Wonder what he'd do if he had only a single shell left and a pair of buffalo came through the grass? Or how he'd feel about a herd of elephant wheeling – trampling his boy – coming on? Or even tigers, eh? If a man's on foot."

Crunch said nothing. There were bigger ones in the Gulf Stream – but none better.

The Viscount seemed to notice, in a vague way, that Crunch was downcast. He clapped him cheerily on the shoulder. "No criticism of you, old fellow!" he said. "Very clever to find one of these creatures! It's just that – my definition of sport involves a spot of hazard, I guess. Risk – and that sort of thing. I dare say a sedentary old duffer like Mac would find all this extremely stirrin'!"

Later in the day, they ran into a school of king mackerel. The Britisher caught six – and gave it up. He was sleepy he said. He took a nap. Crunch waved Des toward the shore, and they went in. At the dock, Cradbey woke. He viewed with mild amusement the enthusiastic rush to see his fish. It was quite clear that he had a low opinion of this American sport. He refused to be photographed with his catch, and when Des suggested having the marlin mounted, he guffawed. "Can you imagine what Ponsley and Ashton and old Douglas would say if they saw that damned mackerel – marlin – among the heads in my den, eh?"

He was on the point of stepping ashore when he caught sight of the *Trident*, moored under the dock. He stopped and peered. "Odd-looking thing. What is it?"

Crunch looked at the man coldly. "A prog boat."

"Prog?"

"For harpooning things. At night."

The Viscount snorted. "Confound it, man, jacking fish with a light is a bad business! We'd hang a man for doing it to a deer!"

"There's a difference," said Crunch huskily, "between a deer and a shark."

"Shark?" The small man's monocle twinkled. "Harpoon sharks? Now – that sounds interestin', young man! Why didn't you mention it? More in my line. I'd like to take a whack at it!"

The merest glimmer of hope shone across the dark panorama of Crunch's mind. A notion formed there – a notion no bigger than a minnow but capable of growth. He shrugged. "It would mean a trip down to the Keys. Pretty uncomfortable country. Mosquitoes – flies – coral snakes – and a few other things."

The Englishman's eyes, for the first time that day, were a little livelier than lumps of blue clay. "You don't say! Well, well! If you'll make the arrangements..."

After he had departed for the Royal Caribbean Hotel, Sari came down the dock. When she saw the white marlin, she smiled. She hurried toward her husband. "Crunch! How perfectly marvelous!"

Crunch stared at her and gave a burlesque. "Active creature – but all dead fish look alike, what? Interestin' sport – for cripples – I dare say!"

"He wasn't – like that!"

Crunch grinned ruefully. "Sari, the guy is an icicle! He caught that marlin as if he were tying up his shoelace! Sportsman – baloney!"

"That's dreadful! What are you going to do? Mr. McLaen will be so disappointed!"

"We're going down to Key Amigo," Crunch said. "Tomorrow."

The pier at Camp Amigo extends into the Bay of Florida for about a hundred feet. At the shore end are comfortable log cabins with electric lights, hot showers, bar service, and beds of a luxury brand. True, two coral snakes, which are beautiful but dangerous, had been found in the summer in the lounge. The scream of a panther could sometimes be heard in the dining room. And the chef had shot a crocodile, once, that was trying to tip over the garbage pails. But, by and large, the camp was an oasis of civilization in the wilderness.

It is a wilderness of nameless trees and unknown vines where a man cannot hack his way fifty feet an hour with a machete. It is a far more sinister wilderness of water – water that extends from the dock north toward the Everglades and west clear to the Dry Tortugas. Islands rise by the thousand in this water – islands covered with pines, with palms, with ferns, with raw jungle – islands a few yards square and islands forty miles long. Between them run labyrinthine tidal creeks which are often miles in length, and around them lie bays and lagoons, charted but untenanted.

In the water there is life – abundant and formidable. It is, for the most part, shallow water. Low tide bares wide acreages of weedy flats. High tide may cover with a scant ten feet of sea limitless gardens of coral and aquatic vegetation in which live monsters longer than elephants, bigger than lions, armed with shocking weapons which disappeared from the earth's surface eons ago but survive still in the huge, horrid things under the waters of the earth. The pier at Amigo Key was a tiny outpost in that wild marine world.

There the *Poseidon* was moored. And there, on the next evening, as the sun was setting in a red-streaked, windless sky, Crunch pushed off the *Trident*. She was armed to the teeth, then, with five-pronged, hand-forged gigs on ten-foot shafts, a lily iron, a turtle peg, a plain harpoon, rope, an eighteen-inch lance, and a smooth-bore large-gauge gun that fired a soft lead slug. Crunch twisted the flywheel and the engine purred. He sat astern, steering toward the low-lying islands in the bay. His guest was perched on one of the stools forward, a gig in his hands, his eyes roaming over the scene.

They moved rapidly along the coast. An echelon of pelicans coasted down the twilight air toward a roost in the mangroves. A man-o'-war hawk teetered and plunged for a last morsel before the coming of night. A bald eagle passed on whispering pinions.

The lights of Camp Amigo vanished around a point on which dead tree trunks stood above the jungle. There was no one in sight, finally. No boats, no lights, only the opalescent water turning gray as the sun withdrew. The disappearance of its last faint bars left a flat, forlorn world that looked utterly silent.

Crunch throttled down the motor. His passenger had stiffened in unconscious reaction to the environment. He, also, sensed its primordial quality, its balefulness. It was a land not meant to be invaded, a land of quietude and teeth and poison. He looked back at Crunch and his smile showed whitely. He gestured with the long shaft in his hand. Crunch nodded in response and pointed. The man saw something dark and triangular moving slowly on the surface of the water.

"Shark." Crunch's voice seemed loud.

"Let's go! ..."

"Little one," Crunch replied casually.

He waited until he was in the exact spot and until the night had closed in, black and hostile. At a creek mouth, some fifty yards from the tangled arches of mangrove root, he touched a switch. The big electric light in the bow went on. The Viscount looked down, saw the transparent water and fishes in it, looked deeper, and gasped. He was no longer on a boat. He was, instead, floating in the air. From his seat he could see for a hundred feet ahead and forty on each side. Underneath him was a fairyland.

Lacy, lavender fans stood stiff in the water. Yellow "plants" without leaves grew high as a man among them. Coral, white as alabaster, lay on the sea floor in brain-shaped lumps, and branched toward the surface like the horns of a herd of stags. Huge niggerheads rose like reefs under their pontoons. Water-plants with bulbous stems writhed in the slow current. There were grottoes, shelves of hard coral, sand pits where shells swirled like snowflakes. On the bottom, spiny black sea urchins moved tentatively, red starfish lay in waiting, rock lobsters half hid, shifting their fringed feelers lazily. Here and there were patches of sponge, moss, sea mats – in sulphur yellow, scarlet, green, blue. And in and out through the caverns and the vegetation and the coral, swam fish of every imaginable color and pattern – black and silver individuals, darting purple schools.

"Jove!" the Viscount said.

Crunch did not answer. He kept his attention focussed on the murky outer fringe of the light. He was looking for several things – mud swirls, gray ghosts in the peripheral gloom, the flash of an eye. The *Trident* crept along. Ahead, near the shore, there was a violent flurry and the dark water was whipped to foam.

"What's that?" The Englishman asked quickly.

"Tarpon. They're chasing a school of bait up against the mangroves. Feeding."

The man, silhouetted against the light, nodded and looked down at the gardens in the sea. There came, from inland, a hoarse, choked cough. A grunt. He turned. "I won't ask about that," he said quietly. "'Gator."

"Croc."

"Didn't know you had 'em here!"

Crunch smiled a little. "Yes. Crocodiles are fairly common on the Keys."

"But – Lord, man – on a flat little thing like this – if one took a notion to swim out! ... Why! I've seen 'em on the Nile thirty feet long!"

"Never saw one that big here. But we have a gun – and a good motor."

The man nodded. Presently he said, "All right for me to spear one of these things? I'd like to try my aim."

"Shoot." Crunch came up and took the stool beside him, then. He had auxiliary controls on a panel there. He watched his passenger sight at a crimson fish that was standing still in the brilliant light. The gig shot into the water.

"Missed!" said the man, with chagrin.

"There's some diffraction. You've got to compensate for it. Next time – slide your spear down toward your fish – and jab. Don't let go. You'll begin to be able to judge the angle, that way."

There was another small fish – blue with yellow spots – a triangular fish with a sharp back, a flat belly, and two tiny horns. The man let the three-pronged spear slide toward it through the water until the tines were only inches behind it. Then he stabbed lightly. He hit the fish. They could see it tip sideways. But it swam away.

"Cowfish," Crunch said. "They have a skeleton on the outside. Good-eating meat inside, though. You didn't hit it hard enough. Try one of those crayfish."

The Viscount tried. A moment later he hauled his spear triumphantly out of the water. He had impaled a large lobsterlike animal that was flapping wildly and emitting a croaking noise. Crunch removed the crayfish, killed it, and dropped it into the live well. "You can have it for lunch," he said.

He started back toward the stern. The Viscount wheeled and grabbed his arm. "That thing – old man!"

"Hit it!" Crunch answered instantly.

The thing was diamond-shaped and about four feet long, not counting a tail that dragged behind it. Sand-colored and flat. A skate of some sort, the Viscount thought. He measured its course with his eye, poised himself, and drove in the spear. He could actually see the tines imbed themselves in the thing's back. The shock galvanized it. Like a boomerang coasting up on the air, it rose in a swift circle. The Viscount leaned over to see, and the shaft of his spear hit him sharply on the head. He slid off the stool and caught himself by grabbing the rail.

"Stupid!" he said. "The demned pole stuck up straight, eh? Here!"

Crunch was paying out line as the ray rushed through the night. The Viscount grabbed the rope. Crunch tilted up the light. They could see the ray leaping and shaking out on the water. Its efforts shook loose the head of the gig – but the line was made fast both to the metal and the wood, so it did not free itself. For a few minutes the Englishman hauled furiously on the line. The ray came closer, plunging and leaping. Crunch put the light on the *Trident's* side and leaned over the rail. With a heave, he tossed the ray aboard. It lay on the deck, its edges rippling with efforts to swim – its tail thrashing. The Englishman stepped toward it fascinatedly.

"Get back!" Crunch yelled.

He jumped. The ray's tail lashed at the deck in the spot where he had been. Crunch went around it gingerly and picked up the lance. He thrust it home. The fish quivered. "Now," he said, "I'll show you why I hollered. See that long spine at the base of the tail? That's his stinger. It's poisonous. It would break off in your leg – a good six inches of it – and stay there, because it's barbed. That would be the end of our party tonight – and all others, for a few weeks."

"Well, well," said the Briton. His voice was bland – but Crunch detected a note of tension in it.

"We'll keep this guy," Crunch continued. "Trophy. Must go a hundred pounds, easy." He swung the light back on the water.

Cradbey went back to his post. He speared a snapper, which Crunch told him was difficult, inasmuch as they were quick. Then he missed a sea robin. Something amorphous and bright green next caught his eye. It was about a yard long. When he struck it, there was no answering quiver in the spear shaft. Instead, the thing vanished and in its place was an inky cloud.

"Octopus," Crunch said. "Little one."

"Hmmmm."

Crunch was going to add that they didn't grow very large in that region. He decided to keep his counsel.

"There's a big fish!"

Crunch looked. It was big – for a barracuda. A five-footer, lying in very shallow water. Motionless, mean, and glittering, it floated there. He headed toward it. His passenger got ready. The barracuda looked with wicked, unblinking eyes into the light. Cradbey plunged. He could feel the spear go home – and he did not let go. It was a mistake. The 'cuda wrenched the spear from his hands, hurting his wrists, and shot under the boat. There was a crack as the shaft snapped – and the fish vanished in the night with the tines in its back.

Cradbey rubbed his wrists. "If I'd let go – let him take it on the line? ..."

Crunch shrugged. "He might have gone under the boat anyhow."

"Hate to think of a fish getting away with that in him!"

Crunch understood that feeling. This, however, was different. "He'll shake it, and heal – or else something will eat him in no time. Besides, I don't like 'cudas. I've seen a man with nothing left of his upper arm but the bare bone from one of those things."

"Hunh!" said the Viscount. "Wouldn't pay to fall overboard, eh?"

"In more ways than one, it wouldn't!"

The Englishman glanced down at the twelve short inches of freeboard. He stepped back a little from the edge. He peered through the thick night toward the shore. He noticed that they were heading into a wide opening that looked like a river mouth. He sat down and glued his eye to the marine wonderland which now seemed more hellish than fairylike. He began to feel a little excited. A ray came by – and he missed it. Then a shark – big and ghostly – but out of range. They chased it, but it put on a burst of speed and vanished.

Crunch steered – searching – hoping. He lighted a cigarette. And suddenly a ripple of cold fear ran down his spine. It was coming toward them. Dark – it looked black – and a good eighteen feet across. Its batlike "wings" propelled it. Its eyes shone. Its tremendous mouth opened and closed. Crunch had never before seen one that close to shore.

Of all the contrivances of nature for swooping and guzzling on the shoals, the manta is the most hideous. It is a ray – a giant ray – that grows to weigh three or four thousand pounds. Usually peaceable, it is fierce and destructive when aroused. Harpoons and guns will not always stop it – and more than one small boat has been crushed in its "wings" or by its weight when it leaped and fell upon it. Crunch stared and gulped – and saw the Viscount reach for the lily iron.

He spoke in time. "No! Not that! Let it alone! We'd need a bigger boat and more men!"

There was a moment of suspended action. The awful fish swam into the light and turned and went away. The Englishman put down the iron. Crunch felt sweat leak down his back.

"The thing did look – dangerous," said the Englishman.

"It could be. They leap – like the little one. Fall on the boat. They like to come up underneath you, too – when you have an iron in 'em. And the *Trident's* only inch cedar ..."

Cradbey took out his handkerchief. He whipped it open in the cool air. He passed it across his brow. "Plenty of game," he said.

Crunch was pointing again. "But there – yonder! The lily iron!"

The Briton turned. "Shark?"

"Look!"

"Great heavens, man! It's got a sword!"

"Saw! We can give it a whirl – if you care to!"

"Do I!" He was standing. His iron was ready – pointing down across the square bow of the raft. The sawfish swam slowly along the edge of a bank. When the light touched him, he stopped for a moment, and then went on – more rapidly. Crunch gunned the motors. The great fish turned toward deeper water. But Cradbey was getting closer. He had a clear view of the thing – its long, toothed beak oscillating, its tail waving. He could see small fish dodging under cover. He had no idea of what would happen. He threw.

The shaft of the harpoon stood quivering for a split second.

"Got him!" Crunch whispered.

Then the line was yanked from Cradbey's hands. It snapped tight on the automobile wheel which had been made into a reel. Crunch rushed forward and pushed on a lever. The wheel whizzed and in a minute the air was rank with the odor of hot brake lining. Far ahead the water went white as the fish's tail broached. The *Trident* was gathering speed. Presently the wheel stopped revolving. Ahead, the creek opened out. There was a bend and then another. The sawfish was pulling them steadily. Crunch tipped up the light. Cradbey could see, far beyond its range, the dark, level horizon on the open sea. They were going straight for it.

"Is it safe to take this thing out there?"

"No!" Crunch answered. "Shall we cut him loose?"

"That's for you to say."

Crunch shook his head. "It's a question of whether or not you want to take the chance. I, for one, hate to cut off a fish – "

"Carry on!"

The fish slowed. They were several hundred yards from shore. The water was glass clear and not deep. Six feet, perhaps. The bottom was grassy. Cradbey saw the line go slack. Crunch began to spin the wheel. "Here!" Cradbey said. "I can do that! You get to the engine!"

Crunch threw the *Trident* in reverse. But the sawfish was coming around fast. You could tell that by the slack. The Englishman was spinning the auto wheel – taking in line – with all his might. For a small man, he had a great deal of power and endurance. They both heard again the sound of the broaching tail. Crunch tipped the light. He caught the blur of the fish – a hundred feet away – as it cut in a circle around the boat. He pushed up the throttle and turned the rudders. The *Trident* was designed for sharp spinning. It swung to face the fish. Cradbey was not getting in the line fast enough with the auto wheel. He gave up and grabbed the rope, pulling it hand over hand. Crunch watched the fish. It charged up and over a submarine bank into very shallow water. It seemed extraordinarily violent for a member of its fairly sluggish breed. Then Crunch saw why: Under the bank, following hard on the bleeding fish, was a big shark. Cradbey got the line tight and heaved with all his might. The saw-fish cut in close to the *Trident*. The shark lashed at it in the darkness.

There was a split second of furious, complex action. The sawfish, trying to slash either at the boat or the shark, reared out of water. Cradbey yanked again. The toothed blade came aboard, cutting right and left. The *Trident* heeled up. The shark broke water and its jaws snapped. The rail of the *Trident* went to smithereens. Pail, automobile wheel, rope, harpoons were ripped loose and tossed overboard. Cradbey lost his balance and slid down the deck. He teetered on the canted edge above the melee of blood, foam, saw and fins. Crunch hooked his leg around a rail stanchion, leaned, grabbed with his powerful right arm, and yanked the man bodily out of danger. The combat churned and gurgled astern. The *Trident* settled back level. Crunch turned the light on the boat. In a moment, everything was quiet again. Not even the engine broke the stillness.

The Viscount spoke. His voice was level – even amused. "Thanks, old man!"

Crunch waved his hand. He had wanted passionately to show the Englishman a little excitement. Even a little danger. But not that much.

"Great sport! Another fish down there, what?"

"Yeah. Shark."

"Thought so. Heard his jaws snap. Rotten sound."

Crunch sat down and lighted a cigarette. The Englishman polished his monocle. Suddenly he stood still. "We're settling a bit, aren't we?"

Crunch nodded. He was digesting the thought that if Cradbey had been six inches farther across the deck – there might have been no Cradbey. "That sawfish holed one of our pontoons."

The Englishman sat down on the opposite bench. "I see," he said quietly. "Tough."

There was a splashing far out on the water. Perhaps the sawfish had escaped. Perhaps the shark was feasting. Perhaps some other voracious drama was being enacted. "We could shoot a few rounds," the Englishman suggested.

Crunch was still thinking about the narrowness of that moment on the water. He shrugged. "Useless." He assumed the Britisher was hoping for his sawfish.

Then it dawned on Crunch. The man from across the sea thought they were going to sink. He had suggested shooting as a signal for help. He didn't know that there were bulkheads in the pontoons. Bulkheads he and Des had carefully built against just such accidents as – a fish charging, or a sharp rock. The Englishman assumed that when the *Trident* went down – a shark – or a barracuda – or perhaps a manta – would come shooting through that limpid, murderous water – and they'd yell once or twice – and that would be finis.

For a moment Crunch felt his flesh creep and tingle. That was what they'd meant when they talked about the British. He wondered how he would feel if he thought he was going to sink into the water out there where the current ran toward the Gulf Stream, and the Stream was alive – with death.

"This is one time," said the Viscount, with a smile that was invisible in the night, but audible, "when we don't seem to rule the waves, what?"

Then Crunch told him.

The Viscount was not angry. He just said, "Splendid, old man! Then – we can still get one of those what-do-you-call-its, eh?"

When Mr. McLaen reached Key Amigo, after flying from Michigan and driving a long way down the Key West road, it was night. He'd had no dinner and he was hungry. Nevertheless he stopped long enough, while his duffel was being unloaded, to look at the thing on the dock. It was like a big bat – fifteen feet from tip to tip. It hung from a block and tackle and had been spread out with spikes. The colored boy who was waiting on him followed his eyes. "That there Crunch Adams and his mate and this Englishman catched it," he said. "In the *Poseidon*. Guess they'd go a-whalin' – if they was any whales outside. He sure is the harpooninest man! Me – if ah even seen one of them devilfish – I'd row right up into the air!"

Mr. McLaen chuckled. "I take it he likes fishing?"

"That Lord Crabbey? Not fishin'! He don't fish! He's a pure proggin' man! He's out right now, Mr. McLaen – tryin' to prog up a 'lectric ray! Ain't rightly got no sense at all. He tells the boss here to tell you he's too busy to talk any more business than to say 'O.K.!' – whatever that means."

"I think I understand."

Mr. McLaen grinned in the dark. He followed the boy to his cabin. He tipped him five dollars. It was a record for the man from Michigan.

Out on the broad smooth bay, near the shore of an island, the *Trident* moved along behind her headlight. Two men stared into the water with breathless concentration. Below them streamed beauty – bizarre beauty – fiendish beauty. They did not talk at all – but it was evident in their gestures and their attitudes that they understood each other extremely well.

The next afternoon was calm. The *Trident* was out to see what could be scared up by daylight. Aboard her were Crunch, who was looking at the Viscount with a continual but secret admiration, Mr. McLaen, who was expertly casting a plug into every likely cove, and the man from England himself, who stood in the bow, holding a harpoon, ready for anything. They slowly rounded a bend in Angelfish Creek. It is a favorite mooring place for private boats of all kinds – sheltered, beautiful and full of fish. Crunch was not surprised, but he was somewhat displeased to see the *Paloma* anchored there.

The Viscount squinted at it. "*Paloma*," he said. "*Paloma, Paloma, Paloma!* Isn't that Terry Walm's boat?"

Crunch nodded.

"Let's go over and put aboard, what? I know the young chappie."

Crunch did not seem eager to turn from his course.

"Anything wrong?" the Viscount asked.

"Wrong? Nothing. The people on that ship, though, have a habit of razzing the devil out of the *Trident*."

The Viscount's eyeglass twinkled. "They do, eh? Don't like the *Trident*, eh? You know, young Walm owes my company about ten thousand pounds. I wasn't aware he had the *Paloma* in commission. I do think we might stop by. I fancy he'd be quite taken with the *Trident* – under the circumstances." He saw Crunch's look of discomfort. "Oh – no mention of the money, old fellow! Not a syllable! I just think we might drift past and solicit the crashing bounder's admiration, don't you? Matter of fact, I insist!"

Crunch grinned, then, and turned the wheel.

LOST IN THE
20th Century

BY TOM DAVIS

Tom Davis, Contributing Editor to *Sporting Classics*,
is a contemporary writer with a special sense of time and
place. Lest you think hunting for prairie chickens and
sharp-tailed grouse is pretty mundane stuff, devoid of
romance save for a possible spot of fine dog-work,
read on. All of us look longingly back to better days and
better ways, and here we follow in the footsteps
of a gifted writer who recreates the endless panorama
of man, bird, dog and gun.

I f you were tilted in that direction already, like Van Gogh, perhaps, sunset on the prairies would drive you mad. It is too much for the mind to comprehend. The colors swirl and mutate impossibly (even Vincent himself could not have painted them); the grasses pulse like charged filaments; the astonished sky expands. You feel yourself diminishing uncontrollably, as if the inventory of your soul, your very being, is escaping your grasp.

112

Once beyond your reach, it joins those distant stars said to be hurtling toward the rubbery walls of the universe.

Such are the thoughts that occur to a nervous system careening on truck stop coffee, and a brain soggy from interstate driving. The pickup is loaded, pointing west. South Dakota, Nebraska maybe: wherever the thunderheads were stacked miles high, and lightning cracked them as if they were brimming ewers. The grass will be good there, the big bluestem pooling its maroon in the meadows, the grama gone yellow against the smooth-backed hills. This is where the birds will be, the prairie chickens and the sharp-tailed grouse, in a place that hasn't changed, a place that cattle and plows and combines haven't used up.

I go as much for the country as for the birds. It's a long trip. Zack will sprawl on the seat beside me, his back paws twitching against my leg and his weary muzzle wedged between the backrest and the door. A cache of Emmylou Harris cassettes will be scattered on top of the dashboard, except for the one in the tape player, with the volume cranked. Her voice reminds me of the faces of Depression-era women frozen in time by Dorothea Lange's photographs. I imagine them, thirty going on eternal, singing to their brave children, their voices clear, proud, and whetted by the gritty stone of despair. They went west too, these women, hearts half-filled with hope, half-filled with dread. The way their husbands talked, a better life was something they would simply find, like a lost calf, or an arrowhead. *Quarter-moon in a ten-cent town, time for me to lay my heartaches down. . .*

So it's a dangerous enterprise, heading west with something in mind, something related to expectations. I know: I've gone chicken hunting with great ones and watched them shatter; I've gone with none and seen the prairies alive with birds, shot them, cradled them in my hand and stroked their soft barred breasts with the backs of my fingers. The survivor's attitude is just to go, and take what comes.

This much I'm sure of: It'll just be the setters and I, eating, sleeping, and hunting out of a tent pitched on the brink of nowhere. Coffee in the morning, sour mash at night. Great looping fervent casts, the dogs tacking upwind like sloops, grass parting in their wakes, their flags like burgees snapping in the wind. Zack will make game first, standing like a monument, and Em will

113

honor instantly, crouched low in front, brown eyes riveted on her kennelmate. Chickens in the air, reports that barely scratch the overwhelming silence, a bird on the ground, setter muzzles whuffing the feathers. Naps in the warm afternoon, and books that can stand the weather: Kittredge, McGuane.

My camp will not be high, but it will be plenty lonesome. If all goes according to plan, the view will encompass no man-made objects whatsoever, other than the tent and the pickup. On second thought, I'd be willing to grant an exception for an abandoned ranch house, curtains still moving behind dark windows, especially one with a creaky windmill off to the side, a windmill that stood up to blizzards and droughts, and accomplished a quantity of work that couldn't be measured. That would seem right, a kind of lighthouse on this sea of grass.

I want to do it the way my friend Jon does, remote and self-sufficient, far from artifice and close to the honest bone. He makes his grouse camp up on the Missouri Coteau, not far from the Canadian border. Like me, Jon runs English setters, but he doesn't tote a shotgun. Instead, he carries a falcon on his fist. It's been said that flying hawks at prairie grouse is the ultimate expression of this ancient sport, the pinnacle of achievement for the falconer. Whether this is true, I'm not prepared to say. But I do know that when one of Jon's birds kills a sharptail – waiting on until the flock rises, then folding its wings, compressing its feathers and stooping, air shrieking through its bells – the moment is luminous. Later, Jon will grill the wine-red breast of the grouse over an open fire, just as the Bedouin falconers of Arabia might roast a bustard, their hooded sakers solemn as statuary. There is a continuum of tradition here, atavistic, pure, and unencumbered by existential baggage. The attraction is powerful. This is the way men should hunt; gun or falcon, it makes no difference.

Ideally, my camp will be as far removed from fences as possible, but this desire may not be realistic. I'll be hunting public land, the primary use of which seems to be the fattening of private cattle. Cattle translate into barbed wire. As I understand it, grazing rights to the public domain are leased under the same brand of sweetheart arrangements that make it cheaper for lumber companies to log the national forests than to harvest timber from their own stands. This land is your land, this land is my land, but no one consulted us when our elected stewards bent over and squealed for the pleasure of cattle interests. I say: Save a prairie chicken, declare open season on range beef.

Obviously, I've been reading far too much Ed Abbey lately.

In fact, it would be easy to recite chapter and verse about the mistreatment these birds have received – particularly the prairie chicken – at the hands of man. For a time in the late 19th century, when the original tallgrass prairies were only partially broken by the plow, chickens were fabulously abundant. There was still enough good grass for nesting, brooding the chicks, and roosting, and, in the form of corn, barley, rye and other cultivated grains, a literal glut of food. It has even been suggested that the decimation of the bison had a salubrious effect on the chicken populations because it left the prairies undisturbed by large herbivores. But cattle soon replaced buffalo, and the inexorable plow left little native sod unturned. As early as the 1920s, one eminent ornithologist would lament that only the passenger pigeon had suffered a crueler fate in the face of "civilization" than the prairie chicken.

They are anachronisms, these grouse of the prairies, living out on the edge of things, where it's too dry to plant and too big to graze to the nub. Perhaps this is why the idea of hunting them is so compelling: Clearly, they do not belong here, in 1990, but to an older era, an era of sod huts and horse-drawn plows, of shocked corn and steam engines, black-powder shotguns and dogs that point with low tails, gunners wearing ties, waxed mustaches, and bowler hats. Think Currier & Ives.

I wonder if I belong there, too. My mother, who puts much stock in such matters, tells me that in a former life I was a genteel sportsman of southern extraction – Virginian, probably – who cottoned to English setters, upland bird hunting, and fast women. If she is correct, the timing would have been right: I envision a Butleresque version of myself clacking west in a handsomely-appointed railroad car, enroute to the prairies for a week of shooting, happily relieving Yankees of their bankrolls in friendly games of poker, each garnered pot a sweet, symbolic act of revenge for the lost war.

Profoundly suspicious of the impulse to assign tidy answers to questions beginning with "Why?," I like Mom's explanation as well as any. And I can't help thinking, whenever I watch a flock of chickens sail out of sight, as they inevitably do, that the reason they disappear has nothing to do with distance, or with the limitations of the human eye. The reason they fly so far, the reason they vanish, is that they are searching for a flaw in the fabric of time, a rent that will ferry them back to the 19th century. They are not looking for a better place; they are looking for a better time.

But enough of metaphysics. The best populations of prairie chickens anywhere occur in Kansas, which also boasts the largest harvest. Statistics, however, lie. The season in Kansas doesn't open until November; by then, the birds have aggregated into extensive flocks, and their nerves are cocked against a hair-trigger. A hunter on foot with a dog has about as much chance of getting close to them as a naked and raving lunatic has of dodging Michael Jackson's bodyguards and getting autographed on the tush. It ain't going to happen. The deal in Kansas is to pass shoot in the afternoons when the chickens are trading between feeding areas (cornfields, mostly) and roosts. It's a little like dove shooting, but colder; very sporty and undeniably effective.

Trouble is, it doesn't appeal to me in the least. I have this perverse need to feel that I've earned my birds, a need that can be satisfied only by walking them up (this ethos applies to all gamebirds except quail, but as John Madson put it, you don't hunt quail, you hunt for the dog that is hunting for the quail). The choice, then, is between the grasslands of central South Dakota, below Pierre, and the eastern half of the Nebraska Sandhills. I generally lean toward Dakota, simply because it has less cactus and is therefore kinder to the dogs. The seasons in both states open in mid-September, when the birds still play fair. Actually, early-season grouse and chickens can be ridiculously easy, especially if they're hunkered down in sloughgrass or other heavy cover. They flush literally off your toe, are casual about getting up to speed, and once the flight plan is established, they don't deviate. In other words, they fly straight and slow (although they are burners at terminal velocity, as any falconer who has watched one pull away from a peregrine will attest).

You almost feel a twinge of guilt at shooting such agreeable birds. Don't worry; they'll soon extract their own peculiar toll, which you'll pay for in the currency of out-of-range flushes, long

116

and staggeringly difficult shots, legs alchemized into lead, and dead-on-your-feet exhaustion. Some number-cruncher once calculated that in a thin year the average chicken/sharptail hunter walks seven miles per bird. That's 21 miles for a three-bird limit, Dr. Einstein. Even in a good year, the distance between birds is measured in miles. This is not a sport for the infirm of body or the weak of heart.

Nor is it a game for soft, short-winded canines. Prairie hunting demands everything a bird dog has to give, and then some. A poorly-conditioned animal will soon be dragging its sorry ass; after a few days of this, you and your dog(s) both will be broken and pathetic. I remember checking on Zack in his truck kennel a couple days into a chicken hunt, just to see how the old boy was doing. A knuckle tapped on the window provoked no response. I called his name; no sign of life. A wave of anxiety crested in my stomach. "Zack!," I cried, rapping furiously on the glass. With excruciating effort, he cracked one eye, a gesture that said, "Let me lie, you pestiferous son of a bitch!"

While September has its virtues, I'll trade its easy marks for the educated birds of October. By then, the frosts will be visiting regularly, and the colors of the prairie will have mellowed to ocher, burnt sienna, and apricot, all streaming beneath a china sky. Besides, the scars incurred on that September trip to the Sandhills a while back remain vivid and painful to the touch. After 850 miles on the road, we – the setters and I – landed in Hell's Kitchen. The heat was ludicrous; I'm talking a hundred degrees. I tried to hunt at dawn, hoping to take advantage of the cool dew, and I damn near killed my dogs. It was the most outrageously ill-fated expedition of my career; there's not even a close second. It reminded me of the Custer joke: Corporal – looks like a pin cushion, so many arrows sticking out of his hide – crawls up to Custer at the Little Big Horn. "General," he gasps, "I've got some good news, and I've got some bad news."

"Tell me the bad news first," Custer orders.

"The bad news is that all our ammunition's gone, most of the horses are four hooves up, we can't run, we can't hide, and after we're dead the Sioux women will cut off our balls."

"What's the good news?"

"We won't have to ride back through Nebraska."

Whether I wind up in Nebraska or South Dakota, the shooting will be mixed, chickens and sharptails both. There are subtle differences in each bird's habitat preferences – sharptails gravitate more to brush than chickens; conversely, chickens do better in straight, undiluted grass – but for all practical purposes you're hunting the same bird. As if to prove the point, they commonly interbreed, and often as not you'll see both species in the same flock. Short course in identification: The birds with the white undersides and the spiky tails are sharptails, the ones that are dark all over and have rounded tails are chickens. The respective DNRs do not ask you to distinguish them on the wing: To the warden, they're both "grouse," and you're allowed three a day.

I confess to a weakness for prairie chickens. They're rarer, for one thing, and, to paraphrase Marlowe, I'm fascinated by their "tragical history." They strike a resonant chord in my soul. In the Sandhills, they'll tell you that chickens are wilder than grouse, but in South Dakota they claim that the opposite is true. What is for certain is that they both adore wide horizons, they both tend to flush "out there," and they fly forever, alternately beating their wings and gliding. Because they are muscled for long flights, their breast is profusely supplied with blood vessels. The meat is dark red, almost purple, the color of Pommard. It is incomparably tender and intensely flavorful: Imagine the finest tournedos of beef, prepared very rare, and you'll have an approximate idea of the taste. Eating the flesh of chickens or sharptails is an event – or should be. Parisians would beg, even weep, for such a delicacy.

It would be preposterous to advocate strategies for hunting these birds. The first bit of advice I received on the subject is still the sagest: "Keep walking – you can get well in a hurry." You need good grass, of course, which is one of those commodities you learn to recognize without being able to define precisely, like style or beauty. An upwind approach will get you closer, and be a huge help to your dog. Use enough gun: nothing less than an ounce of sixes. Some sportsmen like to work the meadows early and late, and concentrate on high ground during the day. Another variation is to hunt the grass in the morning, hit the sloughs and thickets when the heat is on, and then return to the grass just before sunset. Patches of wild rose and buffalo berry are always worth a look. Frankly, I'm convinced that chickens and sharptails operate on a totally random schedule, like wealthy eccentrics. So, I just keep walking.

That man I saw in South Dakota had it right. It was just he, his merry-gaited springer, and prairie enough to swallow them whole. I waved as I passed in the truck; he smiled and nodded. It sounds hopelessly cliche, but he carried a Parker. Hours later, I found myself passing by again. His car hadn't moved, but now there were dishes of food and water resting in the shade of the rear bumper. Suddenly, I had a clear picture of them: the man stretched out on the grass, hands clasped behind his head, cap pulled over his eyes, legs crossed at the ankle; the spaniel curled at his side, the curve of its back fitting into the hollow above the man's hip. When the shadow of a marsh hawk brushed over them, the dog came alert, and the man, without knowing it, laid a reassuring hand on its flank. No, I couldn't really see them, in a physical sense: They were somewhere out on the billowing prairie, searching for birds, waiting for their chance, for the simple opportunity, knowing the rest would take care of itself. I could see this man because I knew his mind. It was the same as my own.

Her voice sustains me, it lifts me up. We roll across the sand counties, thick with deer, of central Wisconsin, then enter the Coulee Country. The glaciers swerved when they got here, leaving the earth squeezed tight into ridges and valleys, like the bellows of an accordion. We bridge the Mississippi, climb the limestone bluffs of eastern Minnesota, top out on the vast tilled plain that stretches all the way to the Missouri. Stultifying, the land too clean, too polished to hold its soil. Dirty clouds curl up from the fields. A cock pheasant peeking from the brome is a revelation; a covey of Hungarian partridge gritting on the parallel gravel road a miracle. At Heron Lake a pang of sadness for the great flocks of canvasbacks that once rafted there, gorging on wild celery. Gone, to come no more. *How I crave the liquor of your song. . .*

My mind races ahead. I won't stop until I catch it, at a place where the land heaves itself up in broad, tan hills, only to fall away in blue vistas that undulate beyond a man's reckoning; a place where I can hunt all day and never retrace my steps, where the setters and I finally merge with the rhythms of the country, becoming as much a part of that music as the white-rumped pronghorns, the twitchy-eared jackrabbits, and the wheeling falcons, following the grouse and the chickens like partners in a dance, a dance that began before any of us were born.

THE OLD BROWN Mackinaw

BY GORDON MacQUARRIE

Gordon MacQuarrie's (1900-1956) stories of the Old
Duck Hunter's Society Inc. are, much like Corey Ford's
tales of The Lower Forty, filled with the camaraderie and
good-natured exchanges you'll find in any hunting camp.
Many of his pieces are humorous, but here we see a
deeper, more reverential side of the outdoors,
one that shows MacQuarrie at his best.

W hen the president of the Old Duck Hunter's Association,
Inc., died, the hearts of many men fell to the ground.

There was no one like Mister President. When the old-
timers go, there is no bringing them back, nor is there any hope
of replacing them. They are gone, and there is a void, and for
many, many years I knew the void would never be filled, for this
paragon of the duck blinds and the trout streams had been the

121

companion of my heart's desire for almost 20 years.

I made the common mistake. I looked for another, exactly like hizzoner. How foolish it is, as foolish as it is for a man to try to find another beloved hunting dog, exactly like the one that's gone.

In the years after Mister President's death I fished and hunted more than before, and often alone. There was a great deal of fishing and hunting, from Florida to Alaska, before a man came along who fit the role once occupied by Mister President. This is how it was:

I was sitting in the ballroom of the Lorraine Hotel in Madison, Wisconsin, covering the proceedings of the unique Wisconsin conservation congress. I became aware that a man carrying one of the 71 labels for the 71 counties of the state was eyeing me.

He held aloft the cardboard label "Iowa" signifying that he was a Big Wheel in conservation from that western Wisconsin county. He looked like Huckleberry Finn, and he grinned eternally. One of the first thoughts I had about him was that he probably could not turn down the corners of his lips if he wanted to.

Each time I glanced at him his eye was upon me. This sort of thing is unnerving. Once he caught my eye and held it and grinned harder. I grinned back, foolishly. The beggar burst out laughing. I felt like a fool. He knew it and laughed at me.

Let me give you the picture more completely. In that room sat more than 300 dedicated, articulate conservationists. They were framing, no less, the fish and game code of this sovereign state for an entire year. Not in silence, you may be sure.

Up at the front table on the platform, as chairman of the congress, sat Dr. Hugo Schneider of Wausau, with a gavel in one hand and – so help me! – a muzzle-loading squirrel rifle in the other. Each time Roberts Rules of Order seemed about to go out the window, Doc would abandon the gavel and reach for the rifle.

In this delightful pandemonium, in this convention of impassioned hunters and fishers and amidst the shrieks from the wounded and dying delegates, Wisconsin evolves its game and fish laws. And if you can think of a more democratic way, suggest it. We may try it.

At one point in the milling commotion and confusion, I saw my grinning friend slip to the floor and on his hands and knees start crawling toward me. By this manner of locomotion he managed to evade the baleful eye and subsequent vengeance of Dr. Schneider, and he crawled up to my chair and handed me a scribbled note. Then still on his hands and knees, he crawled away. The note read:

"I've been reading your drivel for years. See me after school if you want to get some good partridge hunting."

Harry

Since then I suppose I've "seen him" a thousand times – on trout streams, on lakes, in partridge cover, in the deer woods, in the quail thickets, and yes, in the August cow pastures where the blackberries grow as long as your thumb, and in the good September days when you can fill a bushel basket with hickory nuts beneath one tree.

No outdoor event of its season escapes Harry. He is lean and fiftyish. He is a superb shot. He ties his own flies, one a black killer with a tiny spinner at the eye made from special light material he begs, or steals from dentist friends. On a dare, once he shinned up a 12-foot pole and came back down head first. Once he made me a pair of buckskin pants. All in all, he was an unbelievable person.

How natural then, just this last October, that we should rendezvous, not in Iowa County – we save those partridge until December – but at the ancient headquarters of the Old Duck Hunter's Association, two whoops and a holler north of Hayward, Wisconsin.

I got there first. This is not hard for me to do when going to this place. Some things do not change, and this is one of those things. It's exactly like it was before the atomic age. On that particular day, late October's yellow shafts were slanting through the Norways on the old cedar logs of the place. A chipmunk which had learned to beg in summer came tentatively close, then scurried away, uncertain now.

All was in order, down to the new windowpane I had to put in where a partridge in the crazy time had flown through. The label was still pasted to the tiny square of glass. I must scratch it off some day, but there is always so much to do at places like this.

I went to the shed at the rear to check decoy cords and anchors. When you open this shed door one of the first things to catch your eye is a brown, checked-pattern Mackinaw, about 50 years old, I guess. It belonged to the President of the Old Duck Hunters. I like to keep it there. It belongs there.

Flying squirrels had filled one pocket of the Mackinaw with acorns. They always do that, but these avian rodents, so quick to unravel soft, new wool for nests, have never chewed at the threadbare carcass of Mister President's heroic jacket. Perhaps this is because the wool, felted and tough, has lost its softness and flavor. I launched a boat, readied a smaller skiff and screwed the motor on the big boat. I fetched three bags of decoys down the hill and put them in a handy place. I put an ax – for blind building – in the boat with other gear, and when I got back up the hill to the cabin, Harry was there.

On the way – a 300 mile drive – he had hesitated, he said, long enough to slay two pheasant roosters.

"I see," he said, "that you have been here an hour and have killed 'ary a duck or partridge." He explained that he had felt my auto radiator – "She's cooled only about an hour." This man operates like a house detective. I explained that in the remaining hour and a half of daylight I would prepare him a kingly supper.

"An hour and a half of daylight!" He flung two skinned pheasant to me, dashed to his car and returned, running, bearing fishing tackle.

"D'ja soak the boat?" he cried as he passed me. I doubt if he heard my answer for he was soon down the hill and nearing the beach when I replied. Within two minutes he was trolling.

The man never lived who could fill up each moment of a day like this one. Nor was there ever a one who could, once the day was done, fall asleep so fast. He goes, I am sure, into a world of dreams, there to continue the pursuits of fish and game, man's lifeblood – well, his anyway.

I lit the fireplace. No need for the big steel stove, or was there? Late-October weather in the North can be treacherous. I laid the big stove fire, to play safe. The provident Harry had made getting supper easy. You take two pheasant and cut them up. You save the giblets. You steam some wild rice for an hour. . .

It was long after dark when Harry returned. He had a seven- or eight-pound northern, and a walleye half as big – "If we're gonna be here for four days, somebody around here has got to bring home the grub."

I set the table fast for fear he would fall asleep. He stuffed himself with pheasant and wild rice and mentioned that he must not forget to tell his wife how badly I treated him. Then he collapsed on the davenport before the fire, and in one yawn and a short whistle he was gone. I washed the dishes.

No, he was not a shirker. Before sleep afflicts him he will kill himself at any job which needs doing, especially if it pertains to hunting and fishing. To prove his willingness for the menial tasks, I recall a deep camp one night when one of the boys brought in a 300-pound bear – dragged him right through the door and dropped him at Harry's feet.

Harry was wiping the dishes, clad only in a suit of new, red underwear. He had sworn to be the first man in that camp to bring in important game, and because now he obviously had not, he turned, dishcloth in hand, eyed the bear casually and remarked:

"Johnny, that's a mighty-nice little woodchuck you got there."

Even when I turned on the radio for a weather report he did not awaken. His snores, wondrously inventive, competed with the welcome report of changing and colder weather. Outside the wind was coming along a bit, and it was in the northwest. But mostly it was the warm wind hurrying back south ahead of something colder at its back.

Iowa County's nonpareil was bedded down in the far room where his snores joined the issue with the rising wind which keened over the roof. A good fair contest, that.

When I arose I had to light the big heater for the weather had made up its mind. No snow, but a thermometer at 26 degrees and a buster of a wind. I hurried with breakfast because I thought we might have to build a blind on Posey's point. That point, the right one on this day, had not been hunted in the season. When I mentioned the reason for haste he explained:

"Man, I built that blind yesterday. You think I fooled away three hours just catching a couple of fish?"

It is not possible to dislike a man like that. Furthermore, I knew this blind would be no wild dove's nest, but a thing of perfection, perfectly blended with the shoreline.

A lot of people in this country think the old Duck Hunters are crazy when they hunt this lake. We carry so many decoys that we have to tow them behind in a skiff. Fifty is our minimum, half of them oversize balsas, and a scattering of some beat-up antiques more than 120 years old, just for luck.

125

Settling himself for some duck-blind gossip, Harry began, "I was down on the Mississippi at Ferryville last week. Mallards all over the. . ."

"Mark!"

A hundred bluebills, maybe twice that, who knows, came straight in without once swinging, and sat. We never touched a feather as they rose. I have done it before, and I'll do it again, and may God have mercy on my soul.

"This," said Harry, "will become one of the greatest lies in history when I tell my grandchildren about it. I am reminded of Mark Twain. When Albert Bigelow Paine was writing his biography and taking copious notes, he once remarked to Twain that his experiences and adventures were wonderful copy.

" 'Yes, yes,' " replied Mr. Clemens. 'And the most remarkable thing about it is that half of them are true.' "

He then set his jaw and announced he would kill the next three straight with as many shots. This he did, for I did not fire. While I was retrieving them in the decoy skiff, another bundle of bluebills tried to join those giant decoys and were frightened off by me. Walking to the blind from the boat, I saw Harry kill a canvasback.

He was through for the day and not a half hour had passed. Many Badgers will remember that late October day of 1955. Ducks flew like crazy from the Kakagon Sloughs of Lake Superior to sprawling Horicon Marsh, 300 miles away. Only one other day of that season beat it – Wednesday, November 2.

Harry cased his gun and watched. I cannot shoot like Harry, but getting four ducks on such a day was child's play. Many times we had more divers over our decoys than we had decoys. It was pick-and-choose duck hunting. I settled for four bullneck canvasbacks.

Back at the cabin, we nailed their bills to the shed wall, and over a cup of coffee Harry said the divers we'd seen reminded him of the "kin to can't day." Then, he explained, the law let a man shoot the whole day through from as soon "as he kin see until the time that he can't see." I knew a place, Oscar Ruprecht's sugar bush, and we drove the eight miles to it.

This chunk of maple is on an island of heavier soil in an ocean of glacial sand, grown to pines. If its owner had the equipment he could tap 5000 trees. Many know it and hunted it. We separated, for we are both snap shooters, or think we are.

126

The plan was to meet on a high, rocky bluff where the River Ounce passes below, on its way to the Totagatic. Here was no dish like that easy duck-blind venture. These were mature, hunted ruffed grouse, all the more nervous because the wind was high. On one of the tote trails where Oscar's tractor hauls the sap tank I missed my first bird, then missed two more.

A half mile to my right, two calculated shots sounded, well spaced. Perhaps a double. Ah, well. . .My fourth bird was as good as dead when it got out of the red clover in midtrail and flew straight down the road. I missed him, too.

Three times more, and later a couple more times Harry's gun sounded. Then two birds flung themselves out of the yellow bracken beside the two-rut road, and I got one. When I was walking over to pick it up, a third pumped up, and I got it.

It was noon when I got to the high bluff. Deer hunters with scopes on their rifles love this place. From it they overlook almost a half mile of good deer country in three directions. My sandwich tasted good. I lit a little friendship fire and thought about other days on the river below me. It's a pretty good trout stream for anyone who will walk in two miles before starting to fish.

Harry came along. He'd been far up the valley of the Ounce, bucking fierce cover – no sugar-bush tote trails in there, only deer trails. But he had five grouse. We hunted back to the car, and in his presence I was lucky enough to kill my third bird.

It was around 2 p.m. when we pulled into the cabin. My Huckleberry Finn, who I have seen, on occasion, whittle away at a pine stick for 20 minutes without doing anything but meditate, was a ball of fire on this day. He tied into the ducks and partridge. When he had finished cleaning them his insatiable eye fell upon the woodpile.

You can spot those real country-raised boys every time when they grab an ax. They know what to do with it. No false moves. No glancing blows. In no time he had half a cord of fine stuff split and piled for the kitchen range, and he went on from that to the sheer labor of splitting big maple logs with a wedge for the fireplace.

He spotted my canoe and considered painting it, but decided it was too cold, and anyway, it had begun to snow a little. Then he speculated about the weather, and when I said I wish I had a weather vane on the ridgepole, he went into action.

127

He whittled out an arrow from an old shingle, loosely nailed it to a stick, climbed to the roof and nailed it there firmly. I suppose that if I had mentioned building an addition to the back porch he'd have started right in. He came down from the roof covered with snow and said he wished he hadn't killed those four ducks in the morning, so he could go again.

"But, let's go anyway," he suggested. "No guns. Put out the decoys and just watch 'em."

Out there on the point the divers were riding that wind out of Canada. Scores of them rode into and above the decoys. Posey, the owner of the point, came along for a visit and decided we were both crazy when he saw what we were doing. Nevertheless, we had him ducking down as excited as we were when a new band of bluebills burst out of the snow. Only in the big duck years can a hunter enjoy such madness.

Our shore duty at dark that night involved careful preparations against the storm. We pulled up the boat and skiff higher than usual and covered everything with a weighted tarp.

Walking up the hill, I considered how nice it was to have one of the faithful, like Harry, on the premises. He should have been bone-tired. Certainly I was. But before I relit the big heater he took down its 15 feet of stovepipe, shook out the soot and wired it back to the ceiling. He carried in enough wood for the remaining three days, stamping off snow and whistling and remembered such tales as one hears in all properly managed hunting camps.

He spied a seam rip in my buckskin pants and ordered me to take them off. While he mended them he complained bitterly about such neglect on my part – "There's nothing wrong with the workmanship on these pants."

He had made them himself, two months before, from two big chrome-tanned doeskins. He just walked into my house one night with a gunnysack containing the skins, a piece of chalk and some old shears his wife used for trimming plants. He cut the pants out, fitted them to me and took them to the shoemaker's shop where he sewed them up and affixed buttons. I never in my life wore pants that fit so well.

This man should have been born in the same time as a Kit Carson or a Jim Bridger. Turn him loose anywhere in his native heath, which is Wisconsin, and given matches, an ax, a fishhook and some string, he'll never go hungry or cold.

He is a true countryman, a species almost extinct. Each day of the year finds him outdoors for at least a little while. In trout season he hits the nearby streams for an hour or two around sunup. His garden is huge and productive. In the raspberry season you may not go near his home without being forced, at gun point if need be, to eat a quart of raspberries with cream.

He represents something almost gone from our midst. He knows the value of working with his own hands, of being eternally busy, except when sleeping. His last act that snowy evening was to go to his car and return with a bushel of hickory nuts. He set up a nut-cracking factory on a table, using a little round steel anvil he had brought for busting 'em. He had over a quart of hickory nut meats in jars when I put the grub on the table.

He almost fell asleep at the table. Then he yawned and whistled and looked out the door and said he was glad it was snowing hard – "Don't shoot at anything but cans in the morning." He flopped on the davenport and was gone to that far-off land where no trout of less than five pounds comes to a surface fly and the duck season runs all year.

I tidied up and washed the dishes. I smelled the weather and smoked a pipe. The fireplace light danced on the big yellow cedar beams. The snow hissed against the window. The President of the Old Duck Hunter's Association should have been there.

Maybe he was. At any rate, I went out to the shed and took the old brown Mackinaw off its nail and brought it in and laid it over Harry's shoulders. It looked just fine there.

Reprinted from *Stories of the Old Duck Hunter & Other Drivel* published by Willow Creek Press, 801 Oregon Street, Oshkosh, Wisconsin 54901 (paperback $5.95).

Heaven
I S   A   R I V E R

BY SCOTT WALDIE

Waters swift and pure run as so many silver ribbons
through anglers' dreams. In this piece, which originally
appeared in *Sporting Classics*, talented writer Scott
Waldie gives those dreams shape and substance. He
captures in print what many of us feel so strongly in
person, yet find exceedingly difficult to share with
others, especially the uninitiated.

ason was at the rear of the Carrie Creek Boat Works and
Guide Service bent over one of his river dories. It had been a
quiet afternoon. In one hand he moved a small plane along
the gunwhales while the other hand followed, brushing away the
oak shavings and checking his work. Stepping back from the boat
he tried to twist the day's kinks from his back. He shed his apron,
adjusted his suspenders, and leaned against the workbench. The

130

boat was far from finished; he was done for the day.

From there he could look north through the shop's back windows to see a sky filled with threatening clouds. Just in from Canada, it was typical of late September storms: they didn't seem to roll in so much as they liked to bear down. The afternoon sun was making one last appearance from beneath the clouds, and its brilliance was made doubly harsh by the oncoming darkness. Travers Corners was still soaked from a preliminary shower, and its usually dusty streets shone in the light. It set the small Montana town awash in reds and yellows and edged the brick buildings and wooden sidewalks that lined Main Street in white neon.

He pulled a bandana from his hip pocket and wiped the dust from his glasses. Then he added it back into his pocket and wove his glasses back into place through his dark brown, giving way to grey, hair. His movements were slow and precise befitting his trade. If his tired old clothes – flannel shirt, faded Levi's vest, and moccasins – had the energy to make a fashion statement, you would have to read it in the *Mother Earth News*. He pulled an old pocket watch from his vest pocket – 5:25. Jason always imagined that time carried in a pocket watch might travel a little slower.

The sound of someone coming through the front door didn't interrupt Jason's weather watch. On Friday afternoon around quitting time it could only be Henry Albie. He and Henry went back for thirty of Jason's forty years.

Henry hobbled down the wooden ramp that separated what Jason referred to as the retail end of the operation – flies, leaders, and one each of everything else that had to do with fly fishing – from the workshop. As he reached inside a paper bag and handed Jason a beer, he growled, "How am I supposed to take anyone fishing in this shit?" nodding towards the rain, which was gaining momentum.

"What's with the limp?" Jason asked.

"Shoein' old man Kokenauer's mare this morning and she kicked me good, right here on my leg," he said, pointing to a place on his upper thigh. "A couple of inches higher and you could call it my ass.

"I'll be in great shape for rowing tomorrow. Course if this weather keeps up, there ain't going to be any fishing tomorrow. It drops another degree out there and it's apt to snow. They'll cancel sure as hell."

131

Jason took his bitching in stride. He knew that complaint was the road that Henry took to vent his pessimism or to get a laugh. Right now he was doing both. He'd done it since they were kids, so he also knew he wasn't finished.

"I need a couple of day's guiding. I could use the bucks. Shoein's been slow. Hey, how about building a fire in here?" He started to gather wood scraps from the floor. "I ain't ready for winter just yet."

Henry, whose face was as long as a hoe handle, had just recounted a grevious personal injury and predicted bad fishing and financial ruin without moving a wrinkle. His deadpan was divided by a greying mustache set over lips that never seemed to move. Henry was what Will Rogers described as a "close chewer and a tight spitter." He was short and muscular. He was Jason's best friend.

"You can relax about your guide trip," Jason said, trying to soothe him. "Your people called this morning and said they were running a little late. Wanted me to call the Take 'Er Easy and make sure they would hold their room. Henry, I think you could be in real trouble with this one. He was calling from his mobile phone. When I told him it was a little stormy, he said he was going fishing come hell or high water.

"Then he asks me if it's all right if he brings along his shotgun tomorrow. I said there was no real reason to, waterfowl season not starting for another month. He says it wouldn't be the first duck season that he's opened up a little early.

"Then he puts his wife on. She wants to know if we have a vet in town. Seems her poodle has been getting carsick on all our windy roads."

Henry grimaced. "I suppose this all fits in somewhere with getting kicked by that mare. What's their names? Where they from?"

"Wilkinson. Jimbo Wilkinson. From Houston. He's in oil."

"Bingo."

"I've got some good news," Jason offered.

"Better'n rowing two Texans and a poodle down the river in the rain? This is one of those times I wish I were flush. I'd call in sick."

"The Professor called. He's coming out."

You would have to know Albie to be able to observe the change from despair to surprise; everything took place in his eyes. "When's he going to be here?"

"Anytime now. He called from Helena about an hour ago. Now check this out. He's coming today, fishing tomorrow, and going home on Sunday. Then he's coming back in October."

"Well," Henry said, "things must be good in the teachin' business. He was just here two months ago. How long we been guidin' the Professor?"

"Fourteen years, but he's always come in July. He's really going to love the fall fishing. You know," he said with reflection as he lit the fire, "I've guided a lot of people, but I suppose I like taking the Professor the best. Always learn something from him."

"Hope he gets here soon. I gotta leave at six."

As the fire warmed they continued to talk about the Professor. An eavesdropper would soon find out about his expertise with a dry fly and his love of cognac. There would be little chance he would learn that the Professor was known to the rest of the world as Dr. Clark Munroe, a foremost American anthropologist. A noted author. A man who traveled the world and took notes. A fascinating man. A man who had called Margaret Mead "Maggie."

But that was the Professor's other life, and Henry and Jason only knew him within the context of Montana. He was a contrast, to be sure, all tweed, highbrow, and upper crust in the land of denim, down home, and sourdough. He seemed to fit in well in spite of all this, but that was the mark of a great anthropologist, to slip in and out of cultures without making a ripple.

It was 6:15 and still no Professor. Henry had to leave. "Guess I won't be seeing him until Sunday, unless he comes to hear us play tomorrow night. Oh, Peggy's sister is in town. I hear she's a looker."

"Henry, the Mama Juggs band is not exactly Mozart. I'll try to make him come, but you know how he feels about country music."

Henry had been gone two hours when the door swung open again. Jason looked up from his fly-tying desk. "Hello, Professor."

"And hello back to you, Jason." He was a tall man from a distance, but as he came closer you found that his height came more from his being lanky than from endwise. Jason quickly noticed a change in him. He was 74, but never before had Jason seen his age. His walk had lost its nimbleness, but the blue eyes peering over a pair of half glasses were just as sharp.

Jason put the whip finish to the Red Quill in his vise and stood up. They shook hands vigorously. "What kept ya?" Jason asked.

133

"Oh, I am sorry. I know I'm late, but I've been working on a speech. I must have it prepared by Monday evening. The body of the speech came along quite quickly, but I was having trouble finding a closing. As I drove across the summit I was privy to a most spectacular sunset, and I thought, 'What better time to write an ending? So I pulled off and finished. Now I'm unencumbered for the weekend. I have nothing more important on my mind than doing a little fishing. This weather is temporary, I hope."

Jason handed the professor a beer then tipped his own slightly and toasted, "Good to have you back."

"Thank you. I apologize for the short notice, but on Thursday evening it occurred to me that for the amount of time I was wasting lately thinking about coming here, I would probably save time in the long run by being here." He removed his bow tie. "Came straight from work. Had an easy flight from Boston." He pulled a pipe from his sports coat, which fit the same as his slacks, loose almost to the point of looking borrowed.

They spent the next hour deciding on the best spot for tomorrow's fishing. The Professor said that he had been daydreaming about catching a large rainbow. Rainbow trout had narrowed it down to the Elkheart River, and large rainbows pinpointed it. "We'll float from the Webb Ranch down to the Widowmaker," Jason concluded. "There aren't as many fish in that stretch, but it's where the big ones pick up their mail."

"Is there any reason to get away early tomorrow?" the Professor asked. "We septuagenarians have to offset a long day with an equally long night."

"Okay, let's meet at the Tin Cup for breakfast around eight-thirty or nine."

"That sounds good." He started toward the front door, then stopped and pointed to the fly cases. "I'll be needing some Royal Trudes for tomorrow, but I'll get them in the morning. Good night."

"See you in the morning." It was the first time Jason could remember him to ask for a late start, but then, as Jason glanced at his watch, it was the first time he hadn't stayed half the night talking about fishing.

Jason's old Willys, drift boat in tow, started its climb up McCartney Mountain. The aspen groves above the canyon were performing card tricks in the autumn morning. The Elkheart

River, below, paralleled the old two-lane. Jason was at the wheel and the Professor was in heaven.

"What a glorious day." He sat forward in his seat and pointed out the window. "Hey, there's a boat on the river. Could it be Henry?"

"Couldn't hardly be anyone else. His client wanted to be on the river by daybreak, so he could be this far by now." He veered the old jeep off the road and pulled a pair of binoculars from beneath the seat. "This could be good."

They sat down on the guard rail and Jason, through the binoculars, relayed what he could make out. "Okay, in the bow of the boat we have Jimbo, who doesn't look as though he's been missing any meals." Jason paused and watched him cast a few times. "He has what could be described as a desperate style of fishing. No apparent threat to the fish there. In the stern we have the rotund Mrs. Jimbo. Two hundred pounds, no problem. She is – yes it's confirmed – she's bait fishing. A quick note – the Jimbos are wearing matching lime-green jumpsuits. The white fluff bouncing all over the boat would have to be the poodle. And there in the center of things is our boy, Henry, who has had better two-day stretches."

He handed the field glasses to the Professor and tried to control an outburst, but released a chuckle that sounded like a checkvalve on a steam line. But he felt a sense of guilt about laughing. Here he was spending the day with a prince among men while his best friend was trapped in a boat with an oil maggot, a hyperkinetic poodle, and a bait-fishing watermelon.

"Wait a minute," the Professor said after refocusing, "Jimbo has a fish on, and judging by the bend of his rod, Henry's frantic rowing, and the velocity of the poodle, it must be a good one. No. He had a big one. He lost it."

"Well, if Jimbo just hooked one, the fishing has got to be good. Let's go."

Twenty minutes later Jason was standing knee-deep in the Elkheart, holding the drift boat, named the *Lucky Me*, steady in the current. The river gently slapped at her upturned bow. Jason watched as the Professor loaded the last of his equipment. Once he was seated, Jason hopped aboard, grabbed the oars, and rowed out into the river.

Jason oared the boat into position, and the Professor stood up against the knee braces, picked up his old fly rod, stripped off some line, and began to false cast. "Elizabeth gave me this rod, you know."

Jason knew. The Professor had said that or something similar almost every day they had been fishing together. He had heard the whole story. Of how she had bought the bamboo rod from the Winston Rod Company during the '39 World's Fair, just before her death. It still looked good. But then he must have had its old cane refinished half a dozen times.

Satisfied with the length of his line, he let the fly light and watched it float along the branches of a fallen cottonwood. Trout Territory, but no one was home.

For the first hour the fishing was slow, the next two hours were even slower. In a lot of ways Jason didn't mind that the fishing was off. The Professor was a master storyteller and had personal anecdotes from all over the world. They had accumulated enough poor fishing time together over the years for Jason to have heard some wonderful tales.

"Hey, Professor, you just missed a fish."

"Guess my mind was someplace else. How big was he?"

"About fifteen inches. Are you getting hungry? I could go for some lunch."

Jason eddied up the boat at a sharp bend in the river just after they entered the canyon. It was a place where the river folded up against the limestone wall, then flowed away at a right angle, shallowing into a long green glide. The cliffs towered hundreds of feet above, leaving them with a jagged window to the sky. The Professor was leaning against a large piece of driftwood, and Jason was lying on a patch of sand, propped up on one elbow.

"Oh. Henry's band is playing down at the Stompin' Grounds tonight, and he sure wants to see you. With you leaving early tomorrow, guess it'd be his only chance."

"Yee gawds!" exclaimed the Professor. "You know how I feel about that horrific music he plays, but I suppose there could be no harm in it – other than to my auditory nerve. What's the name of his band again?"

"The Mama Juggs band." Jason finished his piece of Tin Cup apple pie. "Hey, I just saw a couple of fish rise in the middle of the run. There's another. And another..."

They agreed to split the run, Jason fishing the bottom half and the Professor the top. Jason still had to set up his rod, and as he did he could look up and watch his companion. He made that old Winston dance, and he sent his fly line floating over the water as softly as a spider's web caught in the wind. Jason was tying on one of his Red Quills when he heard him let out a small whoop. He had his first fish, the old rod jerking and bending while a fair-sized rainbow jumped upstream. By the time Jason had finished greasing his fly, the Professor had hooked a second. Two fish in as many minutes is about all the invitation a fisherman can stand, and in moments Jason had the third.

Satisfied that they had hooked or at least frightened everything in the run, they started wading back to the boat. They had caught plenty of fish between them, so who had caught the most would be secondary. It was sure to be a game of who had caught the biggest. Once they were within earshot of one another they began to compare their catch. It was like listening to two men yelling out a game of draw poker.

"How'd ya do?" Jason opened.

"I did very well, very well indeed," the older man shouted back.

"I did okay. Caught a couple. Lost a real nice one."

"I caught three fifteen inchers and two that hit the sixteen-inch mark," hollered the Professor.

"Well, that certainly beats anything I landed. But I wish you could have seen the fish that I lost. If he was an inch, he was twenty. Had him on for a long time. Surprised you missed it. But you probably had one of your fifteen inchers on. Jumped five times. Had him up to the net twice. But he was just too big and too mean. He finally broke off my hook and I lost him. Best fish I caught all year."

(Poker and fishing are a lot alike. Except in fishing nothing can beat one of a kind.)

In all their years of fishing together, they had each bluffed their way into a lot of pots, but there could never be a clear-cut winner over all. They released every fish they caught – never had to show their cards. Jason waded from the water with a look that said "Drinks all around, Barkeep."

Back in the boat the fishing returned to the morning's slow pace. For long stretches the only sounds were that of the old man's Winston fanning the air and the creaking of Jason's oars against their locks.

The silence was broken by the rumblings of Widowmaker, an ominous name given to an easy rapid. Although Widowmaker Rock, which was roughly the size of a split-level, did sit dead center in the river while two-thirds of the Elkheart roared right into it with enough power to reduce the *Lucky Me* to kindling, it was simple to avoid by staying in the third that didn't. If you put your back into it a little, you could miss the whole rapid. But Jason never liked to do that. He liked to ride a few waves, then pull into safer water.

Showing about as much concern as one might pulling onto a freeway, Jason readied himself at the oars. He had respect for the Widowmaker, even though he could probably row it in his sleep. "Better sit down, Professor. Don't want to lose you." The river was moving faster, the rumble becoming a roar.

The Professor took one more cast, targeted at a small pocket of water completely surrounded by the willows. The fly fell short and was quickly swept beneath the brush. It snagged and drew his line taut. He tried to jerk it loose, then sat down as instructed.

Jason was doing last-minute maneuvering when from the corner of his eye he saw the fly line leave the willows and a flash of silver beneath the surface. "Hey, Professor, I think your snag is trying to swim upstream."

The Professor looked up to see his fish break water. A big fish. Bigger than anything he had hooked in years. Maybe ever. Jason turned to see the fish start its run. Fly line was coiling out of the boat like a harpooner's rope, until it reached the loop pinned under the Professor's foot. He instinctively jumped up, hopping on one foot, trying to shake the line free from his other. He needed slack or he'd lose that fish.

The first wave of the Widowmaker smashed into the bow, throwing him back over his seat and into Jason's lap. Trying to stand he reached for the gunwhale but instead knocked the oar from its lock. The boat turned sideways, and the second wave hit with enough force to loosen Jason's grip so that he lost the oar. With no pulling power on one side, they were in real trouble. They were taking on water.

Jason grabbed for the spare oar, but it was macraméd into place by the fly line.

Outside of expletives, nothing was said. They had floated together for years. They both knew exactly what had to be done. Jason had to get the Professor back into his seat. Get all that damned fly line away from his oar. Get the oar back into its lock. And row his cheeks off if he was going to miss the Widowmaker, if he was going to save his boat.

The Professor knew his role equally well. First he was going to get back to his seat. Get his fly line away from the damn oar. Find his net and straighten out the slack in his line, if he was going to save that fish. They worked feverishly at the oar and by the time Jason had freed it from its lashing, the professor had unravelled it from his fly line. Jason slammed it into place and frantically heaved at the oars, spinning their blades like runaway windmills. The boat didn't budge. It was half-filled with water and taking on more. No chance of missing the Widowmaker.

The Professor was a man lost in sport, his knees frozen in the braces, both hands holding the rod high above his head, and shouting, "He's still on! I still have him!"

There was little chance the *Lucky Me* would actually smash into the Widowmaker, the force of the water curling back off the rock would cushion that. But there was no doubt they were going over.

"Hold on, Professor! Grab your preserver!" Jason screamed.

But in the din of the rapid all he heard was "Hold on, you deserve her." He thought so.

The river hurled the boat directly at the rock, but instead of flipping, it somehow rode the crest of the wave and stalled almost motionless at the top of the curl like a rollercoaster car at the top of a rise just before your belly drops out. Jason's oars were still whirling and he was hoping for a miracle. The Professor wondered if he should give the fish more slack in this chop.

The boat spun, then slipped stern-first around the Widowmaker just as smoothly as a cat takes a corner. They came within inches of the rock. Jason tried to ship his right oar, but it was too late and he heard the sound of cracking wood.

The river suddenly calmed behind the massive rock into a large pool. The *Lucky Me* was all but underwater yet still right side up. The Professor had been knocked down but was scrambling to his feet and yelling, "I still have him!" Jason, having just returned from a trip to his Maker, was slow to share in his enthusiasm. He was glad to see the lost oar had joined them in the eddy.

The fish jumped, shimmering like wet silver. He was a sight. If he were a sound, he'd have been thunder. The third time he left the water he came within 20 feet of the boat, giving them their first close look. He was shaking his head for freedom and tailwalking his crimson sides. The Professor sensed the fish was tiring. "Better get the net."

For the first time Jason really noticed the condition of their gear – now flotsam. Fly boxes, reel bags, and rod tubes bobbed around inside the boat. "Well, I'm sure it's here somewhere."

The Professor brought the weary rainbow to the surface. The fish materialized from the depths like an oncoming ghost. He was sluggish but attempted one last run, right into Jason's net. He lifted him from the water and into the boat, freed the hook, then flipped the fish from the net and let him swim about in the boat.

"Not much fight left in him. Better let him catch his breath," Jason said and looked up to see that the Professor had gone quite pale. "You all right?"

"A little dizzy perhaps," he said and sat down and watched his fish swim near his feet. "Isn't he a beauty? He's the biggest fish I've ever caught. Certainly couldn't have done it without your superb rowing."

"But – "

"What oarsmanship, the way you kept the boat out in the center, keeping me straight to the fish and away from the willows. The way you went through the Widowmaker backwards. Now that was quick thinking."

"But Professor, I couldn't – "

"If you hadn't pivoted the boat at that exact moment, I would have lost him for sure. He was making for the other side of the rock, but when we started backwards, I could really put the butt to him and make him follow us."

"But the boat was completely out of – "

"How much do you think he weighs?"

"Six pounds, maybe a little more." Jason decided to tell him how they really went through the Widowmaker later. Anyway, he could stand to be a hero for a while. Jason started to bail and the Professor began an inspection of their waterlogged cargo.

140

Everything seemed to be unharmed, until he spotted his camera swimming alongside the trout. "Damn, and I wanted to have a photograph of my fish. He's the kind of fish that will require proof."

Jason was ten minutes into the bailing with another twenty to go when the trout started to cruise the length of the boat, circling and picking up speed, searching for an exit.

"Looks like he's ready to go.' He handed the Professor the net. "He's your fish, you have the honors."

He scooped him up and lifted him overboard, easing the net and fish into the river. The current played on the netting, and once the fish sensed the opening, he swam free of the net, shook his tail, and disappeared instantly back into the green.

Jason bailed the water down to the point where the *Lucky Me* could be rowed again. They had only a quarter-mile to go before they reached the takeout, and he was glad. The Professor hadn't seemed to regain his color. "Listen, you sure you want to go to the Stompin' Grounds tonight? You gotta catch the red-eye tomorrow, and it's been a long day."

"Nonsense, a trip to Montana without seeing Henry is simply not a trip to Montana. I have given it some thought, and this is how I envision the evening. First I will return to the Take 'Er Easy and get some rest, then meet you at the Tin Cup for dinner around eight. We can be at the dance by nine, listen to several selections, and I can be back at my room by ten. That will almost give me my eight hours, and I can sleep on the plane."

At the take-out Jason bailed the remaining water from the *Lucky Me*, then trailered her. The Professor, in the meantime, had shaken out and wrung dry all their gear and had spread it all over the boat ramp. Jason turned to see him looking sadly at his dripping camera. "Could be worse, Professor."

"Oh? And how is that?"

"Could be raining."

On the way home the Professor caught his fish four more times for Jason. He dreamed about it twice at the Take 'Er Easy. And then caught it once more for his fellow Tin Cup patrons. The fish grew a little with each telling, and the Professor became more animated, his hands high above his head holding his imaginary Winston. "I wish you all could have seen this fish. Eight pounds if he was an ounce."

After dinner they stood near the cash register waiting to pay their check when Jason asked, "You notice that fish of yours growing any?"

"Why Jason, you know for a fact that fish was just a shade over eight pounds."

"I got a new intro to your story when we get to the Grounds." He deepened his voice, took a dramatic pause, and said, "Call me Ishmael."

The roadhouse was a place time dropped off in '58. Inside it was Copenhagen, punchboards, and Miller Standard Time. The good ole boy to woman ratio was the usual five to one, so everything in a skirt was a queen.

It took a couple of minutes for Jason and the Professor to weave their way to the bar, as Jason knew just about everyone. And the Professor, a renowned visitor for many years, knew his share as well. Finally, they found a table near the dance floor.

There was no sense in trying to talk above the music for the next half-hour. Mama Juggs was starting to cook, and with each number more people crowded onto the floor. Henry had his fiddle wound up, the band was side by side with "Maybelline," and everyone that could grab a partner was swinging her.

At the break Henry joined them at their table. The Professor stood and shook his hand. "Henry, how are you?"

"Well, Professor, I guess I'm not too bad for a fella that just had the worst day of his life." Jason could tell they were in for a story and ordered another round.

Henry started his day at the beginning. "At seven o'clock I pull up at the Take 'Er Easy, and there are two fat and ugly people standing out front with a poodle. Next to them is a mound of fishing equipment. All of it brand new, some still in the box. They are ready, trout to tarpon.

"The guy, Jimbo, waddles over to me, smoking a two-foot cigar and wearing enough turquoise jewelry to support a reservation. He opens the trunk of his Caddy and there's more stuff." Then drawling his best Foghorn Leghorn, Henry mimicked, "Sort through this stuff, boy, pick out the gear we need today.

"His wife, are you ready for this, 'snamed Lulu. And she might have been at one time, but since then her body's gone bad on her. Has pink hair. Talks like Minnie Mouse.

"So, I get them all squared away and loaded up and Lulu comes

142

over and hands me this magnum thermos and says, 'Can't forget our libations now, can we?'

"Just before we get in the truck, Jimbo pulls me over and stuffs a fifty in my pocket and says there's another fifty in it for me if I put him into some nice fish. Then he says there's another hundred in it if I drown the poodle."

Henry painted an image so ridiculous he had the Professor and Jason howling. He continued on without so much as a hairline crack in his great stone face.

"Well, it didn't take too long to figure Jimbo and Lulu hate each other. They didn't say anything to one another unless it's mean. He ain't catching shit. She's catching fish hand over fist. He's pissed. And every time she'd catch one she'd squeal like a stuck pig and all the hairs on his neck would stick straight out and that dog would start yapping.

"I was thinking about striking a deal with Jimbo. I would off the poodle for a hundred and take out Lulu for nothing.

"After every fish, she'd toss down some 'libation', which was straight gin, and say, 'Daddy says that if you want to catch women use diamonds. If you want to catch a fish use a worm.'

"Jimbo turns to me and says, 'Boy, where did I go wrong? I used diamonds and caught a fish.'

"Around ten o'clock Jimbo is pretty well in the bag, but Lulu's a mess. But Jimbo manages to land one, only it's real small. Lulu goes right for the jugular. She goes, 'That's why Daddy won't let you run the company. You think small. Just look at your dick.'

"Jimbo goes sideways, throws down his rod, and starts for her. The poodle bites him, and he smacks the poodle overboard. Lulu goes nuts. I fish the dog out of the drink. Then Jimbo picks up his rod like nothing at all has happened and turns to me and says, 'You ought to see her naked. It'd make you gag.'

"Anyway, Lulu has a three-martini lunch. I had two, myself. And the rest of the day goes along pretty calmly. Lulu is about the closest thing I have ever seen to passed out. She's lying down on the bottom of the boat and every once in a while she would groan something but you couldn't make it out. Sounded like the death rattle of a beached whale.

"So, finally, we get off the river and Jimbo and I try to squeeze Lulu, who is lights out, into the cab of the truck. It couldn't be

143

done, not without a crane and a shoehorn, so we load her and the poodle into the back. On the way into town, and here comes the punchline, Jimbo tips me a hundred bucks and says he wants to go again tomorrow."

Catching his breath from laughter the Professor asked, "Are you going?"

"Hey, Jason, that's Peggy's sister over there. She looks like a sweetheart. Peggy says she's going through a divorce and looking to have a good time. She's sure got a nice butt-and-thigh setup. I know if I weren't playin' tonight I would give her a tumble."

Jason purposely changed the subject and started to tell Henry of their day. He had him as far as the canyon, figuring to let the Professor take over the story at the Widowmaker. In the meantime the Mama Juggs players were tuning up back on stage and growing impatient for their fiddler.

"I'll hear about it after this set."

"I'm afraid I have to go, Henry," said the Professor. "Jason can fill you in on the rest of the story, and I'll be back in a month or so and tell you the truth."

"Wait a minute," Jason asked, "are you taking Jimbo down the river tomorrow?"

Henry hobbled back to the table, still sore from yesterday's kick. "Jason, I learned a little something about myself today. There ain't enough hundred dollar bills or martinis to make me do something like that again," and headed back to the stage. Then he called back, "Jason, let's you and me go fishing tomorrow, and Professor, when you get back, we'll all go."

"Splendid," he said. "See you then, Henry." He stood to put on his jacket, but when Jason did the same, he asked, "And where do you think you're going?"

"I'm a little tired myself," said Jason, "thought I would just head for – "

He pushed Jason back into his chair, then stood over him looking very professorial. "Listen, here is some advice from an old man. Ask Peggy's sister to dance. You can sleep anytime." Then he sat back down.

"In 1948 I was in what is now Zaire, studying and living with the Batwasande. They were typical of Africa's middle tribes. Among the Batwasande, when a young woman comes of age, her

144

family throws a party. Every eligible man in the village must ask her to dance, but she will only dance with one, and the one she chooses will become her husband, if he meets the necessary requirements.

"First the boy must prove himself. He must show the girl his courage by bringing her the heart of a lion. Second he must show his worth by giving her father as many goats as he can afford. And third he must prove his generosity, a very big thing with the Batwasandes, by supplying the family with their meat until the wedding day.

"Now in our culture all the gentleman has to do is tap a girl on the shoulder and they can dance and enjoy each other's company and have fun. No pressures. This is the most logical breakthrough between the sexes since we lost our tails. Now ask her to dance."

The Professor stood again then remembered, "Jason, could you give me a key to the shop? I believe I left a pipe in there yesterday."

"Sure," he said, taking it from his keyring. "Just leave it under the mat."

The Professor patted Jason on the shoulder. "See you soon," he said cheerfully then disappeared into the smoke and crowd.

Jason sat through another number and one more beer, then decided it was probably best just to head on home when Peggy Martin's sister appeared at his table and said, "It's possible."

"What's possible?" Jason asked and they exchanged puzzled looks. She tossed a cocktail napkin on the table. On the back was the Professor's handwriting which read, "I would love to dance with you. Is that possible?"

Jason shyly extended his arm, a bit confused, and not by the Professor's trickery but by the fact that all his fatigue had dissolved. She was pretty. The kind of woman who could give you a second wind. He stopped short of the dance floor, turned to her, and said, "There is something I must know before we can go any further."

Her eyebrows raised in suspicion of an early come on, she asked, "What's that?"

"You're not by any chance Batwasande are you?"

Jason was making coffee when Henry arrived. The morning light was flooding through the windows of the Boatworks, illuminating the sawdust swirls and turning the oak trim on the drift boat gold and the cedar red.

After seeing that Jason was still in last night's clothes and this morning's beard, Henry reckoned, "Well, don't look like I need to ask how last night turned out."

"Yeah. Peggy's sister is really great."

"Yeah, how great?" Henry leered.

"Well, she's fun to look at and she's got a good attitude. She's not going to send you out tracking lions or make you run out and buy a bunch of goats."

"What?"

They went around the workshop gathering what they might need for the day's fishing as Jason explained about the Batwasandes when he spotted the Professor's old Winston leaning against the boat with a note pinned beneath it. Jason unfolded the note and read silently for a moment, then read aloud:

"Jason, what a day it was. I wish Henry could have been a part of it. I feel I must apologize, I wasn't very talkative. Kept thinking about the speech.

"Monday I must make a speech. A retirement speech, I'm afraid. I had no intention whatsoever of retiring, always thought of myself as just fossilizing right there in Anthro 404. But as it turns out, I have contracted acute leukemia instead. It's a quick and sure-handed killer. Most people live four months, old farts like me can go in a month."

Jason paused, cleared his throat, and read on, "Now I have an eternity of some sort to look forward to. I have studied dozens of religions. Every one claims to have the definitive answer for the hereafter, but most of them have it in a different location. The Pope puts it in heaven, the Hindu say you have to come back for it, and agnostics say you might not get one.

"I always thought if there is a true and just God, He would allow you to have a say in your heaven. A graduate attended one of my classes several years ago, wearing a t-shirt which read, 'First you are born. Then you live. Then you die. And when you die you go to Montana.' Always thought that summed it up quite well.

"You and Henry have good fishing today, although if approached with the proper attitude, it's hard to have bad fishing. Good luck."

Jason's voice was a mixture of sorrow and conviction. "Let's go fishing."

THE LADY IN

Green

BY ARCHIBALD RUTLEDGE

Fascination with deer runs as a bright thread through
the fabric of the life of Archibald Rutledge (1883-1973).
Perhaps no American writer has been more successful in
capturing the myriad, and often elusive, meanings of the
hunt for whitetails. In "The Lady in Green," we see
Rutledge at his best – a master of African-American
dialect, a lover of irony, and a man closely attuned to the
sort of endings which always delight readers.

F or a very long time we have had on the plantation a Negro
named Steve. For a generation he worked for us; and he is
with me to this day. While we usually had certain Negroes
who could be counted on to accomplish even difficult material
tasks, in what might be termed the realm of the psychic, Steve
reigned supreme. For some reason, he was at his best when
something esoteric and peculiar had to be accomplished. My

Colonel early recognized Steve's strange talent, and occasionally called on him to exercise it.

Thus when the lady in green came to us for a visit, and came with the hope of killing a regal buck, I felt called upon to enlist the darksome strategy of Steve.

"Steve," I asked my good-for-nothing Negro, "have you ever seen a woman wear pants?"

"I ain't done seen it, Cap'n," he responded, a fervent fire of recollection kindling in his eyes, "but I has done seen some wimmins what act like dey wear dem."

"Has your Amnesia ever worn them?"

"When I is around home," he assured me, "she don't ever wear anything else but."

"Have you two been falling out again, Steve?"

"Cap'n," he answered solemnly, "for yeahs and yeahs we ain't never done fell in."

"I guess she doesn't like your playing around with all these young girls, and leaving her at home."

"I tole her dat woman and cat is to stay home; man and dog is to go abroad. She didn't like dat atall, atall."

"Well," I said, "this is Friday. Monday will be Christmas Day. I know just one way I can get you out of the dog-house where Amnesia has put you. Wouldn't you like to get out for Christmas?"

Steve licked his lips, a sure sign that he is about to take the bait. Besides, as I had beforehand been of assistance to him in the vital matter of domestic reconciliations, he regards me as a kind of magician.

"Tomorrow," I told him "will be Saturday, the day before Christmas Eve. I will help you, but I expect you to help me." I was testing his loyalty in a large way.

Haunted by a sense of his own helplessness and by the mastery of his huge Amnesia, he appeared pathetically eager to do anything. In fact, such was his yielding mood that I had to be careful what I asked him to do, for he would do it. Steve can resist anything but temptation.

"I'm giving a big deer drive tomorrow," I said. "There will be twenty men and one woman – but I hear she wears pants."

"Great Gawd," was Steve's comment.

"Green ones," I went on.

"Jeedus!"

"Now, Steve, you know that old flathorn buck in the Wambaw Corner – the one that has been dodging us for about five years?"

"You mean him what hab dem yaller horns, flat same like a paddle?"

"He's the one."

"Cap'n, dat's a buck what I knows like I knows the way to another man's watermelon patch," Steve assured me grinning. "What you want me to do? And how Amnesia suddenly gwine take me back because of what you is planning for me to do?"

"Well," I told him, "you've got a job, all right. I don't want to be unfair to these men, but ordinary bucks will do very well for them. Your business is to get the buck with the palmated horns to run to the lady in green. If you will do this, I will give you a whole haunch of venison, a ham out of my smoke-house, a dollar in cash and a dress for Amnesia. How about it?"

Steve was stunned. When he came to, he said, "Boss, when I gits to heaben, I ain't gwine ask. 'How 'bout it?' "

"Of course," I told him, "I will put her on the Crippled Oak Stand. You know that is the favorite buck run. Just how you are going to get him to run there I don't know, but you probably can figure it out. Oh, "I added, "I will not hold you responsible for her killing the buck. Being a woman, she'll probably miss it anyway. But I want you to give her a chance to shoot."

I could see that Steve was already deep in his problem. Knowing the woods like an Indian, so familiar with game that he can almost talk with it, familiar also with the likelihood of big game's acting in ways unpredictable, Steve was pretty well equipped for his task. I could also see how he would enjoy this particular job.

"One more thing," I told him: "this lady doesn't shoot a shotgun. She always uses a rifle."

"Cap'n," he sensibly asked, "does you think she knows a deer? If she don't I mustn't get too close to dat rifle."

"I have never seen her," I told him, "and I don't know whether she is a real huntress. All I know about her is what I have been told. But she's the daughter of one of my best friends, a gentleman from Philadelphia. I want her to have a good time. Think of what it would mean if she could kill the crowned king of Wambaw Corner!"

"I sure loves to please wimmins," Steve mused. "But so far I ain't done had too much of luck."

As we parted I kept pounding home his job to him: "Drive the buck with the flat horns to the Crippled Oak Stand. Drive him there if you have to head him off. And remember the haunch and the ham that will be yours if you manage it right."

Not long after daylight the following morning the crowds of Christmas hunters assembled in my plantation yard. As the season was nearing its close, every man I had invited came. And *there* was the lady in green. When I saw her, I was ashamed of the way in which I had bandied words with Steve about the nature of her attire. She was slender, graceful and very lovely. She looked like Maid Marian. Clad in Lincoln green, with a jaunty feather in her Robin Hood's cap, she was the attraction of all eyes. I could see that all the men were in love with her, and I didn't feel any too emotionally normal myself. There was nothing about her of the type of huntress I had described to Steve. She appeared a strange combination of an elf, a child and a woman; and though I do not profess to know much about such matters, that particular combination seems especially alluring, perhaps dangerously so.

While my Negro drivers were getting their horses ready, and while stately deer hounds, woolly dogs and curs of low degree gathered from far and near on account of the general air of festivity and the promise of some break in the general hunger situation, I got everybody together and told them that we planned to drive the great Wambaw Corner; that we had standers enough to take care of the whole place, we had drivers and dogs, we had deer. The great, and really the only question was, can anybody hit anything? That is often a pertinent question in hunting.

Wambaw Corner is peculiarly situated. A tract of nearly a thousand acres, it is bounded on two sides by the wide and deep Wambaw Creek. On one side is the famous Lucas Reserve, an immense backwater, formerly used for waterpower, but now chiefly for bass and bream. In shape this place is a long and comparatively narrow peninsula, with water on three sides. On the south runs a wide road, along which I usually post my standers; but when I have enough (or too many), I post them along the creek. The chance there is excellent, for if a buck is suspicious there's nothing he'll do quicker than dodge back and swim the creek.

150

With the woods still sparkling with dew, and fragrant with the aromas from myrtles and pines, I posted all my standers. I had sent my drivers far down on the tip of the peninsula, to drive it out to the road. I had also had a last word with Steve.

"Only one mistake you might be can is makin', Cap'n," he told me. "I dunno how 'bout wid a gun, but with a rollin'-pin or a skillet or a hatchet a woman don't eber seem to miss. Anyhow," he particularized, "dey don't neber miss me!"

"Have you got your plan made?" I asked him. "You've got five other boys to drive. That just about sets you free to do what you want to."

"I got my plan," he said. "And," he added darkly, "if so happen it be dat I don't come out with de other drivers, you will onnerstand."

In a place like Wambaw Creek there are at times a great many deer. They love its remote quiet, its pine hills, its abundant food, its watery edges. I have seen as many as six fine bucks run out of there on a single drive, a flock of wild turkeys, and heaven knows how many does. I have likewise seen wild boars emerge from that wilderness – huge hulking brutes, built like oversize hyenas, and they are ugly customers to handle.

I knew that there was sure to be a good deal of shooting on this drive, certain to be some missing, and possibly to be some killing. Everybody seemed keyed just right for the sport. I had men with me who had hunted all over the world, grizzled backwoodsmen who had never hunted more than twenty miles from their homes, pure amateurs, some insatiable hunters but rotten shots – and I had the lady in green.

After I had posted the men, there being no stand for me, or perhaps for a more romantic reason, I decided to stand with Maid Marian. She seemed like such a child to shoot down a big buck; yet she was jaunty and serene. When I had explained to certain of the standers as I posted them just how an old stag would come up to them, I could see, from the way they began to sweat and blink, that they were in the incipient stages of nervous breakdowns. But not so my Sherwood Forest girl.

Her stand, by the famous Crippled Oak, was on a high bank in the pinelands. Before her and behind her was a dense cypress swamp, in the dark fastness of which it was almost impossible to get a shot at a deer. If the buck came, she would have to shoot him when he broke across the bank. All this I carefully explained to her. She listened intently and intelligently.

She appeared concerned over my concern. "You need not worry," she assured, for my comfort. "If he comes, I will kill him."

"Have you killed deer before?" I asked.

"No," she admitted lightly but undaunted. "I never even saw one."

My heart failed me. "This one," I told her, hoping that Steve's maneuvering would be effective, "is likely to have big yellow horns. He's an old wildwood hero. I hope you get him."

About that time I heard the drivers put in, and I mean they did. A Christmas hunt on a Carolina plantation brings out everything a Negro has in the way of vocal eminence. Far back near the river they whooped and shouted, yelled and sang. Then I heard the hounds begin to tune up.

Maid Marian was listening, with her little head pertly tipped to one side. "What is all that noise?" she asked with devastating imbecility.

Tediously I explained that the deer were lying down, that the Negroes and the dogs roused them, and that by good fortune an old rough-shod stag might come our way.

"I understand," she nodded brightly. But I was sure she didn't.

Another thing disconcerted me: I could hear the voice of Prince, of Sam'l, of Will and of Precinct; Evergreen's voice was loud on the still air. But not once did I hear the hounddog whoop of Steve. However, his silence did indicate that he was about some mysterious business.

In a few minutes a perfect bedlam in one of the deep corners showed that a stag had been roused. The wild clamor headed northward, toward the creek, and soon I heard a gun blare twice. But the pack did not stop. There was a swift veering southward. Before long I heard shots from that direction, but whoever tried must have failed.

The pack headed northeast, toward the road on which we were standing, but far from us. I somehow felt, from his wily maneuvers, that this was the buck with the palmated horns. Ordinary bucks would do no such dodging, and the fact that he had been twice missed would indicate that the stander had seen something very disconcerting.

Watching the lady in green for any tell-tale sign of a break in nerves, I could discover none. She just seemed to be taking a

152

childish delight in all the excitement. She was enjoying it without getting excited herself.

About that time I heard the stander at the far eastern end of the road shoot; a minute later he shot again. He was a good man, a deliberate shot. Perhaps he had done what I wanted Maid Marian to do. But no. The pack now turned toward us.

Judging from the speed of the hounds, there was nothing the matter with the deer; judging by their direction, they were running parallel to the road, at a little over a hundred yards from it. It was a favorite buck run, and at any moment he might flare across the road to one of the standers at the critical crossings. Ours was the last stand on the extreme west. It seemed very unlikely that he would pass all those crossings and come to us. Now the hounds were running closer to the road. It sounded as if the buck were about to cross.

It is now just fifty years since I shot my first buck, and I have hunted deer every year since that initial adventure. But never in all my experience as a deer hunter have I heard what I then heard on that road, on which I had twelve standers. Judging from the shots, the buck must have come within easy sight, if not within range, of every stander. The bombardment was continuous. Together with the shots, as the circus came nearer, I could hear wild and angry shouts; I thought I heard some heavy profanity, and I hoped the lady in green missed this.

She was leaning against the Crippled Oak, cool as a frosted apple. I was behind the tree, pretty nervous for her sake.

"Look out, now," I whispered. "He may cross here at any minute."

My eyes kept searching for the buck to break cover. Suddenly, directly in front of the stander next to us, I saw what I took to be the flash of a white tail. The stander fired both barrels. Then I saw him dash his hat to the ground and jump on it in a kind of frenzy that hardly indicated joy and triumph.

The next thing I knew, the little rifle of the lady in green was up. I did not even see the deer. The rifle spoke. The clamoring pack, now almost upon us, began a wild milling. Then they hushed.

"All right," said Maid Marian serenely, "I killed him."

Gentlemen, she spoke the truth, and the stag she killed was the buck with the palmated horns. At sixty yards, in a full run, he had been drilled through the heart. On several occasions I had seen his horns, but I had not dreamed that they were so fine – perfect, ten-point, golden in color, with the palmation of a full two inches. A massive and beautiful trophy they were, of a kind that many a good sportsman spends a lifetime seeking, and often spends it in vain.

However, mingled with my pride and satisfaction there was a certain sense of guilt; yet I was trying to justify myself with the noble old sentiment, "Women and children first." "I had told Steve to drive his buck to my lady in green. He had done it – heavens knows how. He would tell me later. But his plan had worked. But now came the critical phase of the whole proceeding. Standers and drivers began to gather, and afar off I could hear many deep oaths. These, I felt sure, would subside in the presence of Maid Marian. They did, but not the anger and the protests.

There seemed to be one general question, asked in such a way that it would be well for the person referred to keep his distance. "Where's that driver?" I heard on all sides. "I mean the big, black, slue-footed driver. I believe you call him Steve. I had a good mind to shoot him."

"I'd have killed that buck if he hadn't got in the way."

"What was that flag he was waving? Looked to me like he was trying to turn the buck from us."

"He was coming right on me when that gorilla jumped out of a bush and started waving that flag."

"Well, after all, gentlemen," I said, "here's the buck, and I must say the lady made a grand shot. Wouldn't you rather have her kill him than do so yourselves?"

Everybody had now gathered but Steve. When questioned, the other drivers disclaimed all knowledge of his whereabouts or his peculiar behavior. But they knew perfectly of both. One artfully sidetracked the whole painful discussion by saying "Steve ain't neber been no good deer driver nohow."

Tyler Somerset, a prince of a backwoodsmen, drew me aside. "Say," he said, "I know what went on back there. You can't fool me. That's the smartest darky I ever did see. More than once he outran that buck. And he sure can dodge buckshot. I wonder where he got that red and white flag he used to turn that old buck?"

We made several other drives that day. Five more stags were

slain. But the buck and the shot of the lady in green remained the records. On those later drives Steve put in no appearance.

When my friends were safely gone, Steve shambled out of hiding to claim his just reward. I loaded him down with Christmas.

"By the way," I said, "some of the standers told me that you headed that buck with a red and white flag. Where did you get that?"

Steve grinned with massive shyness, as he does only when anything feminine comes to his mind. "Dat's de biggest chance I took – wusser dan dodging buckshot. Dat was Amnesia's Sunday petticoat."

"Huh," I muttered with gloomy foreboding. "If she finds that one out, I'll have to take you to the hospital."

"Cap'n, I done arrange it," he told me – the old schemer! "I did tore seven holes in it with all that wavin' but I tole Amnesia I was ashamed to have my gal wear a raggety petticoat, and you was gwine give me a dollar, and I was gwine give it to her to buy a new one for Christmas."

Reprinted courtesy of Irvine H. Rutledge, Hagerstown, Maryland.

Hasselborg's
HANGOUT

BY FRANK C. HIBBEN

North America has no predator more dangerous and challenging to hunt than the Alaskan brown bear. In this selection from *Hunting American Bears*, veteran big game hunter Frank Hibben offers a story of a memorable Admiralty Island hunt. It is a tale well told, a plausible picture of just what close-range hunting in the bush involves, and a conclusion in which the hunter's adrenalin races at breakneck pace.

A dmiralty Island and brown bears are synonymous. It is not that Admiralty is any different from a dozen other Alaskan islands. It is but one of the many that lie like the disarticulated pieces of a jigsaw puzzle, along the coast of southern Alaska. Admiralty is also not the only island inhabited by brown bears. Some people swear by Chichagof or Baranof islands. But usually when the talk is of big brown bears, it is

Admiralty every time.

Admiralty Island is an extensive place too, but you can hardly visit there without meeting Old Man Hasselborg. He's as much a part of the life of the place as the brown bears that live around him, and he has been there almost as long. Allen Hasselborg homesteaded on Admiralty Island in 1900 and he has been there ever since. He staked out 160 acres on the shores of Mole Harbor, on the side of the island toward the mainland and the city of Juneau. This area was a lush meadow clearing where the Tlingit Indians had long ago built a village. There still remained the outlines of their communal houses, and ancient stone implements lay beneath the grass roots. But of the Northwest Coast Indians that had raised their totem poles there, only two survivors remained when Allen Hasselborg grounded his small boat on that beach at the turn of the century. These two Tlingit Indians and the new settler, Hasselborg, developed differences among themselves; and, in a few years, only Hasselborg was left as the sole possessor of the whole island of Admiralty.

In the clearing by Mole Harbor he built himself a cabin of cedar logs and roofed it well with straight-grained shakes split from the same wood. Over the pits and ruined communal houses of the departed Indians, Hasselborg spaded his garden and raised potatoes and cabbages that would be the envy of a county fair anywhere.

Each summer the salmon crowded up Mole Creek in the running season. First the dog salmon came, then the humpbacks and finally the pink-meated cohos. On each of these Hasselborg took his toll. From the doorstep of his cabin it was a short stone's throw to the water where the salmon crowded the shallows so thickly. In a week Allen Hasselborg could catch and split and smoke enough salmon to last him for the rest of the year.

The countless thousands of one and two pound Dolly Varden trout that also inhabited this stream and the fifteen-inch cutthroats that lay in the riffles of Mole Creek were unnoticed and unused. The steelheads too gathered in the tide slack at the mouth of the creek during their spawning season. Flounders skittered across the sand bars and cod and halibut fed on the seaweed banks at the entrance to Mole Harbor.

Nor was this all. In the evening when the shadows of the Sitka spruces were long across the wet grass of the meadow, the black-

157

tailed deer would come out of the heavy trees to feed in the open. Canned venison was a staple item of diet at Mole Harbor and was a welcome change, during the long winter months, from dried salmon. Alaska is the land of plenty. No one could starve there who had even one hand to carry food to his mouth.

Along the waterfront at Juneau the purse seiners and halibut men whispered that Allen Hasselborg had come to Alaska because of a love affair. Others told us that he came to hunt bear for the fur trade. Whatever the underlying reasons were, there is no doubt that he did prefer solitude. Practically the only inhabitant of Admiralty Island for almost fifty years, Old Man Hasselborg had rested secure in his snug cabin. In the winter he trapped for marten and mink and with the proceeds bought the few necessities that a lonely man might need. In the spring and again in the fall he traveled the many watery miles to Juneau, making the trip in a small boat he had constructed himself. On the return trip he loaded his homemade craft mostly with books. Allen Hasselborg was well read. He was better versed on government matters, history and science than you and I. But then we don't have salmon running past our door to provide a certain source of food.

One winter Hasselborg fell on the ice and broke his hip. He set the bone himself and fed and nursed himself as well during his convalescence. Ordinarily this hermit saw no one after the salmon fishers left in the fall until the boats went out again in the spring of the year. It was a full life, this Admiralty Island existence. There were few vexations and most of the noise and hubbub of the avaricious world citizens jostling one another did not reach to the wet shores of Admiralty Island. Allen Hasselborg sat secure in his cabin, read his many books and railed against the government. All the ills that did reach into his remote world were government-sponsored difficulties. With each passing year of progress, the government men imposed more hunting and fishing regulations, each of which Hasselborg scrupulously observed and violently complained about.

But there were villains, too, on the island of Admiralty. There were black-hearted rogues who skulked in the shadows and killed when they could. There were terrors by night and by day on the forest trails. Even the most self-confident of the native Alaskans were armed when he visited Admiralty Island. This evil element in an Alaskan paradise was indigenous. The brown bear had been there even before Allen Hasselborg, even prior, perhaps, to the Tlingit Indians themselves.

My wife and I first visited Hasselborg in his island cabin some years ago. He despised most "yachting parties," as he called anybody who came by boat, no matter what that boat might be. For some reason he tolerated us. It may have been that we appreciated the birds and the flowers and the other wild things that lived in his meadow. Or it may have been that we were more naive than the rest.

We showed Allen Hasselborg great deference. Everyone did, of course. His was a personality that demanded respect. And like everyone else who visited Admiralty Island, we came to see the brown bears that lived along the salmon streams and wooded mountains of this fascinating place.

I remember very vividly how Hasselborg looked the first time I saw him. He leaned in the door of his cabin looking out toward us as we came up the path from the beach. His face was kindly but with a peculiar alertness, a certain air of questioning as though he were awaiting our next move, or perhaps watching for a mistake. Allen Hasselborg wore a black spade beard of generous proportions, and his dark ringlets of graying hair hung down over generous ears. He always wore a round canvas hat and the button on top of this headgear usually sported an irregular cud of half-used chewing gum. Around his neck hung an old-fashioned telescope in a leather case. I remember my first reaction upon learning that this cylindrical object was a spyglass. I wondered how he got it out of the case without the thing tangling in his beard. Allen Hasselborg wore the gray wool shirts and the lumbermen's pants of any normal Alaskan. His gum boots were "half-masted" and he only pulled them up over his hips when he crossed the stream in front of his house.

The people of Juneau had told us that Hasselborg was peculiar. All those old-timers get "bushed" sooner or later, they said, and eventually get dangerous. But we noticed none of these things in him. He waved us into his cabin with all the grave courtesy of a king ushering a subject into his castle.

The cabin itself was scrupulously clean and invitingly neat. Of course there were peculiarities, but then anyone has a right to these in his own house.

159

In one corner of the cabin was the stove. It was of antiquarian make and the wood-burning variety. In this corner also were piled the dishes and utensils that constitute a kitchen. In this place was the eating establishment and all such offices were performed there. In the next corner was the library. It was well stocked with a hundred-odd volumes bearing the numbers of the library at Juneau. Beside the book shelf was an easy chair amply lighted by a generous window that looked out on the lush meadow of the old Tlingit clearing. Seated here with his books at his elbow, Allen Hasselborg could survey all his domain.

Even as we examined the library for the first time, I saw a movement outside the house through this windowpane. It was a bear, a great, dark-colored monster who was splashing noisily through the shallows of Mole Creek not a hundred yards from the house. By heaven! Those bears were big! This fellow obviously was an average of his kind, but there must have been a thousand pounds of meat and muscle that circled idly in the stream, looking for a passing salmon.

"Mr. Hasselborg!" I said excitedly with half-raised finger, pointing tentatively to where the gray Alaskan morning shone through the window.

Hasselborg dipped his head and glanced quickly out from beneath his canvas hatbrim. "Why, certainly," he said, as though explaining to a small child. That's Dark Pants. He lives here."

I looked again, but was careful to make no more exclamations. The bear in the stream did seem to be darker-colored in his hindquarters.

Trying to assume some of the casualness I did not feel, I inspected the rest of Hasselborg's house. In the far corner across from the stove was the bed, well-made as everything else in this establishment, and with a neat covering smoothed over it. And in the fourth corner, near the door, was the gun rack. Here were the axes, the packboards, and lastly the rifles which Hasselborg used so little.

I had spent but half a day in Hasselborg's cabin when I learned that each of these divisions was separate and immutable. Woe to him who took a plate of venison stew from the kitchen and walked the four steps that would seat him on the bed. If you read a book, you stayed in the library. If you cleaned a rifle, you didn't do it in the kitchen. Such is the law of things at Hasselborg's.

In the several successive years that my wife and I visited Mole Harbor, it was always the same. Mr. Hasselborg was at home constantly and ever received us with the quiet courtesy which he always showed. The path up from the harbor seemed never to change. The camas plants on the tide flats showed silver under the advancing water, with just the same sparkle and gleam that they had had on our previous visits. Mr. Hasselborg brought us into his cabin and seated us in the immaculate library with the air of one who had expected us that very day and very hour. Actually he didn't know when we were coming, from May to September. And if Dark Pants wasn't catching salmon in the shallows, there was some other bear of this domain lumbering heavily through the wet grass of the clearing or skirting the woods.

Twice on these visits to the marvelous kingdom of Admirality Island, we came to photograph the brown bears that lived there. On each occasion it was Hasselborg who showed us the best streams up and down the coast where we could set the camera. It was always he who told us whether a bear was good or bad as soon as he saw him. He knew these bears and they knew him. It seemed a well-integrated community.

But like all willful humans who came from "outside" – as the Alaskans call the United States – I wanted to shoot a bear. "Don't you ever save any bearskin, Mr. Hasselborg?" I asked with incredulity. My tone implied that he must have collected some marvelous ones in the many years he had actually lived among the animals. "Why, certainly not," he said with his characteristically clipped accents. "Why would I ever keep a bearskin, to collect ants and fleas? I haven't killed a bear since 1918." The old man chuckled to himself as though at some distant recollection. I hoped I would get the story later on. "But, Mr. Hasselborg," I continued, "don't these bears ever hurt you?"

"We've learned to get along," he said quietly, and I wondered at his few, simple words. These were the same brown bears which had such a vicious reputation that no one else went unarmed among them. It had been an Admiralty Island bear that had pulled a timber cruiser out of the limbs of a tree and quietly chewed his legs off while the poor man yet lived. Only the year before a fisherman at Eliza Harbor on the southern coast of Admiralty had met his death at the hands of one of these ferocious monsters.

161

And yet Allen Hasselborg had lived in their very midst unharmed and unafraid for half a century.

The disbelief must have shown on my face. "You don't believe I can shoot a bear, do you?" Mr. Hasselborg asked. "You know," he added reflectively, "I believe I might shoot another one. They killed and ate four of my fawns this spring and some stranger has been digging my potatoes." By "stranger" I presume Hasselborg meant some other bear that didn't belong at Mole Harbor. As for the deer, it seemed to me that their children were their own responsibility. But Hasselborg was rising to his subject with more fervor. "If I don't stop them," he continued, "they'll kill every deer on the island. The government keeps shooting the deer and protecting the bears. I can't understand such stupidity."

Allen Hasselborg railed against the government for most of the evening. I did not fall in with most of his views, but the conversation was inevitably leading me toward a bear hunt, which was my object. "But, Mr. Hasselborg," I said, for perhaps the fifth time. "I'd like to get a really big bear. A monster; one that would be a record."

"So Dark Pants isn't big enough for you," he answered with a twinkle in his eye. I knew instinctively that he would never let me kill Dark Pants or any other bear friend that lived around Mole Harbor. "All right, Hibben," he said with finality as he rose from the easy chair. "I'll take you up to the hangout and we'll get a really big bear from there." He emphasized the word "really" as he looked at me keenly with his dark eyes. I knew what he was thinking. If I got close to even a small bear, he would look as big as a ten ton truck and be just as hard to stop.

We returned to our small boat anchored well out in Mole Harbor. All that night I turned in my bunk and thought of the great adventure of the morrow. The turn of the tide was making small choppy waves that slapped against the hull of our craft with the regularity of clicking wheels under a Pullman sleeper. Hasselborg's hangout – I was actually going to see the interior of the island and in company with the most famous bear man of them all. Monster bears danced through my dreams. They waved mighty paws at me and always they melted before the end of my rifle.

At daylight the next morning I came in alone in the canoe. I brought a sleeping bag and such food and provisions as I was sure a frugal camper such as Allen Hasselborg would approve of. My pack was a light one lashed in a professional manner which I had carefully copied from some Alaskan sourdough friends. As I approached the cabin door the old man eyed me with all of the hostility he would lavish on a Tlingit Indian. My first thought was that the people in Juneau were right – Hasselborg was as mad as a hatter and had forgotten all about the projected trip to the hangout which I anticipated so keenly. But Hasselborg was looking at my pack and not at me. "Do you expect to take all that stuff?" he asked with rising incredulity.

"But Mr. Hasselborg," I answered feebly, "I only have a little pancake flour, some sugar, coffee and a few other things."

"In the first place, you'll need no bed," the old man said as he turned back into the cabin. "And I have all the food we'll need for six weeks." I followed Hasselborg into the kitchen corner of the cabin.

"If he carries that mountain of stuff," he was muttering to himself, "he'll hang in the first patch of devil's club we come to." As I ate a meager dish of venison near the stove, I thought it best to remain silent and let events shape themselves.

Hasselborg strapped a pack frame onto his own back and began to pour dry oatmeal into his trousers pocket. When he had filled this to his satisfaction, he turned toward me. Without a word he pulled open my own pocket and first extracted some odd articles of trout-fishing gear I had hoped to carry with me into the interior of this fabulous island. Then he poured my pocket full of dry oatmeal as he had his own. "That's our provisions," he said with finality. My heart sank at the prospect of a dry oatmeal diet. He next handed me a pack frame of the conventional Alaskan variety, with ropes crisscrossed over a stout wooden framework. The thing was as bare as it had been when Hasselborg's axe first fashioned it. Strapping our empty packboards on our backs, Hasselborg led the way out of the cabin.

As we passed my duffle by the door, I looked longingly at my sleeping bag. Then with a single note of rebellion I stooped and picked up a small sack of pancake flour and stuffed it into my pocket. I glanced furtively at Hasselborg to see if he had noticed this dastardly act. But he simply dipped his fingers into his pocket and threw a little of the dry oatmeal into his mouth as a starter. I picked up my rifle and we were off.

For armament, Hasselborg carried an old .38-.40 of ancient vintage. I was still smarting under the indignities of the spurning of my camping equipment. Nonetheless it was good to be with Hasselborg. I noted with satisfaction the rifle that he carried. The octagonal barrel and the sharp curve of the butt-plate looked ancient, it is true, but heavy and effective just the same. I would be safe with Hasselborg.

It seemed that astonishing things would never cease on this strange expedition. We had walked the few yards to the bank of Mole Creek and Hasselborg waded unhesitatingly in. The floor of the stream was set with round boulders of large and small sizes that made an uncertain footing. The mosses and algae of the brackish water made these surfaces even more treacherous. To offset these difficulties Hasselborg thrust the butt and mechanism of his ancient rifle down into the water as a supporting staff. Here the salt waters of the tide made the mouth of the stream death on hardware, but this seemed to bother the old man not at all. Some steelhead trout in the shallows skittered away before our booted legs, but I was too disturbed to notice them. If Hassleborg used his rifle in salt water like that, I could guarantee that the thing wouldn't fire when the crucial moment came.

With a pocketful of dry oatmeal and a bare packframe on my back, I followed Old Man Hasselborg toward his fabulous hangout. If our equipment was like this, what could I expect of the hangout?

On the far side of the Mole Creek meadow, the Alaskan forest swallowed us completely. The islands of southern Alaska are densely wooded and Admirality Island is foremost among these. Sitka spruce and Douglas firs stand almost trunk to trunk. Red cedars and yellow cedars vary the forest monotony with here and there a solid stand of hemlock and alder. The forest floor is so damp and dark that few things grow there. Only dead-colored mosses and certain parasitic plants that suck their life from the fallen trunks and exposed roots of other forest growth can exist in the dark. There is ever the lush drip of moisture in these shadowed places. Even when the sun shines, which is seldom, few of its rays penetrate to the actual earth of the Admirality forests.

Through these wooded places the brown bears have made trails. Thousands of generations of these ponderous animals have walked in the same places and I daresay for the same reasons. They move from salmon streams on the coasts to the mountain meadows of the interior. The bears eat grass in the spring when there are no fish, and salmon when the spawning time is on. These bear trails are actually worn a foot or so deep into the spongy earth. They wind among the trees for a few hundred yards with the certainty of a well-cleared road. Then beyond, in the next thicket, as though the bear's tenacity of purpose had failed him, the trail fades away into nothingness. In places also, succeeding brown bears had actually stepped in the footprints of their predecessors so as to produce a measured series of deep impressions, each the stride of a bear's legs apart. But after a few yards, these too fade into dimly marked treads and then again to the untouched forest floor.

But at the dead ends and the places where the bear trails ceased, Hasselborg never hesitated. He had tracked these trails before and, as ample evidence of this, he pointed out the places where he had set his traps the preceding winter. He showed me rather proudly the crotch of a certain tree where he had caught two marten together in the same trap set. He turned occasionally, too, to point out with some laconic remark a fresh bear track in the trail we were following. Each time he did so I glanced apprehensively around and especially behind me. What if some monster like Dark Pants should come up noiselessly in the soft mud along this same trail? But Hasselborg showed no apprehension whatever. He walked unhesitatingly with a quick step from one bear trail to another and we trended generally west into the interior of Admiralty Island. From time to time he threw small handfuls of oatmeal into his mouth as though stoking an inward fire.

The thickest tree growth was on the lower slopes of the hills near tidewater. As we gradually worked our way upward, the trees seemed to thin somewhat and occasionally along some little creek or semi-open spot, there grew a clump of skunk cabbage plants. The leaves of these were as tall as a man, and Hasselborg showed me how to break off and fold a leaf skillfully into a drinking cup. There were also in these semi-clearings solid stands of the awful devil's club – the scourge of the Alaskan forests. This plant looks like a castor-oil bean and from some distance away is rather decorative. But the stalks and stems of the stuff are thickly

165

studded with needle spines as dangerous and painful as any cholla cactus on a southern desert. Even the leaves of the devil's club are a pincushion of points and each one is coated with an irritant as aggravating as a bee sting if it punctures the human skin. And who can brush by these stems without a few such penetrations? Before we had gone many miles on the trail to the hangout, my hands and elbows were tingling unpleasantly from intimate association with devil's club clumps.

About the middle of the morning we came out on the bank of a considerable stream that flowed downward through skunk cabbage marshes and occasional open grassy spots. Mr. Hasselborg told me this was the headwaters of Mole Creek itself and ahead were the beaver ponds. I had seen beaver workings before, but none like these. These ponds were lakes and the destruction and desolation caused by the dark-skinned beavers of Admiralty Island extended for miles. Like everything on Admiralty Island, it was on a lavish scale. There were dead forest trees where the flood waters had killed them. There were tangled masses of felled alder and hemlock. The tapered cones of dead stumps showed where the voracious animals had gnawed whole groves of trees down and, in most cases, let them lie where they fell, crisscrossed and rotting in the mud and ooze and the beaver meadows. For the first time I was happy that I did not have a heavy pack to hold me down in these places. We balanced on precarious feet across beaver dams and even on single-log bridges that had been left, here and there, across the waterways.

Once as we passed an alder thicket there was a sudden rush of sound, a gigantic crash in the underbrush and the breaking of smaller branches and twigs as some heavy animal forced its way through the heavy growth. Hasselborg never broke his stride. "Probably a bear," he flung back over his shoulder. It probably was, I thought, and shivered with apprehension. On the lip of the beaver dam we were passing at that moment was a bear track as big as my two hands put together. It would dwarf to insignificance the hugest grizzly track I ever saw in my life, and yet Hasselborg never even turned his head toward the thrashing in the alders. I hurried my steps to be certain I kept close behind him.

It was early afternoon when we skirted the last of the beaver ponds and came out into open meadows. These had been formed

166

centuries ago by other beaver that had flooded these places and killed out the trees there. These ancient beaver places were now filled in and grasses grew lushly and as tall as a man's waist. At that time of year the cotton grass was in bloom and white puffs of the feathery stuff bounced and danced over the grass stems before the wind from the mountain.

We walked with caution for occasionally in these old beaver meadows there were "bathtubs" or deep holes filled with dark brown water ready to trap the unwary. On the edge of one of these places Hasselborg stopped and pointed at the ground with his gun barrel. There was a spotted thing in the shadow and I made out the form of a small body and a tiny head with a pair of long ears laid flat on top. It was a little fawn quite alive, but playing as dead as could be. I smiled at the little rascal and could hardly keep from stooping to put my hand upon it. Hasselborg held me back with his rifle placed against my chest. "Don't touch him or his mother may not come back."

As we climbed higher through these open places the clouds seemed lower over our head. Wisps and spangles of gray moisture hung over the tops of the trees and moved steadily down toward us. It seemed in a few more yards we would enter the clouds themselves. The country grew more open too as we progressed. The slopes grew steeper and the trees grew only in scattered clumps in some places. We apparently were making our way up a mountain valley which was the top of the Mole Creek watershed. There were high mountains towering above us, but for the most part we felt them rather than saw their summits. The ragged gray clouds obscured all things above and most of the forms around us. Occasionally an opening in the overcast showed a steep mountain ridge for a few moments, with clumps of alders clinging precariously to the incline. Late in the afternoon we began to cross occasional patches of snow in deep pockets or on northern slopes. It was the first week in June, but the winter lingered yet on these mountains of Admirality Island.

By mid-afternoon we were walking in clouds. Streamers of thick mist like ghost banners hung on the tips of the stunted evergreens around us. The white wisps wavered in the light wind and I had the impression that Hasselborg and I were walking under water and that the cloud streamers around us were strips of kelp and seaweed in a fantastic submarine landscape. Those parts of our clothing which had escaped the wet grasses of the beaver meadows were now soaked through. My rifle barrel felt clammy to the touch and water dripped from the muzzle.

This high in the Admirality mountains the timber grew only on the east slope and in the very steepest of the pockets and ravines that crevassed the side of the mountains. For the most part we slipped and stumbled in our booted feet on wet grasses and sphagnum mosses that covered the ground. Hasselborg steadily breasted the rising ground and showed no hesitation of direction, although I couldn't see any landmarks fifty feet away in the mists. We diagonaled upward along the slope of what seemed to be a single mountain peak although it was divided into small valleys with ridges in between. Even here on the mountain slopes we still saw bear tracks and occasionally over a single ridge or shoulder a short stretch of terrain would show the bare earth-scar of a trail that the brown bears had trodden out.

It must have been suppertime when we dropped down over the lip of a small pocket or valley. I had the feeling, too, that we were close to the hangout for the steady scrape-scrape of Hassleborg's heavy boots as we walked seemed to quicken in tempo. There was timber in this high valley. We walked among the boles of majestic cedars of a size which we had not seen since we left the lower slopes of the island. Bracken ferns grew as high as my head and brushed at my neck and cheeks like paintbrushes dipped in cold water. The darkness was almost terrifying in this hidden little place, but at the same time it seemed a refuge. No streamers of mist came through the trees. We seemed secure from the wet and the wild elements of the open mountainsides.

I don't know what I had expected Hasselborg's hangout to be, but it wasn't that. I could have cried in disappointment. As I stood and looked at the place, the water in my rubber boots suddenly felt cold. My sodden shirt, too, seemed to freeze in my back. Night was coming on.

"Well, here we are," said Hasselborg with a show of briskness. He chuckled into his black beard, but I do not know whether he laughed at my doleful face or whether he simply felt joyful at seeing his beloved hangout again. The prospect was awful to contemplate. The hangout was a lean-to, nothing more. It was one of those triangular affairs that hardy woodsmen throw up as a temporary shelter against the wind. It was made of poles leaned against a single fallen tree. The chinks between these slanting poles were rudely filled with moss and occasional flat slabs of lightning-split cedar. The whole structure was flimsy in the extreme and casual in every detail, and yet in these rainy regions a man needed all the shelter he could find. I had to think hard to remember that Hasselborg had slept and lived in this lean-to in the dead of winter when he tended his trap line.

If the structure of the hangout itself had been disappointing, the contents of this haven were heart-rending. As I drew close to the place, Hasselborg was bending over something on the ground. "Contemptible monsters," he was mumbling to himself. "Steal behind my back, will they?" The bundle before him looked like a shapeless mass of rags and, indeed, it was. I could see, however, as I picked up one end of the tattered thing that I had once been a sleeping bag of the Hudson Bay variety. The cover was ripped to shreds and the feather filling, oozing out of a hundred rents and tears, was now sodden with the dripping moisture. Streaks of rust ran away from the metal clasps that had once made this a snug envelope for warm sleeping.

But the tragedy of the sleeping bag was not all. Two or three coffee cans lay scattered before the lean-to and a splintered wooden box of the kind that carries two five-gallon gasoline tins. The cans and the box too had several gaping holes in them as big as my thumb. Even a rusty tin cup had a rent through it as though it had been hung on a post and shot through with a heavy rifle. That was it. Some vandal hunter had torn Hasselborg's bedroll to shreds. Some Tlingit Indian, perhaps, had fired with a vengeful rifle through these meager belongings.

Hasselborg was running a tentative forefinger through one of the holes in the side of a coffee can. "Those contemptible ones!" Bears – those awful holes must be tooth marks. A shiver of apprehension passing over me seemed to make my wet shirt even colder on my spine. I looked fearfully around the little patch of woodland that shielded Hasselborg's hangout from a wet world. The shadows beneath the cedars were deepening to complete dark. I could hear the moisture dripping from the fern fronds and there was no sound but the steady splash of these little droplets as they added to the puddles on the ground below. With no sleeping bag and no food, Hasselborg's hangout was completely lacking in appeal. My pampered stomach, accustomed by several years to steady meals, cramped at the prospect of another handful of dry oatmeal.

It was at this instant that Hasselborg, behind me, chuckled with satisfaction. I turned to see him pulling a white rag out of the debris in the back of the lean-to. This piece of cloth was torn and full of holes like everything else in the hangout. Obviously a family of mice had spent last winter in it and probably raised some children there. But Hasselborg carefully shook it and caressed it with his gnarled hands as though content with that his greatest treasure had not been destroyed by the bears. With a single gesture he hung his wet canvas cap on a protruding pole of the lean-to and slipped this white rag over his dark hair. It was a sort of stocking cap, obviously made out of one leg of some discarded set of long underwear. It was ludicrous and dirty, but somehow it seemed to make things all right with Allen Hasselborg. It restored my own humor too, and I caught myself smiling at the old man as he sat on the battered gasoline box and looked around him at his domain.

We built a small fire which added to the cheerfulness and I even attempted to wring out and dry my socks before the blaze. Hasselborg filled one of the rusty cans with dark-colored water from a small trickle near the lean-to. He could only use the can halfway up, for the same vicious bear that had destroyed his other things had sunk a pointed canine tooth completely through the can. Hasselborg straightened the top of this improvised kettle with his powerful fingers. "I'll bet I know who did this too," he said, half to me.

The water was stained red with cedar roots and the rust made it even darker, but perhaps the combination contained healthful ingredients unknown to ordinary scientists in spotless labratories. Two handfuls of oatmeal in this brew made our supper. It was done when the brown mess boiled up through the tooth hole in the side of the can. Without salt, sugar or other ingredients of any kind it tasted delicious. We ate it with the tips of our fingers as soon as it had cooled a little.

The bears had destroyed the one sleeping bag in the hangout and the tattered stuffing lay in sodden patches in the mud in front

170

of the lean-to. As it was we both slept Admiralty Island style. There are ways of doing things on this island, unknown in ordinary places. First Hasselborg built a large fire and spread it over a considerable area. Next he set me to gathering armloads of bracken ferns that grew in wet clumps along the little rivulet that flowed among the cedars. These I brought back to the firelight before the lean-to, where Hasselborg carefully shook the water from them and laid them in neat piles. After I had gathered a sufficient quantity he scraped the fire back into a small pile. The ground over a considerable area then was dry and warm to the touch of my hand. On this place Hasselborg fixed our beds. The bracken ferns he laid in a generous covering with their stems feathered under like a regular fir-bough bed. When two places had been arranged to his satisfaction there still was a pile of bracken ferns left over. Apparently these were to be the covering of this novel arrangement. I shivered at the anticipation of a sleepless night.

I dried my rifle off as best I could with one end of a damp hand-kerchief. When I had finished Hasselborg had already retired. He lay at full length on the bracken bed and was carefully piling other ferns over him. There was nothing else to do but follow his example. As I lay on the green stuff, it did feel fairly soft and had a certain springiness, almost as acceptable as a thin mattress. But how could any one expect a covering of damp ferns to keep him warm in Alaskan mountains? Still it did.

I found that the serrated fronds of the bracken interlaced to a certain extent so that the individual leaves did not disintegrate when I moved my body. Lastly I placed a wad of the stuff under my head for a pillow and I felt remarkably snug. Of course there was a disconcerting draft on one foot where I hadn't piled enough of the fern, but then I couldn't disturb my whole bed to fix that one spot. I drew the foot up underneath the rest of the bed and drifted off. "What an awful place for insomnia," I was thinking as I fell asleep.

I woke with a start in the middle of black night. I must have slept some time for I now felt chilled and several of the ferns had fallen from over me where I had moved a restless shoulder in my sleep. But it was not the creeping chill which had awakened me. There was something else there in the darkness. I could not tell

171

whether it was a noise, a smell or a movement. It was as black with my eyes open as it had been before with them closed. There was a clammy stickiness to the air. I cautiously reached out my hand and began to pull the ferns over my exposed shoulder. "Thud! thud! thud!" There it was again! I could feel the reverberation in the earth beneath my fern pillow. "Thud! Thud!" Again the noise echoed through that still place. It sounded like a heavy mallet driving a stake at no great distance. There was a shifting, too, among the cedars on the far side of the lean-to.

I heard Hasselborg stirring beneath his ferns. He was groping for something in the darkness beside his bed. I knew he was fully clothed, even to his wet boots and I had retired the same way. We had both left our rifles in the comparative dryness of the lean-to a few yards away. The thudding noise came again and I thought I could hear with it a low growl, the same sound a dog makes when another approaches too close to his food. Hasselborg was thrusting something into the fire. I could see out of the corner of my eye several spots of red as he stirred the embers. But the glowing coals made no light and the starless night was wet black among the trees. I still looked toward the sound as though expecting some awful shape to materialize there. I did think I could hear a sniffing now, as though some gigantic nose were taking in long draughts of the damp air.

Suddenly there was a blaze of light by the dead fire and Hasselborg sprang into black outline. He was thrusting a splintered piece of wood into the embers and blowing on them. He held the stick up in his hand like a torch and it flared before his face in long streamers of blue and yellow flame. The heat of the lightning bolt had opened out the grain of the wood into a thousand tiny splinters which now blazed and crackled in Hasselborg's hand.

"Get up, Hibben, and build that fire." There were no hesitant explanations and it never occurred to me to hesitate. I piled other pieces of cedar on the glowing embers and blew them into flame. I turned to see Hasselborg stalking off among the trees waving his torch in front of them. The red light threw his face into moving relief. His black beard made his features appear enormous and the pointed stocking cap on his head gave him a peaked, gnomelike appearance that was sinister and ludicrous too. "Scat! Get out, you!" he said to the shadows and waved his torch furiously before him. The sparks fanned from the billet and fell hissing to the damp earth in a cascade of fireworks. Hasselborg stamped his heavy boot on the wet earth twice, then held his torch still and appeared to be listening. I thought I could hear the faint thud-thud of a reply to this challenge, but it was certainly farther away than it had been. Hasselborg again dashed forward, with his torch making a black plume of smoke behind him. Then he turned and came back to the fire.

"It's a male," he told me in a matter-of-fact manner. "They stamp like that when they challenge another male." Then as an afterthought Hasselborg added: "Well, we're both males, aren't we?" He opened his mouth in his black beard and laughed uproariously. He stopped only when his upper dental plate slipped a little and he had to catch it in one hand.

"You mean it was a bear?" I gasped. "A male bear that close to us?"

"Well, what did you think it was?" Hasselborg snapped. "A chipmunk?" Hasselborg glanced sideways at me with that discon-certing expression of his. What would I do when I actually met one of these Admiralty monsters?

Hasselborg and I spent the rest of the night huddled around the fire of cedar wood. The male bear had stamped his foot at us about three in the morning. For the rest of that dreadful night the old man regaled me with stories of other bears. He told of bear hunts on the mainland and on other Alaskan islands. He told especially of one monster brown bear that had left him for dead. So absorbed was I in these stories, that the rest of the darkness passed quickly and the dawn came almost without my noticing it.

When it was light enough to distinguish the trunks of the cedar trees in the grove around us I got out the little bag of pancake flour that I had secreted for just this occasion. I sorted out the lid of an old kerosene can that lay among the debris in Hasselborg's hangout. In this I poured a mixture of pancake flour and water and prepared to manufacture at least a small semblance of civilized food. I placed the rusty lid on the embers at the edge of the fire to bake the thick mass into some kind of hoecake or super-flapjack. The crackling cedar of the blaze kept dropping embers into the dough as it baked. I picked these out carefully with charcoal-stained fingers.

I was so absorbed in my cookery that I had momentarily forgotten Allen Hasselborg and his habits. Now he laid a hand on my shoulder and his black beard brushed against me as he leaned over to look at my breakfast. "Ashes never hurt anybody," he said with finality. To emphasize this pronouncement he raked a handful of wood ashes from the edge of the fire and deliberately threw them into the soft dough of my pancake.

I cooked the thing, ashes and all, and when it was ready gave Hasselborg half. The only thing that can be said of this Admiralty hotcake was that it didn't taste like dry oatmeal. The ash-filled dough had baked into a heavy sodden mass, pervaded by the taste of stinging lye.

The strangeness of these things had many hours ago been lost upon me. Anything seemed natural at Hasselborg's hangout. I wiped the spots of rust from the barrel of my rifle and stood ready to go. Hasselborg led off without glancing back to see if I followed. Even with the dismal lye-cake feeling like a lump of lead in my stomach, there was a thrill of anticipation at the start of the hunt. Who would not endure a thousand discomforts such as these to hunt Alaskan brown bear with Allen Hasselborg? Perhaps on the very edge of the cedar grove we might come face to face with the male bear that had challenged our sleep. Bears might be anywhere in those misty wastes. I checked my rifle carefully and put dry shells into the magazine.

The early morning was clearer than the afternoon before. The misty clouds had lifted and to the left we could see the naked peak of a stony mountain rising high against the lead-colored sky.

"Dish Tuk Mountain of the Tlingits," Hasselborg explained, waving his ancient rifle in that direction. There were other peaks around us too. There was one especially, with a dark, rocky crest that stuck out of the clouds directly before us. "I named that one after myself," said Hasselborg with a pleased expression.

We stood for a moment there on the slopes of Hasselborg Mountain. My famous companion took out the telescope that all this time had hung around his neck in its leather case. Squinting his eye he looked through this antiquated spyglass at the slopes around us. He swung, slowly, pivoting on one foot, pausing now and again to examine more closely some ravine or timbered nook on the mountainside. The open slopes wore a fairy's covering in

174

the growing morning light. Silver drops of water tipped every grass blade and glistened on the blueberry leaves. There was a streak of silver near my feet where a giant slug had trailed his body the night before. An unknown bird sang behind us in the cedars. It was a misty but glorious world.

"There's one," said Hasselborg calmly. His telescope was fixed on a slope perhaps half a mile away. There, a group of alders hung precariously on the steep incline. There were open patches and grassy glades around them. I could see nothing. The old man handed me the spyglass and I leveled it at the spot he indicated. I adjusted the eyepiece to my vision and the alder clump sprang closely into view. There was nothing there. "Wh – " I began to say. The top of one of the alders had thrashed violently in the still air. Then a neighboring tree bent down and jerked sideways. A bulky body was moving unseen within the alder stems. Then something red appeared among the green of the alder leaves. There was a round thing, then another. They were ears and between them was a head that looked as big as a full moon even at that distance.

The bear was not looking at us, but seemed to be sweeping his Teddy bear nose in all directions above the alder leaves. I watched with growing excitement as the ponderous animal swept his black nostrils in all directions. Then as suddenly as he had appeared, he withdrew his head into the verdure. As before only the twitching of the alder branches showed that an Admiralty bear walked beneath.

"It's a beautiful red one, Mr. Hasselborg!" I gasped excitedly. "He's a monster!"

"He is nothing of the sort," said Hasselborg with asperity. "That bear is a two-year-old and the fur on his rump is badly rubbed. You certainly don't want that one." The old man emphasized the word "that" with such contempt that I did not even answer. I glanced again at the alder clump in the distance and I could see with my naked eye a spot of mahogany color moving among the green. Hasselborg was already moving on.

As we moved farther up the mountain slopes, the clouds descended to meet us. As before, we sometimes walked through solid walls of mist where I could barely make out the dark form of Hasselborg before me, and could scarcely see the ground beneath my boots. There were open places, too, between the clouds. In each one of these spots, Hasselborg paused and swept the mountainside

175

with his telescope. But each time he collapsed the thing and returned it to its case with never a word. By noon I was growing apprehensive. Perhaps I should have stalked the red bear after all. We might not find any among these cloud-covered mountain peaks. After several hours we paused to eat some more dry cereal. I voiced my fears to Old Man Hasselborg. "Are you afraid you won't get any bear?" he asked me quizzically. "I've seen four this morning and none of them were any good. Absolutely no good." I remained silent at this. I didn't want to admit that I hadn't spotted these other bears at all, and yet I considered myself quite a hunter.

It was mid-afternoon, perhaps, and I was plodding along mechanically. The first thrill of the hunt had passed and a despairing mood had come over me. I would have settled everything for a hot cup of coffee and a dry bed. I had bent my neck forward to keep the cold mist out of my collar. In my clumsiness I rammed Hasselborg in the back with my lowered head. He turned and looked at me with a sorrowing glance, such as one bestows on an ignorant puppy. Hasselborg was standing stock-still, looking up at the slope above us. Here as everywhere, wisps of clouds drifted low on the ground. Stunted blueberry bushes appeared and disappeared as the white moisture enveloped them and passed on. There was nothing but ghostly stillness around us. Hasselborg and I were alone in the wild mountains of Admiralty Island. The wet and the cold discouraged even the birds. There was no other living thing. But wait! On the slope above was a large rock jutting into the mists from the low bushes round about. It was a squarish-shaped thing, dark in color and absolutely still. A feathery fold of cloud whitened this shape to nothingness, then it appeared again. There it was plainly now – but we had seen stones before.

As the trailing streamers of mist made an opening for an instant, the stone seemed to move, or perhaps change shape. That was it. On one end of the squarish thing, a projection appeared. This protrusion swept upward and out. There were two round objects on its end. I stared, fascinated by a pair of enormous black nostrils as the animal raised its head and looked full at us. "There's your bear," Hasselborg said, as calmly as ever.

It was indeed a bear, a monster of his kind. The wet fur on the animal's back was the color of old burlap. Only his nose glistened as he wriggled it toward us. From his half-open mouth there hung a few sprigs of blueberry stems upon which the animal had been feeding when we came up. The bear's feet and those awful claws were hidden in the blueberry bushes in which he stood. The ponderous body was broadside to us and the hump above his shoulder showed plainly. "Good gosh!" I muttered under my breath. The bear craned his head upward as though squinting at us down the sloop through a pair of invisible bifocals.

"You'd better get to shootin'," muttered Hasselborg out of the side of his beard. "He's getting ready to charge."

"Why, he looks like a great big Teddy bear, Mr. Hasselborg," I said in wonderment. The animal was only a hundred yards away and straight up the slope from us. I could see every nuance of expression on that brown bear face and it didn't look at all fierce.

"Aim for the shoulder," Hasselborg was saying. "Don't wait till he turns straight toward us, and don't miss," he continued, underlining each word heavily as he hissed through his teeth. Suiting his actions to his words he raised his own rifle to his shoulder and I thought momentarily of the salt-corroded shells in the chamber. I hoped my own gun was in better shape.

I pulled back the hammer on my rifle and squinted through the sights. All I could see was wet brown fur in a solid mass. They had told me at Juneau that these bears could run a hundred yards in five seconds and could do it with a dozen shots in their bodies if the bullets weren't placed just right. Just right – I raised my head over the sights to pick again the spot on the bear's shoulder where the bullet must strike. "Shoot!" Hasselborg said with rising inflection. The bear had raised one paw from the ground and was turning toward us. Here came the charge.

With no time then for careful squinting or calculation, I drew the sights down on the point of his shoulder and pulled back the trigger. Can't miss, I thought. Can't miss. The blast of the gun almost jerked me off my feet. My boot slipped in the wet grass and I dropped to one knee. Automatically I levered another shell into the chamber, even as I went down. I had a momentary flash of the vast bulk of the bear hurtling down toward us. Was he charging or falling? "Look out!" Hasselborg screamed. The bear was upon us. It was a mountain of brown fur with ponderous legs and paws thrashing out toward us. We were gone. Instinctively I

177

rolled to the side and blanched into the grass, still holding the cocked rifle above me.

There was a thrashing of leaves and the terrifying noise of grunts and snarls only a yard away. The brown bulk of the bear flashed between Hasselborg and me, not a yard from either of us. By some miracle the infuriated animal had charged between us and was gone down the slope in a flurry of torn bushes and flying droplets of blood. Blood! I must have hit him after all. I raised on one knee and looked down the slope after the bear. He wasn't running at all, but was rolling over and over like a gigantic sack of stones. The powerful legs of the bear flopped out in all directions as he rolled, and he hit the bottom of the slope all in a heap and lay still.

My heart was pounding wildly in my neck and I found myself clutching the rifle till my knuckles were white. I glanced at Hasselborg and he was just picking himself up from the wet grass where he had thrown himself as the bear had passed. There was a set expression to his black beard and I didn't know whether he was glad or sorry.

"Don't stand there gawking – Close your mouth and for God's sake shoot him again before we're both killed." I looked down the slope again where the bear had fallen in a heap of lifeless fur. Instinctively I jerked the rifle around. The monster brown bear was standing at full height on both hind feet. The bottom of the slope was perhaps only thirty or forty yards below us and I could see clearly the blood-colored eyes of the bear fixed on me with a look of hatred that spanned the space between us. Clots of blood were oozing out of the corner of his mouth and dropping unheeded on the fur of his belly. The animal waved his front paws as though in anticipation of gathering us in to those murderous teeth. Standing erect on his hind legs the height of the bear was so great that he seemed at a level with us in spite of the steepness of the slope.

It was only a second, I think, that I stared at the infuriated animal. He looked like the cover of a lurid magazine I had seen once which I never thought could be real. I remember noticing that the bear swayed a little as he weaved toward us and his right forepaw seemed to be broken at the shoulder. Again I raised the rifle and brought the sights instinctively down on the bear's throat. The animal opened his cavernous jaws wide and a flood of blood rushed forth, staining the whiteness of his teeth. Just as the bear lurched forward, I fired. The noise was deafening in that cloud-enclosed space, but even with the recoil of the weapon I saw the bullet hit and carry away a wisp of fur from the bear's neck. Even as the echoes rolled back from the unseen mountain peaks around us, the gigantic animal stayed erect. He shifted with difficulty, first one hind foot and then another. Suddenly something seemed to snap and the huge head and the bloody mouth sank forward on his chest at a sickening angle. Without a sound the great body slumped forward and lay still on the blood-spattered grass.

"He's about a twelve-footer," Hasselborg was saying as we started to skin the animal. "It's a good skin, too, if you want such things," he added.

It was late the next evening when we came out of the woods on the shores of Mole Harbor. Carrying the green skin and the skull of the monster bear had been a Herculean task on those wet trails. I understood then why we had carried empty pack boards into the mountains.

I thought as I loaded the limp hide into the canoe that the whole adventure in the clouds was unreal. Nightmares have backgrounds such as this and hallucinations also involve charging monsters with bloodshot eyes.

But as I turned to wave good-bye to Allen Hasselborg, he was standing in the doorway of his cabin with the light of a kerosene lamp outlining him from behind. His head had a pointed look. I smiled as I turned and shoved the canoe into deep water. Hasselborg had brought back his stocking cap from the hangout.

"Hasselborg's Hangout" from HUNTING AMERICAN BEARS by Frank C. Hibben. Copyright 1950 by Frank C. Hibben. Copyright renewed 1978 by Frank C. Hibben. Reprinted by permission of HarperCollins Publishers.

ON
Dry-Cow Fishing
A S   A   F I N E   A R T

BY RUDYARD KIPLING

No representative collection of tales exemplifying the
sporting experience would be complete without at least
one rollicking piece of humor, and famed English writer
Rudyard Kipling (1865-1936) provides it. Originally
published in the December, 1890, issue of *The Fishing
Gazette*, this light, lively story serves as a rib-tickling
reminder that fly fishermen need to be constantly on
guard against taking themselves too seriously.

It must be clearly understood that I am not at all proud of this
performance. In Florida men sometimes hook and land, on
rod and tackle a little finer than a steam-crane and chain, a
mackerel-like fish called "tarpon," which sometime run to 120
pounds. Those men stuff their captures and exhibit them in glass
cases and become puffed up. On the Columbia River sturgeon of
150 pounds weight are taken with the line. When the sturgeon is

hooked the line is fixed to the nearest pine tree or steamboat-wharf, and after some hours or days the sturgeon surrenders himself, if the pine or the line does not give way. The owner of the line then states on oath that he has caught a sturgeon, and he, too, becomes proud.

These things are mentioned to show how light a creel will fill the soul of a man with vanity. I am not proud. It is nothing to me that I have hooked and played seven hundred pounds weight of quarry. All my desire is to place the little affair on record before the mists of memory breed the miasma of exaggeration.

The minnow cost eighteen pence. It was a beautiful quill minnow, and the tackle-maker said that it could be thrown as a fly. He guaranteed further in respect to the triangles – it glittered with triangles – that, if necessary, the minnow would hold a horse. A man who speaks too much truth is just as offensive as a man who speaks too little. None the less, owing to the defective condition of the present law of libel, the tackle-maker's name must be withheld.

The minnow and I and a rod went down to a brook to attend to a small jack who lived between two clumps of flags in the most cramped swim that he could select. As a proof that my intentions were strictly honorable, I may mention that I was using a little split-cane rod – very dangerous if the line runs through weeds, but very satisfactory in clean water, inasmuch as it keeps a steady strain on the fish and prevents him from taking liberties. I had an old score against the jack. He owed me two live-bait already, and I had reason to suspect him of coming upstream and interfering with a little bleak-pool under a horse-bridge which lay entirely beyond his sphere of legitimate influence. Observe, therefore, that my tackle and my motives pointed clearly to jack, and jack alone; though I knew that there were monstrous big perch in the brook.

The minnow was thrown as a fly several times, and, owing to my peculiar, and hitherto unpublished, methods of fly throwing, nearly six pennyworth of the triangles came off, either in my coat-collar, or my thumb, or the back of my hand. Fly fishing is a very gory amusement.

The jack was not interested in the minnow, but towards twilight a boy opened a gate of the field and let in some twenty or thirty cows and half-a-dozen cart-horses, and they were all very much interested. The horses galloped up and down the field and shook the banks, but the cows walked solidly and breathed heavily, as people breathe who appreciate the Fine Arts.

By this time I had given up all hope of catching my jack fairly, but I wanted the live-bait and bleak-account settled before I went away, even if I tore up the bottom of the brook. Just before I had quite made up my mind to borrow a tin of chloride of lime from the farmhouse – another triangle had fixed itself in my fingers – I made a cast which for pure skill, exact judgement of distance, and perfect coincidence of hand and eye and brain, would have taken every prize at a bait-casting tournament. That was the first half of the cast. The second was postponed because the quill minnow would not return to its proper place, which was under the lobe of my left ear. It had done thus before and I supposed it was in collision with a grass tuft, till I turned round and saw a large red and white bald-faced cow rubbing her withers with her nose. She looked at me reproachfully, and her look said as plainly as words: "The season is too far advanced for gadflies. What is this strange disease?"

I replied, "Madam, I must apologize for an unwarrantable liberty on the part of my minnow, but if you will have the goodness to keep still until I can reel in, we will adjust this little difficulty."

I reeled in very swiftly and cautiously, but she would not wait. She put her tail in the air and ran away. It was a purely involuntary motion on my part: I struck.

Other anglers may contradict me, but I firmly believe that if a man had foul-hooked his best friend through the nose, and that friend ran, the man would strike by instinct. I struck, therefore, and the reel began to sing just as merrily as though I had caught my jack. But had it been a jack, the minnow would have come away. I told the tacklemaker this much afterwards and he laughed and made allusions to the guarantee about holding a horse.

Because it was a fat innocent she-cow that had done me no harm the minnow held – held like an anchorfluke in coral moorings – and I was forced to dance up and down an interminable field very largely used by cattle. It was like salmon fishing in a nightmare. I took gigantic strides, and every stride found me up to my knees in marsh. But the cow seemed to skate along the squashy green by the brook, to skim over the miry backwaters, and to float like a mist through the patches of rush that squirted black filth over my face. Sometimes we whirled through a mob of her friends – there were no friends to help me – and they looked scandalized; and sometimes a young and frivolous cart-horse would join in the chase for a few miles, and kick solid pieces of mud into my eyes; and through all the mud, the milky smell of kine, the rush and the smother, I was aware of my own voice crying: "Pussy, pussy, pussy! Pretty pussy! come along then, puss-cat!" You see it is so hard to speak to a cow properly, and she would not listen – no, she would not listen.

Then she dropped, and the moon got up behind the pollards to tell the cows to lie down; but they were all on their feet, and they came trooping to see. And she said, "I haven't had my supper, and I want to go to bed, and please don't worry me." And I said, "The matter has passed beyond any apology. There are three courses open to you, my dear lady. If you'll have the common sense to walk up to my creel I'll get my knife and you shall have all the minnow. Or, again, if you'll let me move across to your near side, instead of keeping me so coldly on your off side, the thing will come away in one tweak. I can't pull it out over your withers. Better still, go to a post and rub it out, dear. It won't hurt much, but if you think I'm going to lose my rod to please you, you are mistaken." And she said, "I don't understand what you are saying. I am very, very unhappy." And I said. "It's all your fault for trying to fish. Do go to the nearest gate-post, you nice fat thing, and rub it out."

For a moment I fancied she was taking my advice. She ran away and I followed. But all the other cows came with us in a bunch, and I thought of Phaeton trying to drive the Chariot of the Sun, and Texas cowboys killed by stampeding cattle, and *"Green Grow the Rushes, O!"* and Solomon and Job, and "loosing the bands of Orion," and hooking Behemoth, and Wordsworth who talks about whirling round with stones and rocks and trees, and "Here we go round the Mulberry Bush," and "Pippin Hill," and "Hey Diddle Diddle," and most especially the top joint of my rod. Again she stopped – but nowhere in the neighborhood of my knife – and her sisters stood moonfaced round her. It seemed that she might, now, run towards me, and I looked for a tree, because cows are very different from salmon who only jump against the line, and never molest the fisherman. What followed was worse than any direct attack. She began to buck-jump, to stand on her head and her tail alternately, to leap into the sky, all four feet together, and to dance on her hind legs. It was so violent and improper, so desperately unladylike, that I was inclined to blush, as one would blush at the sight of a prominent statesman sliding down a fire escape, or a duchess chasing her cook with a skillet. That flopsome abandon might go on all night in the lonely meadow among the mists, and if it went on all night– this was pure inspiration – I might be able to worry through the fishing line with my teeth.

Those who desire an entirely new sensation should chew with all their teeth, and against time, through a best waterproofed silk line, one end of which belongs to a mad cow dancing fairy rings in the moonlight; at the same time keep one eye on the cow and the other on the top joint of a split-cane rod. She buck-jumped and I bit on the slack just in front of the reel; and I am in a position to state that that line was cored with steel wire throughout the particular section which I attacked. This has been formally denied by the tackle-maker, who is not to be believed.

The *wheep* of the broken line running through the rings told me that henceforth the cow and I might be strangers. I had already bidden goodbye to some tooth or teeth; but no price is too great for freedom of the soul.

"Madam," I said, "the minnow and twenty feet of very superior line are your alimony without reservation. For the wrong I have unwittingly done to you I express my sincere regret. At the same time, may I hope that Nature, the kindest of nurses, will in due season..."

She or one or her companions must have stepped on her spare end of the line in the dark, for she bellowed wildly and ran away, followed by all the cows. I hoped the minnow was disengaged at last; and before I went away looked at my watch, fearing to find it nearly midnight. My last cast for the jack was made at 6:23 p.m. There lacked still three and a-half minutes of the half-hour; and I would have sworn that the moon was paling before the dawn!

"Simminly someone were chasing they cows down to bottom o' Ten Acre," said the farmer that evening. "Twasn't you, sir?"

"Now under what earthly circumstances do you suppose I should chase your cows? I wasn't fishing for them, was I?"

184

Then all the farmer's family gave themselves up to jam-smeared laughter for the rest of the evening, because that was a rare and precious jest, and it was repeated for months, and the fame of it spread from that farm to another, and yet another at least three miles away, and it will be used again for the benefit of visitors when the freshets come down in spring.

But to the greater establishment of my honor and glory I submit in print this bald statement of fact, that I may not, through forgetfulness, be tempted later to tell how I hooked a bull on a Marlow Buzz, how he ran up a tree and took to water, and how I played him along the London-road for thirty miles, and gaffed him at Smithfield. Errors of this kind may creep in with the lapse of years, and it is my ambition ever to be a worthy member of that fraternity who pride themselves on never deviating by one hair's breadth from the absolute and literal truth.

THE
Georgia Breeze

BY DAN O'BRIEN

Quail are the soul of the sporting South, and as Havilah
Babcock once put it, a fine pointer is more precious than
rubies and pearls. The Georgia Breeze was such a pointer,
the dog of a lifetime every devoted hunter deserves.
Fickle fate dealt this incomparable wizard of broomsedge
fields and fence-rows an indifferent hand, but his end is a
fitting one. This is a story to move all but the flintiest of
hearts, and anyone who has been a party to the demise of
a faithful canine companion will conclude it with a catch
in his throat and dampness in his eyes.

From this rocking chair I can see the whole place. My house
is on the highest ridge in the country and beneath me I can
see everything that ever meant anything to me. The ridge
that I'm on is hardwood and rolls down to the dairy pastures
where the gray-brown cows with black eyes stand chewing, staring
into the thickets at the edge of the pasture like there might be
something in there. And past them are the five- and ten-acre

patches of corn and cotton, all of them connected by horse paths and ringed with brush. I can see the buildings and the house, probably two miles off, as much a part of what I see as the trees, or the grass, or the red clay that's under it all.

Sometimes I sit here and dream. And if I sit long enough, I can see the Georgia Breeze again, casting out around those field edges, running downwind of the fence lines, holding his head high. He's reading this place like it's all painted in black and white. I can see him glancing back over his shoulder, staying out in front, and sometimes I can see him swing into the wind and freeze, as if that instant God had turned him to stone. But mostly when I see him I see him running, long and smooth, covering the ground, running. Running like nothing else matters.

Like nothing else mattered. Like that was all that mattered. All that mattered to Mr. Morgan, frail and gray. Moving slowly now, down the steps of the house that has been in his family since before the Civil War. Waving away the women who try to help him. Walking with a cane to shake the hands of the men who have worked for him since they were boys. Old and sick but the brightness still there, sunken in wrinkled sockets. He nods to each man. Then he comes to me, but not taking my hand, just reaching out and touching me and I follow him away from the rest and we walk the same way we've walked a thousand times. Through the break in the hedge and out to the kennels. And together we walk down the concrete path past each run and the pointers paw and force their noses through the wire at us.

Mr. Morgan touches them all, all except the big old brown-ticked pointer in the last run. When we get to him we stop. Mr. Morgan tells me, Jessie, the Morgan plantation is quite a place. I don't say a word, and he says, We got us a herd of registered dairy cattle, a lumber mill, a gin of our own, and some of the best crops in the state. I'm standing there nodding, not looking up, and he says, But the best thing is right here. We both look down the line at the dogs. Straight legs, loose skins, shiny eyes, and high, cracking tails. Without saying it we are both thinking back to the mountain curs that Mr. Morgan bred them from.

Then he puts his thin hands through the wire of the last run and holds the old pointer's big square head and says, Take care of the Georgia Breeze, Jessie. He's the best pointer that ever pointed a quail, he says.

The best you got, he says. Go get the best you got, and I drop the manure fork and I'm back before he has time to bring them big walking horses out of the barn. Wonderful day, scent's just right, he says. And he smiles as he swings up into the saddle. And I think, Lord God, if I could only ride like that. Sitting tall, back straight as a fence post, glued to that little flat saddle like it's part of him. And the horse, sliding those feet out like he's glad to be doing it.

Mr. Morgan says, Let's try the new bitch and Sam. So I unsnap their leads and they're gone. The two other dogs that I brought out jump and tug at their lead ropes wanting to go with them. But once I'm in the saddle they quiet to a steady strain on the ropes and we head out, riding side by side, me holding the second pair of dogs and Mr. Morgan singing to the brace that's down so they know where we are and can stay out in front.

Sometimes I watch him, if I'm not watching one of the dogs, and I can tell when one comes into sight and I can tell if it's running like he likes to see them run. By Mr. Morgan's eyes or mouth I can tell if that dog is keeping its head and tail high. Like now, I can tell that the young white bitch is casting out, running the edge of the beans and I can tell that she's running good. I can see in Mr. Morgan's face that he's happy with her. I knew it was a test 'cause he put her down with Sam. He wants to know what she's made of. And by watching his eyes, even from the side, I know an instant before he takes his hat off and holds it high and shouts, Point, that she's found a covey and I lean forward and let that walking horse rock me across the bean field, flat out, the mud from Mr. Morgan's horse splattering us and the wind ripping at my clothes.

We're getting closer and I can see that the bitch is on an incline, her head lower than her rear and her whole body curved. She's pointing a covey that's beside her, hiding twenty feet away in the brush of the bean field edge. The dogs on the leads stiffen up when they see her and refuse to take another step. Mr. Morgan smiles as we dismount and before he takes the shotgun from the saddle he strokes the two dogs who have honored the bitch's point. I look to where the quail should be and deep in the thicket I see another patch of white. It's Sam, pointing the same covey from the brush. Mr. Morgan, I say, and nod toward where Sam

stands motionless. They got them quail plumb bottled up, I say.
Mr. Morgan nods and steps up beside the white bitch, who has
moved nothing, not even an eyelid. He strokes her along the back
and steps forward into the covey.

The birds erupt, twisting and turning between the trees and the
shrubs, the sound of a hundred horses snorting, and Mr. Morgan
fires the shotgun into the air, not even watching the quail but
keeping an eye on each dog. They are both stock still, only raising
their heads slightly to see where the quail are going. I tie the
second pair of dogs and now I'm in snapping a lead onto the little
bitch and Mr. Morgan goes into the thicket to bring Sam out.

He hands Sam's lead to me and steps back to look at the two
dogs. He's always trying to come up with something better and I
know what he's thinking. He's thinking she's strong, thinking that
it's the mixture of blood that counts. Thinking about blood.
Blooded dogs, blooded horses, even people.

New people. New blood for the plantation. A new boss Mr.
John Landeen, walking down the scrubbed bricks between the
thick oak stalls asking me what Mr. Morgan had kept the saddle
horses for. For running the dogs, I tell him, and he looks at me
and smiles. For running dogs? he asks. He swings his hand
around the barn and ends up at the glass-windowed tack room,
the brass-fitted harness and the polished saddles. It's a museum,
he says, and looks at me and makes me feel old. There's just no
place for it now, he says. And I'm knowing he'll be sorry come
quail season and I'm wondering how I'll get them dogs ready
without a horse. But I say, Yes sir, to what he says and, Yes sir, to
doing the kitchen chores. And, Yes sir, to will a tractor fit in the
barn, and, Yes sir, yes sir.

Yes sir. I know what happens this Thursday. I heard it from one
of the girls in the house. Thursday you got people coming from
town to go quail hunting, I say. Mr. Morgan nods at me and I tell
him, Yes sir, I know what that means. That means them dogs best
be looking good, and Mr. Morgan smiles.

And come Thursday those dogs are looking good. I'm out front
scouting up the dogs and Mr. Morgan is riding with his guests and
they're talking and Mr. Morgan is singing to the dogs and they're
putting on a show. They're everywhere and finding more quail
than there could ever be out in those patches and I'm scouting

189

them up, finding them pointing in places they just couldn't be. I'm finding them dogs where they might have never been found, and once in a while I catch one lollygagging around behind the hunters and I quick make him heel behind the horse and we scoot up through the woods to where I can send him out in front and the people don't ever know the truth and they think that dog has been running out there where he belongs all along. Today I know I'm earning my keep.

I'm scouting up a storm and it's all different. I'm right out here with the dogs. I'm thinking like a dog. I'm figuring where those quail are going to be and I'm making up my mind just like a dog, where to go after I cast through that patch of beggar-lice. And I'm always keeping in mind that no dog ever smelled a quail by running upwind of it. And I'm knowing that those dogs know all of that, better than me, and I got to think fast to keep up with them and I can't see the eyes so I can't tell what is happening like I can when I'm riding with Mr. Morgan so I stay one step behind. It's all different out here in the brush. Everything is faster.

Even the singing sounds different. From out here it sounds like it must sound to the dogs. It's distant, a kind of whining language that tells you where you are and means, if you can hear it at all, that everything is still all right.

And later they are all in the kennel talking about what a good hunt they had and what good dogs they are and I'm feeding the dogs and, when I open the last pen, five fat wiggling pointer pups tumble out onto the ground and one of the men says to Mr. Morgan, They're wonderful, and picks one up. The man picks them all up, one by one, and finally he says, Could I buy one. And Mr. Morgan says, No, but I'll give you one. Then he leans over and picks up a male pup that is sitting by itself. Anyone but this one, Mr. Morgan says, anyone but this one.

Anyone at all. Take them all if you want, anyone at all. And he swings that arm again, right down the line. These kennels are going, he says. The man says, Thank you, Mr. Landeen, and I just got to say, Mr. Landeen, I got two of them ready for you to go hunting and that old dog on the end ain't no good to nobody. Mr. Landeen says, The kennels have to go, Jessie. And I remind him that his boy wanted to go quail hunting. He'll be home from college any day, I say, and Mr. Landeen says, Okay, anyone but those three, and the man thanks him and right away I start working them two dogs like they ain't never been worked so when the day comes I am ready.

Ready for Thomas Landeen and his young friend to take them out quail hunting. But they get drunk, imagine that, drunk when guns and the dogs are right. They're running right, sucking up the ground and nobody watching but me. Mr. Tom and his friend don't want to walk and they get the pickup stuck and I know them dogs are piled up somewhere on point waiting for us and we never get there and all I get is, Where are them damn dogs of yours, Jessie?

And after that, when I'm putting the dogs up them boys are drinking more on the porch and pretty soon I hear a shot and come on the run. I stop right beside the Georgia Breeze, who's watching to see about the shooting. I see them two boys walking down the steps of the house laughing and they look into a bush just off the lawn and they wave to me to come. And when I do, Thomas says, Jessie, this here is what we was looking for this afternoon. And he hands me a quail that he shot. That's what they look like, Jessie. And all I can say is, You shot it on the ground. That chasing dogs is crazy, Jessie. That little bastard was almost in the yard. Another minute and it would have run over there and bit that sorry old hound of yours. He points at the Georgia Breeze and they laugh. But the Georgia Breeze pays no attention. He yawns, lays stiffly down, and stretches out in the afternoon sun.

Stretches out. Look at him stretching out, taking in an acre at a breath. And Mr. Morgan sitting that horse, watching him run and showing me that he's watching the best dog that he's ever had on this place. He's only two years old and already they're saying that there ain't never been a dog like him. And I ride right beside Mr. Morgan and I know it sure as he does that the Georgia Breeze is the greatest bird dog that ever there was. But nobody's surprised. That dog couldn't do nothing else. He was born to run them thicket edges, built to quarter a field into the wind, and he can't help covering twelve feet of Georgia dirt with every bound.

And when he swings onto point Mr. Morgan's eyes flash and I can see something I never saw with any other dog. I can see a touch of amazement, like Mr. Morgan is finally seeing something he's never seen before, or maybe something he's only seen in his

191

dreams. And when I look myself I feel it too, I wonder what could make a dog freeze like that, every muscle taut to the point of trembling, but not trembling, solid, the head as high as it can be and the tail arched, absolutely still over his back. When I touch him, he is like living stone. I walk past him to flush the birds and looking back I see his face, drawn up, motionless, the nostrils flared and the eyes wide, almost frightened. I wonder just for a moment if it could be the devil hidden in the brush at my feet.

Twenty feet. Not a good concrete run like he deserves. Twenty feet. Twenty feet of chain and a house to tie it to and that's all that's left of the bird dogs. Just the Georgia Breeze, tied out there in the sun getting older, like me, too old to do any work and out to pasture. Up here in this house and knowing that they'd bulldoze it flat without me and knowing that no one wants that old dog and knowing every bit of it is wrong. And Mr. Tom teasing me and saying nasty things and calling me over and telling me that his dad is going to have the Georgia Breeze put away by the vet. And me, I don't know whether to believe him or not but I get to thinking up here and then I can't remember if Mr. Tom even said it and finally I can't sit here another minute and I head on down the hill. And I creep the best I can up to where the Georgia Breeze is chained and I unsnap him and tie a piece of rope to him and we come back here. And that night I feed him just enough and pet his old head and show him the shotgun to make him feel good and we talk till I fall asleep in the chair and he falls asleep with his head flat on the floor and touching my foot. We dream the same dream and it feels like brush in our faces and smells like horses and gunpowder. And in the night I lean down to touch him, lean down to know that he is there.

Lean down to unsnap him and he looks straight ahead, like I wasn't even there, and I run my hand down each side. I can feel his muscles, strong as a horse's neck. Then Mr. Morgan tells me to let him go and I let go of that collar and he explodes, hitting the ground again twenty feet in front of us and I watch for a minute and then I hear Mr. Morgan telling me to get on my horse. By the time I'm in my saddle Mr. Morgan is singing to him and the Georgia Breeze is running like his life depended on it.

He casts out along the edge of the cotton and makes the whole loop around the field. He crosses into the next field just as we get

192

to where the horse path leads through the woods to the field he's in and by then he's covered almost half of it. I'm watching Mr. Morgan and the Georgia Breeze is going fine. Then we turn downwind and he runs a lane to get in front of us before he takes to the thicket, and I can see him raise his head breathing in, finding no birds and turning again. And I can see that he's running hard, putting his heart into it, pouring his soul into the Georgia ground.

I am on the ground. I can't see. I cannot keep up. I run to where he must have gone and I am right. The sun is hot and I can see that his tongue is out, washing his shoulders with saliva. His head is lower now but he is still running, hunting, doing what he must. He is hard to follow and I have lost him again, but when I stop I can hear him, moving ahead of me, panting, whining sometimes, but then he is gone. I hear no sound and I begin to search. Slowly from thicket to thicket and finally I see him, standing tall, solid as a rock pile, somehow holding back his panting. Intent on the quail, invisible to us both, but there, so very real to us. And I bring up the shotgun, walk to his side, and hold the barrel an inch from his head. I take one more step and the covey crashes from the brush around me, they explode, fifty strong, ascending, flying in every direction. The Georgia Breeze swells that much taller and I pull.

Pull at the arms of this old rocking chair and think about it all. All of it there below me. I watch it. The cropland, the pastures, the stock, the house, and the buildings in the distance and I study it. I try to think where they would be at this time of day. I try to learn what it all means, what my seventy years haven't taught me. And through it all, the honeysuckle and brome, the pigeon grass, the thistles the sorghum the hardwood and the pines I can see the Georgia Breeze touching everything. I can see him moving in it all, knowing what I will never know. At home now. Running. Running long and smooth, covering the ground, running. Running like nothing else matters.

Reprinted from EMINENT DOMAIN by Dan O'Brien by permission of the University of Iowa Press. Copyright 1987 by Dan O'Brien.

THE
Panar Leopard

BY JIM CORBETT

Jim Corbett (1875-1955) is a name synonymous with tales of man-eaters. His books recounting harrowing experiences with rogue leopards and tigers in India enjoyed immense popularity when they were published, and they remain in constant demand among devoted readers and book collectors. This hair-raising adventure was first published in Corbett's *The Temple Tiger* and *More Man-Eaters of Kumaon* and was subsequently included in *Jim Corbett's India* (edited by R. E. Hawkins). This is writing on real-life experiences that rivals the most imaginative of fiction.

W hile I was hunting the Champawat man-eater in 1907, I heard of a man-eating leopard that was terrorizing the inhabitants of villages on the eastern border of the Almora district. This leopard, about which questions were asked in the House of Commons, was known under several names and was credited with having killed four hundred human beings. I knew the animal under the name of the Panar man-eater, and I

194

shall therefore use this name for the purpose of my story.

No mention is made in Government records of man-eaters prior to the year 1905 and it would appear that until the advent of the Champawat tiger and the Panar leopard, man-eaters in Kumaon were unknown. When therefore these two animals – who between them killed eight hundred and thirty-six human beings – made their appearance, Government was faced with a difficult situation for it had no machinery to put in action against them and had to rely on personal appeals to sportsmen. Unfortunately there were very few sportsmen in Kumaon at that time who had any inclination for this new form of sport which, rightly or wrongly, was considered as hazardous as Wilson's solo attempt – made a few years later – to conquer Everest. I myself was as ignorant of man-eaters as Wilson was of Everest and that I succeeded in my attempt, where he apparently failed in his, was due entirely to luck.

When I returned to my home in Naini Tal after killing the Champawat tiger, I was asked by Government to undertake the shooting of the Panar leopard. I was working hard for a living at the time and several weeks elapsed before I was able to spare the time to undertake this task, and then just as I was ready to start for the outlying area of the Almora district in which the leopard was operating I received an urgent request from Berthoud, the Deputy Commissioner of Naini Tal, to go to the help of the people of Muktesar where a man-eating tiger had established a reign of terror. After hunting down the tiger, I went in pursuit of the Panar leopard.

As I had not previously visited the vast area over which this leopard was operating, I went via Almora to learn all I could about the leopard from Stiffe, the Deputy Commissioner of Almora. He kindly invited me to lunch, provided me with maps, and then gave me a bit of a jolt when wishing me goodbye by asking me if I had considered all the risks and prepared for them by making my will.

My maps showed that there were two approaches to the affected area, one via Panwanaula on the Pithoragarh road, and the other via Lamgara on the Dabidhura road. I selected the latter route and after lunch set out in good heart – despite the reference to a will – accompanied by one servant and four men carrying my luggage.

My men and I had already done a stiff march of fourteen miles from Khairna, but being young and fit we were prepared to do another long march before calling it a day.

As the full moon was rising we arrived at a small isolated building which, from the scribbling on the walls and the torn bits of paper lying about, we assumed was used as a school. I had no tent with me and as the door of the building was locked, I decided to spend the night in the courtyard with my men, a perfectly safe proceeding for we were still many miles from the man-eater's hunting grounds.

There was plenty of fuel in the jungle behind the school and my men soon had a fire burning in a corner of the courtyard for my servant to cook my dinner on. I was sitting with my back to the locked door, smoking, and my servant had just laid a leg of mutton on the low wall nearest the road and turned to attend to the fire, when I saw the head of a leopard appear over the wall close to the leg of mutton. Fascinated, I sat motionless and watched – for the leopard was facing me – and when the man had moved away a few feet the leopard grabbed the meat and bounded across the road into the jungle beyond. The meat had been put down on a big sheet of paper, which had stuck to it, and when my servant heard the rustle of paper and saw what he thought was a dog running away with it, he dashed forward shouting, but on realizing that he was dealing with a leopard and not with a mere dog he changed direction and dashed towards me with even greater speed. All white people in the East are credited with being a little mad – for other reasons than walking about in the midday sun – and I am afraid my good servant thought I was a little more mad than most of my kind when he found I was laughing, for he said in a very aggrieved voice, 'It was your dinner that the leopard carried away and I have nothing else for you to eat.' However, he duly produced a meal that did him credit, and to which I did as much justice as I am sure the hungry leopard did to his leg of prime mutton.

Making an early start next morning, we halted at Lamgara for a meal, and by evening reached the Dol dak bungalow on the border of the man-eater's domain. Leaving my men at the bungalow I set out the following morning to try to get news of the man-eater. Going from village to village, and examining the connecting footpaths for leopard pug-marks, I arrived in the late evening at an isolated homestead consisting of a single stone-built slate-roofed house, situated in a few acres of cultivated land and surrounded by scrub jungle. On the footpath leading to this homestead I found the pug-marks of a big male leopard.

As I approached the house a man appeared on the narrow balcony and, climbing down a few wooden steps, came across the courtyard to meet me. He was a young man, possibly twenty-two years of age, and in great distress. It appeared that the previous night while he and his wife were sleeping on the floor of the single room that comprised the house, with the door open for it was April and very hot, the man-eater climbed on to the balcony and getting a grip of his wife's throat started to pull her head-foremost out of the room. With a strangled scream the woman flung an arm round her husband who, realizing in a flash what was happening, seized her arm with one hand and, placing the other against the lintel of the door, for leverage, jerked her away from the leopard and closed the door. For the rest of the night the man and his wife cowered in a corner of the room, while the leopard tried to tear down the door. In the hot unventilated room the woman's wounds started to turn septic and by morning her suffering and fear had rendered her unconscious.

Throughout the day the man remained with his wife, too frightened to leave her for fear the leopard should return and carry her away, and too frightened to face the mile of scrub jungle that lay between him and his nearest neighbour. As day was closing down and the unfortunate man was facing another night of terror he saw me coming towards the house, and when I had heard his story I was no longer surprised that he had run towards me and thrown himself sobbing at my feet.

A difficult situation faced me. I had not up to that time approached Government to provide people living in areas in which a man-eater was operating with first-aid sets, so there was no medical or any other kind of aid nearer than Almora, and Almora was twenty-five miles away. To get help for the woman I would have to go for it myself and that would mean condemning the man to lunacy, for he had already stood as much as any man could stand and another night in that room, with the prospect of the leopard returning and trying to gain entrance, would of a certainty have landed him in a mad-house.

The man's wife, a girl of about eighteen, was lying on her back when the leopard clamped its teeth into her throat, and when the man got a grip of her arm and started to pull her back the leopard – to get a better purchase – drove the claws of one paw into her breast. In the final struggle the claws ripped through the flesh, making four deep cuts. In the heat of the small room, which had only one door and no windows and in which a swarm of flies was buzzing, all the wounds in the girl's throat and on her breast had turned septic, and whether medical aid could be procured or not the chances of her surviving were very slight; so, instead of going for help, I decided to stay the night with the man. I very sincerely hope that no one who reads this story will ever be condemned to seeing and hearing the sufferings of a human being, or of an animal, that has had the misfortune of being caught by the throat by either a leopard or a tiger and not having the means – other than a bullet – of alleviating or of ending the suffering.

The balcony which ran the length of the house, and which was boarded up at both ends, was about fifteen feet long and four feet wide, accessible by steps hewn in a pine sapling. Opposite these steps was the one door of the house, and under the balcony was an open recess four feet wide and four feet high, used for storing firewood.

The man begged me to stay in the room with him and his wife but it was not possible for me to do this, for, though I am not squeamish, the smell in the room was overpowering and more than I could stand. So between us we moved the firewood from one end of the recess under the balcony, clearing a small space where I could sit with my back to the wall. Night was now closing in, so after a wash and a drink at a near-by spring I settled down in my corner and told the man to go up to his wife and keep the door of the room open. As he climbed the steps the man said, 'The leopard will surely kill you, Sahib, and then what will I do?' 'Close the door', I answered, 'and wait for morning.'

The moon was two nights off the full and there would be a short period of darkness. It was this period of darkness that was worrying me. If the leopard had remained scratching at the door until daylight, as the man said, it would not have gone far and even now it might be lurking in the bushes watching me. I had been in position for half an hour, straining my eyes into the darkening night and praying for the moon to top the hills to the

198

east, when a jackal gave its alarm call. This call, which is given with the full force of the animal's lungs, can be heard for a very long distance and can be described as 'pheaon', 'pheaon', repeated over and over again as long as the danger that has alarmed the jackal is in sight. Leopards when hunting or when approaching a kill move very slowly, and it would be many minutes before this one – assuming it was the man-eater – covered the half mile between us, and even if in the meantime the moon had not risen it would be giving sufficient light to shoot by, so I was able to relax and breathe more freely.

Minutes dragged by. The jackal stopped calling. The moon rose over the hills, flooding the ground in front of me with brilliant light. No movement to be seen anywhere, and the only sound to be heard in all the world the agonized fight for breath of the unfortunate girl above me. Minutes gave way to hours. The moon climbed the heavens and then started to go down in the west, casting the shadow of the house on the ground I was watching. Another period of danger, for if the leopard had seen me he would, with a leopard's patience, be waiting for these lengthening shadows to mask his movements. Nothing happened, and one of the longest nights I have ever watched through came to an end when the light from the sun lit up the sky where, twelve hours earlier, the moon had risen.

The man, after his vigil of the previous night, had slept soundly and as I left my corner and eased my aching bones – only those who have sat motionless on hard ground for hours know how bones can ache – he came down the steps. Except for a few wild raspberries I had eaten nothing for twenty-four hours, and as no useful purpose would have been served by my remaining any longer, I bade the man goodbye and set off to rejoin my men at the Dol dak bungalow, eight miles away, and summon aid for the girl. I had only gone a few miles when I met my men. Alarmed at my long absence they had packed up my belongings, paid my dues at the dak bungalow, and then set out to look for me. While I was talking to them the Road Overseer came along. He was well mounted on a sturdy Bhootia pony, and as he was on his way to Almora he gladly undertook to carry a letter from me to Stiffe. Immediately on receipt of my letter Stiffe dispatched medical aid for the girl, but her sufferings were over when it arrived.

No matter how full of happiness our life may have been, there are periods in it that we look back to with special pleasure. Such a period for me was the year 1910, for in that year I shot the Muktesar man-eating tiger and the Panar man-eating leopard.

My first attempt to shoot the Panar leopard was made in April 1910, and it was not until September of the same year that I was able to spare the time to make a second attempt. I have no idea how many human beings were killed by the leopard between April and September, for no bulletins were issued by Government and beyond a reference to questions asked in the House of Commons, no mention of the leopard – as far as I am aware – was made in the Indian Press.

Accompanied by a servant and four men carrying my camp kit and provisions, I set out from Naini Tal on 10 September on my second attempt to shoot the Panar leopard. The sky was overcast when we left home at 4 a.m. and we had only gone a few miles when a deluge of rain came on. Throughout the day it rained and we arrived at Almora, after a twenty-eight-mile march, wet to the bone. I was to have spent the night with Stiffe, but not having a stitch of dry clothing to put on, I excused myself and spent the night at the dak bungalow. There were no other travellers there and the man in charge very kindly put two rooms at my disposal, with a big wood fire in each, and by morning my kit was dry enough for me to continue my journey.

It had been my intention to follow the same route from Almora that I had followed in April, and start my hunt for the leopard from the house in which the girl had died of her wounds. While I was having breakfast a mason by the name of Panwa, who did odd jobs for us in Naini Tal, presented himself. Panwa's home was in the Panar valley, and on learning from my men that I was on my way to try to shoot the man-eater he asked for permission to join our party, for he wanted to visit his home and was frightened to undertake the journey alone. Panwa knew the country and on his advice I altered my plans and instead of taking the road to Dabidhura via the school where the leopard had eaten my dinner, I took the road leading to Pithoragarh. Spending the night at the Panwa Naula dak bungalow, we made an early start next morning and after proceeding a few miles left the Pithoragarh road for a track leading off to the right. We were now in the man-eater's territory where there were no roads, and where the only communication was along footpaths running from village to village.

Progress was slow, for the villages were widely scattered over many hundreds of square miles of country, and as the exact whereabouts of the man-eater were not known, it was necessary to visit each village to make inquiries. Going through Salan and Rangot *pattis* (*patti* is a group of villages), I arrived late on the evening of the fourth day at Chakati, where I was informed by the headman that a human being had been killed a few days previously at a village called Sanouli on the far side of the Panar river. Owing to the recent heavy rain the Panar was in flood and the headman advised me to spend the night in his village, promising to give me a guide next morning to show me the only safe ford over the river, for the Panar was not bridged.

The headman and I had carried on our conversation at one end of a long row of double-storied buildings and when, on his advice, I elected to stay the night in the village, he said he would have two rooms vacated in the upper story for myself and my men. I had noticed while talking to him that the end room on the ground floor was untenanted, so I told him I would stay in it and that he need only have one room vacated in the upper story for my men. The room I had elected to spend the night in had no door, but this did not matter for I had been told that the last kill had taken place on the far side of the river and I knew the man-eater would not attempt to cross the river while it was in flood.

The room had no furniture of any kind, and after my men had swept all the straw and bits of rags out of it, complaining as they did so that the last tenant must have been a very dirty person, they spread my groundsheet on the mud floor and made up my bed. I ate my dinner – which my servant cooked on an open fire in the courtyard – sitting on my bed, and as I had done a lot of walking during the twelve hours I had been on my feet it did not take me long to get to sleep. The sun was just rising next morning, flooding the room with light, when on hearing a slight sound in the room I opened my eyes and saw a man sitting on the floor near my bed. He was about fifty years of age, and *in the last stage of leprosy*. On seeing that I was awake this unfortunate living death said he hoped I had spent a comfortable night in his room.

201

He went on to say that he had been on a two-days' visit to friends in an adjoining village, and finding me asleep in his room on his return had sat near my bed and waited for me to awake.

Leprosy, the most terrible and the most contagious of all diseases in the East, is very prevalent throughout Kumaon, and especially bad in the Almora district. Being fatalists the people look upon the disease as a visitation from God, and neither segregate the afflicted nor take any precautions against infection. So, quite evidently, the headman did not think it necessary to warn me that the room I had selected to stay in had for years been the home of a leper. It did not take me long to dress that morning, and as soon as our guide was ready we left the village.

Moving about as I have done in Kumaon I have always gone in dread of leprosy, and I have never felt as unclean as I did after my night in that poor unfortunate's room. At the first stream we came to I called a halt, for my servant to get breakfast ready for me and for my men to have their food. Then, telling my men to wash my ground-sheet and lay my bedding out in the sun, I took a bar of carbolic soap and went down the stream to where there was a little pool surrounded by great slabs of rock. Taking off every stitch of clothing I had worn in that room, I washed it all in the pool and, after laying it out on the slabs of rock, I used the remainder of the soap to scrub myself as I had never scrubbed myself before. Two hours later, in garments that had shrunk a little from the rough treatment they had received, I returned to my men feeling clean once again, and with a hunter's appetite for breakfast.

Our guide was a man about four foot six inches tall with a big head crowned with a mop of long hair, a great barrel of a body, short legs, and few words. When I asked him if we had any stiff climbing to do, he stretched out his open hand, and answered, 'Flat as that.' Having said this he led us down a very steep hill into a deep valley. Here I expected him to turn and follow the valley down to its junction with the river. But no. Without saying a word or even turning his head he crossed the open ground and went straight up the hill on the far side. This hill, in addition to being very steep and overgrown with thorn bushes, had loose gravel on it which made the going difficult, and as the sun was now overhead and very hot, we reached the top in a bath of sweat. Our guide, whose legs appeared to have been made for climbing hills, had not turned a hair.

Down and up we went and down and up again, and then away down in a deep valley we saw the Panar river Panwa. After my men had linked arms and safely crossed, I decided to call it a day and spend the night on the river bank. Panwa, whose village was five miles farther up the river, now left me, taking with him the guide, who was frightened to attempt a second crossing of the river.

Next morning we set out to find Sanouli, where the last human kill had taken place. Late in the evening of that day we found ourselves in a wide open valley, and as there were no human habitations in sight, we decided to spend the night on the open ground. We were now in the heart of the man-eater's country and after a very unrestful night, spent on cold wet ground, arrived about midday at Sanouli. The inhabitants of this small village were overjoyed to see us and they very gladly put a room at the disposal of my men, and gave me the use of an open platform with a thatched roof.

The village was built on the side of a hill overlooking a valley in which there were terraced fields, from which a paddy crop had recently been harvested. The hill on the far side of the valley sloped up gradually, and a hundred yards from the cultivated land there was a dense patch of brushwood, some twenty acres in extent. On the brow of the hill, above this patch of brushwood, there was a village, and on the shoulder of the hill to the right another village. To the left of the terraced fields the valley was closed in by a steep grassy hill. So, in effect, the patch of brushwood was surrounded on three sides by cultivated land, and on the fourth by open grass land.

While breakfast was being got ready, the men of the village sat round me and talked. During the second half of March and the first half of April, four human beings had been killed in this area by the man-eater. The first kill had taken place in the village on the brow of the hill, and the fourth in Sanouli. All four victims had been killed at night and carried some five hundred yards into the patch of brushwood, where the leopard had eaten them at his leisure, for – having no firearms – the inhabitants of the three villages were too frightened to make any attempt to recover the bodies. The last kill had taken place six days before, and my informants were convinced that the leopard was still in the patch of brushwood.

I had purchased two young male goats in a village we passed through earlier that day, and towards evening I took the smaller one and tied it at the edge of the path of brushwood to test the villagers' assertion that the leopard was still in the cover. I did not sit over the goat, because there were no suitable trees near by and also because clouds were banking up and it looked as though there might be rain during the night. The platform that had been placed at my disposal was open all round, so I tied the second goat near it in the hope that if the leopard visited the village during the night it would prefer a tender goat to a tough human being. Long into the night I listened to the two goats calling to each other. This convinced me that the leopard was not within hearing distance. However, there was no reason why he should not return to the locality, so I went to sleep hoping for the best.

There was a light shower during the night and when the sun rose in a cloudless sky, every leaf and blade of grass was sparkling with raindrops and every bird that had a song to sing was singing a joyful welcome to the day. The goat near my platform was contentedly browsing off a bush and bleating occasionally, while the one across the valley was silent. Telling my servant to keep my breakfast warm, I crossed the valley and went to the spot where I had tied up the smaller goat. Here I found that, some time before the rain came on, a leopard had killed the goat, broken the rope, and carried away the kill. The rain had washed out the drag-mark, but this did not matter for there was only one place to which the leopard could have taken his kill, and that was into the dense patch of brushwood.

Stalking a leopard, or a tiger, on its kill is one of the most interesting forms of sport I know of, but it can only be indulged in with any hope of success when the conditions are favourable. Here the conditions were not favourable, for the brushwood was too dense to permit a noiseless approach. Returning to the village, I had breakfast and then called the villagers together, as I wanted to consult them about the surrounding country. It was necessary to visit the kill to see if the leopard had left sufficient remains for me to sit over and, while doing so, I would not be able to avoid disturbing the leopard. What I wanted to learn from the villagers was whether there was any other heavy cover, within a reasonable distance, to which the leopard could retire on being disturbed by me. I was told that there was no such cover nearer than two miles, and that to get to it the leopard would have to cross a wide stretch of cultivated land.

At midday I returned to the patch of brushwood and, a hundred yards from where he had killed it, I found all that the leopard had left of the goat – its hooves, horns, and part of its stomach. As there was no fear of the leopard leaving the cover at that time of day for the jungle two miles away, I tried for several hours to stalk it, helped by bulbuls, drongos, thrushes, and scimitar-babblers, all of whom kept me informed of the leopard's every movement. In case any should question why I did not collect the men of the three villages and get them to drive the leopard out on to the open ground, where I could have shot it, it is necessary to say that this could not have been attempted without grave danger to the beaters. As soon as the leopard found he was being driven towards open ground, he would have broken back and attacked anyone who got in his way.

On my return to the village after my unsuccessful attempt to get a shot at the leopard, I went down with a bad attack of malaria and for the next twenty-four hours I lay on the platform in a stupor. By the evening of the following day the fever had left me and I was able to continue the hunt. On their own initiative the previous night my men had tied out the second goat where the first had been killed, but the leopard had not touched it. This was all to the good, for the leopard would now be hungry, and I set out on that third evening full of hope.

On the near side of the patch of brushwood, and about a hundred yards from where the goat had been killed two nights previously, there was an old oak tree. This tree was growing out of a six-foot-high bank between two terraced fields and was leaning away from the hill at an angle that made it possible for me to walk up the trunk in my rubber-soled shoes. On the underside of the trunk and about fifteen feet from the ground there was a branch jutting out over the lower field. This branch, which was about a foot thick, offered a very uncomfortable and a very unsafe seat for it was hollow and rotten. However, as it was the only branch on the tree, and as there were no other trees within a radius of several hundred yards, I decided to risk the branch.

As I had every reason to believe – from the similarity of the pug-marks I had found in the brushwood to those I had seen in

April on the path leading to the homestead where the girl was killed – that the leopard I was dealing with was the Panar man-eater, I made my men cut a number of long blackthorn shoots. After I had taken my seat with my back to the tree and my legs stretched out along the branch, I made the men tie the shoots into bundles and lay them on the trunk of the tree and lash them to it securely with strong rope. To the efficient carrying out of these small details I am convinced I owe my life.

Several of the blackthorn shoots, which were from ten to twenty feet long, projected on either side of the tree; and as I had nothing to hold on to, to maintain my balance, I gathered the shoots on either side of me and held them firmly pressed between my arms and my body. By five o'clock my preparations were complete. I was firmly seated on the branch with my coat collar pulled up well in front to protect my throat, and my soft hat pulled down well behind to protect the back of my neck. The goat was tied to a stake driven into the field thirty yards in front of me, and my men were sitting out in the field smoking and talking loudly.

Up to this point all had been quiet in the patch of brushwood, but now, a scimitar-babbler gave its piercing alarm call followed a minute or two later by the chattering of several white-throated laughing thrushes. These two species of birds are the most reliable informants in the hills, and on hearing them I signalled to my men to return to the village. This they appeared to be very glad to do, and as they walked away, still talking loudly, the goat started bleating. Nothing happened for the next half-hour and then, as the sun was fading off the hill above the village, two drongos that had been sitting on the tree above me, flew off and started to bait some animal on the open ground between me and the patch of brushwood. The goat while calling had been facing in the direction of the village, and it now turned round, facing me, and stopped calling. By watching the goat I could follow the movements of the animal that the drongos were baiting and that the goat was interested in, and this animal could only be a leopard.

The moon was in her third quarter and there would be several hours of darkness. In anticipation of the leopard's coming when light conditions were not favourable, I had armed myself with a twelve-bore double-barrelled shotgun loaded with slugs, for there was a better chance of my hitting the leopard with eight slugs than with a single rifle bullet. Aids to night shooting, in the way of electric lights and torches, were not used in India at the time I am writing about, and all that one had to rely on for accuracy of aim was a strip of white cloth tied round the muzzle of the weapon.

Again nothing happened for many minutes, and then I felt a gentle pull on the blackthorn shoots I was holding and blessed my forethought in having had the shoots tied to the leaning tree, for I could not turn round to defend myself and at best the collar of my coat and my hat were poor protection. No question now that I was dealing with a man-eater, and a very determined man-eater at that. Finding that he could not climb over the thorns, the leopard, after his initial pull, had now got the butt ends of the shoots between his teeth and was jerking them violently, pulling me hard against the trunk of the tree. And now the last of the daylight faded out of the sky and the leopard, who did all his human killing in the dark, was in his element and I was out of mine, for in the dark a human being is the most helpless of all animals and – speaking for myself – his courage is at its lowest ebb. Having killed four hundred human beings at night, the leopard was quite unafraid of me, as was evident from the fact that while tugging at the shoots, he was growling loud enough to be heard by the men anxiously listening in the village. While this growling terrified the men, as they told me later, it had the opposite effect on me, for it let me know where the leopard was and what he was doing. It was when he was silent that I was most terrified, for I did not know what his next move would be. Several times he had nearly unseated me by pulling on the shoots vigorously and then suddenly letting them go, and now that it was dark and I had nothing stable to hold on to I felt sure that if he sprang up he would only need to touch me to send me crashing to the ground.

After one of these nerve-wracking periods of silence the leopard jumped down off the high bank and dashed towards the goat. In the hope that the leopard would come while there was still sufficient light to shoot by, I had tied the goat thirty yards from the tree to give me time to kill the leopard before it got to the goat. But now, in the dark, I could not save the goat – which, being white, I could only just see as an indistinct blur – so I waited until it had stopped struggling and then aimed where I thought the leopard would be and pressed the trigger. My shot was greeted with an angry grunt and I saw a white flash as the leopard went over backwards, and disappeared down another high bank into the field beyond.

For ten or fifteen minutes I listened anxiously for further sounds from the leopard, and then my men called out and asked if they should come to me. It was now quite safe for them to do so, provided they kept to the high ground. So I told them to light pine torches, and thereafter carry out my instructions. These torches, made of twelve to eighteen inches long splinters of resin-impregnated pine-wood cut from a living tree, give a brilliant light and provide the remote villages in Kumaon with the only illumination they have ever known.

After a lot of shouting and running about, some twenty men each carrying a torch left the village and, following my instructions, circled round above the terraced fields and approached my tree from behind. The knots in the ropes securing the blackthorn shoots to the tree had been pulled so tight by the leopard that they had to be cut. After the thorns had been removed men climbed the tree and helped me down, for the uncomfortable seat had given me cramps in my legs.

The combined light from the torches lit up the field on which the dead goat was lying, but the terraced field beyond was in shadow. When cigarettes had been handed round I told the men I had wounded the leopard but did not know how badly, and that we would return to the village now and I would look for the wounded animal in the morning. At this, great disappointment was expressed. 'If you have wounded the leopard it must surely be dead by now.' 'There are many of us, and you have a gun, so there is no danger.' 'At least let us go as far as the edge of the field and see if the leopard has left a blood trail.' After all arguments for and against going to look for the leopard immediately had been exhausted I consented against my better judgement to go as far as the edge of the field, from where we could look down on the terraced field below.

Having acceded to their request, I made the men promise that they would walk in line behind me, hold their torches high, and not run away and leave me in the dark if the leopard charged. This promise they very willingly gave, and after the torches had been replenished and were burning brightly we set off, I walking in front and the men following five yards behind.

Thirty yards to the goat, and another twenty yards to the edge of the field. Very slowly, and in silence, we moved forward. When we reached the goat – no time now to look for a blood trail – the farther end of the lower field came into view. The nearer we approached the edge, the more of this field became visible, and then, when only a narrow strip remained in shadow from the torches, the leopard, with a succession of angry grunts, sprang up the bank and into full view.

There is something very terrifying in the angry grunt of a charging leopard, and I have seen a line of elephants that were staunch to tiger, turn and stampede from a charging leopard; so I was not surprised when my companions, all of whom were unarmed, turned as one man and bolted. Fortunately for me, in their anxiety to get away they collided with each other and some of the burning splinters of pine – held loosely in their hands – fell to the ground and continued to flicker, giving me sufficient light to put a charge of slugs into the leopard's chest.

On hearing my shot the men stopped running, and then I heard one of them say, 'Oh, no. He won't be angry with us, for he knows that this devil has turned our courage to water.' Yes, I knew, from my recent experience on the tree, that fear of a man-eater robs a man of courage. As for running away, had I been one of the torch-bearers I would have run with the best. So there was nothing for me to be angry about. Presently, while I was making believe to examine the leopard, to ease their embarrassment, the men returned in twos and threes. When they were assembled, I asked, without looking up, 'Did you bring a bamboo pole and rope to carry the leopard back to the village?' 'Yes,' they answered eagerly, 'we left them at the foot of the tree.' 'Go and fetch them,' I said, 'for I want to get back to the village for a cup of hot tea.' The cold night-wind blowing down from the north had brought on another attack of malaria, and now that all the excitement was over I was finding it difficult to remain on my feet.

That night, for the first time in years, the people of Sanouli slept, and have continued to sleep, free from fear.

From *The Temple Tiger and More Man-Eaters of Kumaon* by Jim Corbett. Copyright® 1954 by Jim Corbett, renewed 1982, 1983 by The Standard Bank Ltd. Reprinted by permission of Oxford University Press, Inc.

Dead Fish

T E L L   N O   L I E S

BY FREDERICK PFISTER

*Frederick Pfister is a self-styled entrepreneur who owns
three businesses in Lexington, Kentucky, among them
The Sporting Tradition, a shop specializing in fly
fishing and upland shooting equipment. Pfister and his
wife hunt and fish around the world, and he is an
avowed "connoisseur of reading." He wrote this little
yarn for the May/June, 1987, issue of Sporting Classics,
not long after hearing a similar story at a meeting of
The Tall Tales Club of America. As you'll see, he's not
only a good listener, but an adept storyteller.*

Post mortem jurisprudence. I believe that's what they call it.
This "executor of a will" responsibility is indeed an objec-
tionable bit of business.

"Damn it, Harry," I said as I folded the document and slipped it
into my coat pocket. I was completely surprised when I read the
letter at the law offices of Baker, Hohns and Baker. It was apparent
that the late Harold F. Johnson, former friend, fishing partner and

club member had requested that I be the executor of the sporting portion of his will. In his brief letter Harry requested that I divide his collection of hunting and fishing equipment among our club members, and he asked only that I perform my task fairly.

"Fritz, I have chosen you for this job because I know that you won't let me down."

Harry had died of a heart attack suddenly, but happily. He had to have been happy. He was doing what he loved to do most of all – fishing for Atlantic salmon on the George River in Quebec. And although it proved to be his last fishing trip, at least it had been a lucky one.

The night before he died, Harry telephoned us at the club. Certainly he was not calling all the way from Canada just to apologize for missing our monthly meeting. As Harry told it, he had caught a mammoth Atlantic salmon. The fish weighed nothing less than 33 pounds and was easily the biggest salmon taken from the river in recent years. Harry said that the fish made a spectacular run, stripping line off his reel, swam in circles, sounded, repeated the performance for the better part of an hour, and then succumbed to the net. A local Canadian taxidermist had volunteered to mount the record fish and would be shipping it to Harry's house as soon as it was completed.

"You should see this fish," exclaimed Harry. "It's longer than a pulled leg."

"I don't believe a word of it," cried Thomas as he hung up the phone. "Harry's lying about this fish like he lied about all the others. He always calls with stories of record catches and strings of fish. But have we seen any of 'em? Never! Just wait until Harry gets back. He'll have another wild tale about what happened to his record fish en route to the taxidermist. You mark my word. I don't believe a word of it."

When it came to stretching the truth, Harry was better than the best, and he was never without a tall tale to tell when he returned from a fishing trip.

You see, it was Harry who first introduced me to the fraternal oath of all fishermen. Never be caught telling the whole truth about how big or how many fish were caught. Always lie about the catch.

An understandable wave of grief ran through our club when we received word of Harry's death. But we knew that he would have preferred to go the way he did. You could say that Harry died with his waders on.

But there was another element to our anxiety – Harry's fish. With Harry gone, how would we ever know whether or not he had really caught his record salmon? We all knew him to be a top-notch fisherman. And so we eagerly awaited the arrival of his mounted salmon, secretly knowing that it was just possible he had caught the fish. It's true that the only thing at which Harry was more proficient than fishing was lying about fishing. But with Harry gone, how would we ever know?

About six months after the funeral, I arranged to meet his niece at Harry's old house. There were a few final items which needed to be retrieved from the attic and disbursed to friends.

I must admit that the business at hand could have been attended to at some later date. But a rumor was out that a wooden box had arrived from Canada addressed to Harry, and that his niece had ushered the crate into the attic where it sat to this very day.

To think that this box might hold Harry's legendary Atlantic salmon was too much for the club members to bear. There was talk of breaking into Harry's house to rip open the crate and reveal the truth which we all longed to know. After all, a record salmon given up by the George River in Quebec can play strange tricks on the mind. Besides, this was no ordinary fish; this was Harry's fish.

Fearful of where this irrational thinking might lead, I volunteered, as executor of Harry's sporting will, to solve the mystery of the unopened crate and relay to my fellow club members an appropriate description including, if applicable, the length and weight inscribed.

By the time I arrived, Harry's niece, Diane, was already busy sorting things out. It was the first time that I had actually met her, although we had conversed by phone quite often over the past few months. She was a pleasant girl, married, with a family living in Fayetteville.

We exchanged social pleasantries and suffered the usual nervous small talk as I helped her carry a number of large clothing boxes into the garage. After moving the last of Harry's clothing, we sat down on the back porch while I took a moment to smoke my pipe.

"There is something that I must tell you," she volunteered. "Uncle Harry didn't speak often about his friends or business associates, but he did mention your name when visiting us last Christmas."

"Oh?" I said.

"Yes, he was describing his latest fishing adventure on which you had accompanied him, and he simply referred to you as 'a fishing companion indeed.'

"Harry said that the only man who caught more fish than he caught was you," (in truth, neither of us had caught any) "and that you were one of the few individuals who truly understood the nature of the sport.

"Harry thought highly of you, and I am sure that is the reason he chose you to help me assign what he left behind."

Her accounting of our friendship so reminded me of the man who was no longer with us that I became rather melancholy and decided to retire to the local pub to reminisce about past fishing experiences with Harry. All the while his words kept ringing in my ears, ". . .a fishing companion indeed. . .truly understood the nature of the sport."

I had left Harry's house without violating the mysterious crate containing his alleged salmon. I simply no longer felt the need to validate his catch. I didn't even enter the attic to confirm that the crate was there.

Well, I had been drinking Harry's favorite libation, scotch on the rocks, for a long evening which seemed quite short, when in from the cold winter night came the club members making fast tracks toward my table. Shaking off the cold, each ordered a drink and then stared intently at my face, eagerly awaiting my report.

"Well, man, come on," urged Thomas. "Did you see the fish?"

Gazing across the room, a faint smile came across my face as I contemplated the fisherman's fraternal oath, taught to me by Harry himself.

"Yes," I answered, and the club members fell back in their seats. "The fish is 33, maybe 34 pounds, and longer than a pulled leg. Its color is a most mysterious blue-black dorsally with radiant silver sides. He has a crooked jaw sporting a Jock Scott I recognized as one of Harry's ties. The fish had been sea-run, wild and free, and if Harry were here today he would want you all to

213

see his fish in all of the splendor with which he described it to us, his closest friends."

To this day I carry the torch, the legacy that Harry left me as executor of his sporting will.

Harry, you old liar, I hope I haven't let you down.

Stolen Hunts

BY ALDO LEOPOLD

Aldo Leopold (1887-1948) became, in the course of his extraordinary career, the conscience of American conservation. A man who loved remote, quiet places, he wrote from a philosophical perspective that earned him enduring recognition as the father of modern wildlife management. *A Sand County Almanac*, his best-known book, helps us to understand man the hunter. These exquisite passages from "Stolen Hunts" reveal another side of Leopold – as a writer of power and probity.

There are two kinds of hunting: ordinary hunting and ruffed-grouse hunting. There are two places to hunt grouse: ordinary places, and Adams County.

There are two times to hunt in Adams: ordinary times, and when the tamaracks are smoky gold. This is written for those luckless ones who have never stood, gun empty and mouth agape, to watch the golden needles come sifting down, while the

215

feathery rocket that knocked them off sails unscathed into the jackpines.

The tamaracks change from green to yellow when the first frosts have brought woodcock, fox sparrows, and juncos out of the north. Troops of robins are stripping the last white berries from the dogwood thickets, leaving the empty stems as a pink haze against the hill. The creekside alders have shed their leaves, exposing here and there an eyeful of holly. Brambles are aglow, lighting your footsteps grouseward.

The dog knows what is grouseward better than you do. You will do well to follow him closely, reading from the cock of his ears the story the breeze is telling. When at last he stops stock-still, and says with a sideward glance, 'Well, get ready,' the question is, ready for what? A twittering woodcock, or the rising roar of a grouse, or perhaps only a rabbit? In this moment of uncertainty is condensed much of the virtue of grouse hunting. He who must know what to get ready for should go and hunt pheasants.

Hunts differ in flavor, but the reasons are subtle. The sweetest hunts are stolen. To steal a hunt, either go far into the wilderness where no one has been, or else find some undiscovered place under everybody's nose.

Few hunters know that grouse exist in Adams County, for when they drive through it, they see only a waste of jackpines and scrub oaks. This is because the highway intersects a series of west-running creeks, each of which heads in a swamp, but drops to the river through dry sand-barrens. Naturally the north-bound highway intersects these swampless barrens, but just above the highway, and behind the screen of dry scrub, every creeklet expands into a broad ribbon of swamp, a sure haven for grouse.

Here, come October, I sit in the solitude of my tamaracks and hear the hunters' cars roaring up the highway, hell-bent for the crowded counties to the north. I chuckle as I picture their dancing speedometers, their strained faces, their eager eyes glued on the northward horizon. At the noise of their passing, a cock grouse drums his defiance. My dog grins as we note his direction. That fellow, we agree, needs some exercise; we shall look him up presently.

The tamaracks grow not only in the swamp, but at the foot of the bordering upland, where springs break forth. Each spring has become choked with moss, which forms a boggy terrace. I call

216

these terraces the hanging gardens, for out of their sodden muck the fringed gentians have lifted blue jewels. Such an October gentian, dusted with tamarack gold, is worth a full stop and a long look, even when the dog signals grouse ahead.

Between each hanging garden and the creekside is a moss-paved deer trail, handy for the hunter to follow, and for the flushed grouse to cross – in a split second. The question is whether the bird and the gun agree on how a second should be split. If they do not, the next deer that passes finds a pair of empty shells to sniff at, but no feathers.

Higher up the creeklet I encounter an abandoned farm. I try to read, from the age of the young jackpines marching across an old field, how long ago the luckless farmer found out that sand plains were meant to grow solitude, not corn. Jackpines tell tall tales to the unwary, for they put on several whorls of branches each year, instead of only one. I find a better chronometer in an elm seedling that now blocks the barn door. Its rings date back to the drought of 1930. Since that year no man has carried milk out of this barn.

I wonder what this family thought about when their mortgage finally outgrew their crops, and thus gave the signal for their eviction. Many thoughts, like flying grouse, leave no trace of their passing, but some leave clues that outlast the decades. He who, in some unforgotten April, planted this lilac must have thought pleasantly of blooms for all the Aprils to come. She who used this washboard, its corrugations worn thin with many Mondays, may have wished for a cessation of all Mondays, and soon.

Musing on such questions, I become aware of the dog down by the spring, pointing patiently these many minutes. I walk up, apologizing for my inattention. Up twitters a woodcock, batlike, his salmon breast soaked in October sun. Thus goes the hunt.

It's hard on such a day to keep one's mind on grouse, for there are many distractions. I cross a buck track in the sand, and follow in idle curiosity. The track leads straight from one Jersey tea bush to another, with nipped twigs showing why.

This reminds me of my own lunch, but before I get it pulled out of my game pocket, I see a circling hawk, high skyward, needing identification. I wait till he banks and shows his red tail.

I reach again for the lunch, but my eye catches a peeled popple. Here a buck has rubbed off his itchy velvet. How long ago? The

217

exposed wood is already brown; I conclude that horns must therefore be clean by now.

I reach again for the lunch, but am interrupted by an excited yawp from the dog, and a crash of bushes in the swamp. Out springs a buck, flag aloft, horns shining, his coat a sleek blue. Yes, the popple told the truth.

This time I get the lunch all the way out and sit down to eat. A chickadee watches me, and grows confidential about his lunch. He doesn't say what he ate, perhaps it was cool turgid ant-eggs, or some other avian equivalent of cold roast grouse.

Lunch over, I regard a phalanx of young tamaracks, their golden lances thrusting skyward. Under each the needles of yesterday fall to earth building a blanket of smoky gold; at the tip of each the bud of tomorrow, preformed, poised, awaits another spring.

Too Early

Getting up too early is a vice habitual in horned owls, stars, geese, and freight trains. Some hunters acquire it from geese, and some coffee pots from hunters. It is strange that of all the multitude of creatures who must rise in the morning at some time, only these few should have discovered the most pleasant and least useful time for doing it.

Orion must have been the original mentor of the too-early company, for it is he who signals for too-early rising. It is time when Orion has passed west of the zenith about as far as one should lead a teal.

Early risers feel at ease with each other, perhaps because, unlike those who sleep late, they are given to understatement of their own achievements. Orion, the most widely traveled, says literally nothing. The coffee pot, from its first soft gurgle, underclaims the virtues of what simmers within. The owl, in his trisyllabic commentary, plays down the story of the night's murders. The goose on the bar, rising briefly to a point of order in some inaudible anserine debate, lets fall no hint that he speaks with the authority of all the far hills and the sea.

The freight, I admit, is hardly reticent about his own importance, yet even he has a kind of modesty: his eye is single to his own noisy business, and he never comes roaring into somebody else's camp. I feel a deep security in this single-mindedness of freight trains.

218

To arrive too early in the marsh is an adventure in pure listening; the ear roams at will among the noises of the night, without let or hindrance from hand or eye. When you hear a mallard being audibly enthusiastic about his soup, you are free to picture a score guzzling among the duckweeds. When one widgeon squeals, you may postulate a squadron without fear of visual contradiction. And when a flock of bluebills, pitching pondward, tears the dark silk of heaven in one long rending nose-dive, you catch your breath at the sound, but there is nothing to see except stars. This same performance, in daytime, would have to be looked at, shot at, missed, and then hurriedly fitted with an alibi. Nor could daylight add anything to your mind's eye picture of quivering wings; ripping the firmament neatly into halves.

The hour of listening ends when the fowl depart on muted wings for wider safer waters, each flock a blur against the graying east.

Like many another treaty of restraint, the pre-dawn pact lasts only as long as darkness humbles the arrogant. It would seem as if the sun were responsible for the daily retreat of reticence from the world. At any rate, by the time the mists are white over the lowlands, every rooster is bragging *ad lib*, and every corn shock is pretending to be twice as tall as any corn that ever grew. By sun-up every squirrel is exaggerating some fancied indignity to his person, and every jaw proclaiming with false emotion about suppositious dangers to society, at this very moment discovered by him. Distant crows are berating a hypothetical owl, just to tell the world how vigilant crows are, and a pheasant cock, musing perhaps on his philanderings of bygone days, beats the air with his wings and tells the world in raucous warning that he owns this marsh and all the hens in it.

Nor are all these illusions of grandeur confined to the birds and beasts. By breakfast time come the honks, horns, shouts, and whistles of the awakened farmyard, and finally, at evening, the drone of an untended radio. Then everybody goes to bed to relearn the lessons of the night.

Red Lanterns

One way to hunt partridge is to make a plan, based on logic and probabilities, of the terrain to be hunted. This will take you over the ground where the birds ought to be.

219

Another way is to wander, quite aimlessly, from one red lantern to another. This will likely take you where the birds actually are. The lanterns are blackberry leaves, red in October sun.

Red lanterns have lighted my way on many a pleasant hunt in many a region, but I think that blackberries must first have learned how to glow in the sand counties of central Wisconsin. Along the little boggy streams of these friendly wastes, called poor by those whose own lights barely flicker, the blackberries burn richly red on every sunny day from first frost to the last day of the season. Every woodcock and every partridge has his private solarium under these briars. Most hunters, not knowing this, wear themselves out in the briarless scrub, and, returning home birdless, leave the rest of us in peace.

By 'us' I mean the birds, the stream, the dog, and myself. The stream is a lazy one; he winds through the alders as if he would rather stay here than reach the river. So would I. Every one of his hairpin hesitations means that much more streambank where hillside briars adjoin dank beds of frozen ferns and jewelweeds on the boggy bottom. No partridge can long absent himself from such a place, nor can I. Partridge hunting, then, is a creekside stroll, upwind, from one briar patch to another.

The dog, when he approaches the briars, looks around to make sure I am within gunshot. Reassured, he advances with stealthy caution, his wet nose screening a hundred scents for that one scent, the potential presence of which gives life and meaning to the whole landscape. He is the prospector of the air, perpetually searching its strata for olfactory gold. Partridge scent is the gold standard that relates his world to mine.

My dog, by the way, thinks I have much to learn about partridges, and, being a professional naturalist, I agree. He persists in tutoring me, with the calm patience of a professor of logic, in the art of drawing deductions from an educated nose. I delight in seeing him deduce a conclusion, in the form of a point, from data that are obvious to him, but speculative to my unaided eye. Perhaps he hopes his dull pupil will one day learn to smell.

Like other dull pupils, I know when the professor is right, even though I do not know why. I check my gun and walk in. Like any good professor, the dog never laughs when I miss, which is often. He gives me just one look, and proceeds up the stream in quest of another grouse.

Following one of these banks, one walks astride two landscapes, the hillside one hunts from, and the bottom the dog hunts. There is a special charm in treading soft dry carpets of Lycopodium to flush birds out of the bog, and the first test of a partridge dog is his willingness to do the wet work while you parallel him on the dry bank.

A special problem arises where the belt of alders widens, and the dog disappears from view. Hurry at once to a knoll or point, where you stand stockstill, straining eye and ear to follow the dog. A sudden scattering of whitethroats may reveal his whereabouts. Again you may hear him breaking a twig, or splashing in a wet spot, or plopping into the creek. But when all sound ceases, be ready for instant action, for he is likely on point. Listen now for the premonitory clucks a frightened partridge gives just before flushing. Then follows the hurtling bird, or perhaps two of them or I have known as many six, clucking and flushing one by one, each sailing high for his own destination in the uplands. Whether one passes within gunshot is of course a matter of chance, and you can compute the chance if you have time: 360 degrees divided by 30, or whatever segment of the circle your gun covers. Divided again by 3 or 4, which is your chance of missing, and you have the probability of actual feathers in the hunting coat.

The second test of a good partridge dog is whether he reports for orders after such an episode. Sit down and talk it over with him while he pants.Then look for the next red lantern, and proceed with the hunt.

The October breeze brings my dog many scents other than grouse, each of which may lead to its own peculiar episode. When he points with a certain humorous expression of the ears, I know he has found a bedded rabbit. Once a dead-serious point yielded no bird, but still the dog stood frozen; in a tuft of sedge under his very nose was a fat sleeping coon, getting his share of October sun. At least once on each hunt the dog bays a skunk, usually in some denser-than-ordinary thicket of blackberries. Once the dog pointed in midstream: a whir of wings upriver, followed by three musical cries, told me he had interrupted a wood duck's dinner. Not infrequently he finds jacksnipe in heavily pastured alders, and lastly he may put out a deer, bedded for the day on a high streambank flanked by alder bog. Has the deer a poetical weakness for singing waters, or a practical liking for a bed that cannot be approached without making a noise? Judging by the indignant flick of his great white flag it might be either, or both.

Almost anything may happen between one red lantern and another.

At sunset on the last day of the grouse season, every blackberry blows out his light. I do not understand how a mere bush can thus be infallibly informed about the Wisconsin statutes, nor have I ever gone back next day to find out. For the ensuing eleven months the lanterns glow only in recollection. I sometimes think that the other months were constituted mainly as a fitting interlude between Octobers, and I suspect that dogs, and perhaps grouse, share the same view.

Red Legs Kicking

When I call to mind my earliest impressions, I wonder whether the process ordinarily referred to as growing up is not actually a process of growing down; whether experience, so much touted among adults as the thing children lack, is not actually a progressive dilution of the essentials by the trivialities of living. This much at least is sure: my earliest impressions of wildlife and its pursuit retain a vivid sharpness of form, color, and atmosphere that half a century of professional wildlife experience has failed to obliterate or to improve upon.

Like most aspiring hunters, I was given, at an early age, a single-barreled shotgun and permission to hunt rabbits. One winter Saturday, en route to my favorite rabbit patch, I noticed that the lake, then covered with ice and snow, had developed a small 'airhole' at a point where a windmill discharged warm water from the shore. All ducks had long since departed southward, but I then and there formulated my first ornithological hypothesis: if there were a duck left in the region, he (or she) would inevitably, sooner or later, drop in at this airhole. I suppressed my appetite for rabbits (then no mean feat), sat down in the cold smartweeds on the frozen mud, and waited.

I waited all afternoon, growing colder with each passing crow, and with each rheumatic groan of the laboring windmill. Finally, at sunset, a lone black duck came out of the west, and without even a preliminary circling of the airhole, set his wings and pitched downward.

222

I cannot remember the shot; I remember only my unspeakable delight when my first duck hit the snowy ice with a thud and lay there, belly up, red legs kicking.

When my father gave me the shotgun, he said I might hunt partridges with it, but that I might not shoot them from trees. I was old enough, he said, to learn wing-shooting.

My dog was good at treeing partridge, and to forego a sure shot in the tree in favor of a hopeless one at the fleeing bird was my first exercise in ethical codes. Compared with a treed partridge, the devil and his seven kingdoms was a mild temptation.

At the end of my second season of featherless partridge-hunting I was walking, one day, through an aspen thicket when a big partridge rose with a roar at my left, and, towering over the aspens, crossed behind me, hell-bent for the nearest cedar swamp. It was a swinging shot of the sort the partridge-hunter dreams about, and the bird tumbled down in a shower of feathers and golden leaves.

I could draw a map today of each clump of red bunchberry and each blue aster that adorned the mossy spot where he lay, my first partridge on the wing. I suspect my present affection for bunchberries and asters dates from that moment.

If I Were the Wind

The wind that makes music in November corn is in a hurry. The stalks hum, the loose husks whisk skyward in half-playful swirls, and the wind hurries on.

In the marsh, long windy waves surge across the grassy sloughs, beat against the far willows. A tree tries to argue, bare limbs waving, but there is no detaining the wind.

On the sandbar there is only wind, and the river sliding seaward. Every wisp of grass is drawing circles on the sand. I wander over the bar to a driftwood log, where I sit and listen to the universal roar, and to the tinkle of wavelets on the shore. The river is lifeless: not a duck, heron, marshhawk, or gull but has sought refuge from wind.

Out of the clouds I hear a faint bark, as of a faraway dog. It is strange how the world cocks its ears at that sound, wondering. Soon it is louder: the honk of geese, invisible, but coming on.

223

The flock emerges from the low clouds, a tattered banner of birds, dipping and rising, blown up and blown down, blown together and blown apart, but advancing, the wind wrestling lovingly with each winnowing wing. When the flock is a blur in the far sky I hear the last honk, sounding taps for summer.

It is warm behind the driftwood now, for the wind has gone with the geese. So would I – if I were the wind.

THE SPECTRE OF
Tiger Creek

BY ARCHIBALD RUTLEDGE

Archibald Rutledge (1883-1973) was a grand storyteller in the finest Southern tradition. Long South Carolina's Poet Laureate, he is today primarily remembered for his deer and turkey hunting tales. Rutledge, however, wrote wisely and well on a variety of subjects, including rattlesnakes, cottonmouth moccasins, alligators and wild hogs which were a daily part of life around his beloved Hampton Plantation in the Palmetto Low Country. Here, he describes a chilling encounter with a shark, an incident that very nearly ended in tragedy.

A fter passing the winter on the plantation, we moved, in the spring, down to a house on the coast, where we spent the summer, safe from malaria and other swamp-fevers. It was there that we did our salt-water fishing, and there that we had this adventure with a huge shark in Tiger Creek.

One of the most popular forms of fishing along the Southern coast is the taking of mullets at night, either with a cast-net or with a gill-seine. They cannot be taken with a hook and line, and only rarely can they be caught in the daytime with a net.

One day in August my brother Tom and I, on our return home from a trip after school-bass along the marshes, ran into a big school of mullets near the mouth of Tiger Creek, a deep estuary that withdraws from the main channel and winds a sinuous way up into the marsh-fields. We could do nothing with the mullets then, but we reasoned that they might be there on the next flood, which would be about midnight, and we decided to try for them with the gill-seine.

At eleven o'clock we left the glimmering shell wharf and dropped silently down on the late ebb.

We had a ten-foot cypress *bateau*, light but steady, and capable of carrying a good load. Tom rowed, and I well remember that the star-light and the silent ranks of green cedars on the shore and the strange noises in the marshes made us feel very adventurous.

A pull of half an hour down the channel brought us to Tiger Creek, the surface of which glittered frostily in the starlight with the myriads of small fish that were playing on it. By this time the young flood was beginning to creep in; so, running the boat up under the lee shore, we waited there, and listened with pleasurable assurance to the telltale thudding of the water – a certain sign of mullets. As we had expected, they were going into Tiger Creek; we had only to wait until they got well up the stream before stopping the mouth with the seine.

When it was evident that the school had passed us, we rowed quietly up the creek for a little distance. Then, while my brother pulled slowly, I staked one end of the seine and paid out the length over the stern. The creek was forty feet wide, and our net only thirty; so we staked the boat at the short end, which made an apparent, although not a perfect, shut-off.

As I was the younger, it usually fell to me to run the fish down, while Tom tended the net; but this time he asked me, much to my delight, if I would not like to take the fish out when they struck the net. Making me promise not to let the big ones get away, he splashed off through the marsh with an oar over his shoulder.

Having made the boat fast between the seine and the shore, I let myself down into the warm, sparkling water and began to feel my way out along the seine. I wanted to make sure that the corks were all floating right side up, and that the lead-line was set true. The water was not so deep as I thought it would be, for it came only a little above my waist by the boat and at the middle of the net; but the bottom was very soft and sticky, so that several times I had to take hold of the seine to pull my feet out of the mud. Consequently, I did not venture so far as the narrow channel that ran close to the shore at the other end of the net. There, I knew, the water was deeper. I found the net hanging right; and as it was a new one, with no holes and no weak places, I felt sure that we would make a large catch.

Before long I heard Tom begin to shout, and then came the sound of his oar spanking the water near the head of the creek. Soon I heard mullets jumping; then the water about me began to murmur, and a big fish struck the seine and gilled himself. The corks bobbed and the water foamed, while I waded toward the fish, took him out, and threw him into the boat. Before I could turn, several had gilled themselves, and one had jumped into our *bateau*. The hurrying fish, fleeing for open water, bumped against me. They rushed here and there, huddled against the seine, jumped over it, gilled themselves, or buried themselves in the mud beneath it.

I was so busy and so eager to reach a certain fish that was making a great froth near the middle of the seine that I did not at first notice the decided lull in the general noise, and, anyway, my ears were pretty well engaged with Tom's shouting and his pounding with the oar. But I soon realized that something unusual in the water had frightened the mullets even more than our seine. Yet, well as I knew the salt creeks and the real dangers that lurk there, I did not move from the spot where, with my feet bogged in the sucking mud, I was feeling out along the seine and lifting it here and there to take out the fish that had gilled themselves.

I was holding the seine up with my right hand, and my left hand was hanging by my side in the water, when I suddenly felt a big wave rise to my shoulder, and in front of it, moving sluggishly past me along the downstream side of the seine, I saw the fin of a great shark. He had come in with the flood, and was prowling about for a kill.

Of all the creatures that infest salt waters, none are more sinister than the sharks, especially the hammerheads and the tigers.

Moving like shadowy specters just beneath the surface, they appear suddenly, seize their prey, and rending it with their needle-like teeth, dart away to devour it. They are crafty in their movements, usually cowardly about noises, sinister in their silent and deadly approach.

The hammerheads never grow very large in these waters, but the gray, racing body of the tiger I had seen as long as twelve feet. The shark that was now so near me was – as I guessed from the height of his fin and the size of the wave it carried – ten feet long.

Just now he had turned away from the seine, and was making a semicircle in the creek. It is said that when a shark begins to circle on the surface, with his fin cutting the water faster and faster as he turns, it is time to look for trouble. That is exactly what I saw there on the surface of that placid creek, and I believed I knew what it meant. He had wind of me, and was circling to find and close in on me. There was something fascinating about his bloodhound tactics; sometimes he would stop as if listening, or as if thinking the puzzle out in his crafty mind; then he would move deliberately off with insolent assurance.

At first I was merely surprised that such a big shark should be near Tiger Creek, and provoked that he should have spoiled our seining, for there was now no sight or sound of a fish anywhere. But when I saw the alertness of the creature, the terrible intensity in that rigid fin, that sweeping hither and thither of the lithe body, my feelings changed; I wanted to get out of his way as quickly as I could. There was nothing between us but open water, for I was on the outside of the seine.

Having stood so long in one place, my feet had gradually become set in the heavy mud, so that when I tried to move toward the boat I could not take a step. Hitherto, with the help of the seine, I had pulled myself along; but now, although I tugged vehemently, the only result was the giving of the stake on the farther shore. I could not budge an inch. I think the rapidly rising tide, now well up toward my shoulders, kept me from getting the proper leverage with my knees. At any rate, I was as fast to the bottom as if I had been tied.

Meanwhile, Tom, eager to get down to the seine, where he imagined I was having great sport, had ceased his shouting and beating. He was still a good way off, and I could hear him tramping

228

along through the crackling marsh. I struggled with the dull trap that had locked its soft jaws on my feet, but I only made my knees ache with the strain, and apparently sank myself deeper into the water.

The shark had now come up to the end of the seine next to the boat. He stopped for a moment by it, evidently puzzled. But I felt certain that his next turn would be toward me. With that, losing my nerve, I shouted for Tom, and heard him answer me. He was having a tussle of his own trying to cross a boggy inlet that the incoming tide had filled; evidently, he thought I was calling him to hurry so as to help take the mullets out of the net.

When I heard him floundering in that mudhole, I gave up the idea that he could help me out of my difficulty. Perhaps it was better so; for when I felt entirely thrown on my own resources, when I knew that, single-handed, I must try conclusions with the huge creature that was hunting me, I knew that I must act; and act at once. Weapon of any kind I had none. I was alone and defenseless, in water almost up to my neck, and a ten-foot shark was within two boat-lengths of me, looking for me. For the first time since I had been fishing in those waters I was unnerved.

But my thinking was clear enough until I saw that big creature turn slowly away from the boat and come toward me through the dark water. Then I lost my head. I cried out wildly for Tom. I beat the water with my hands and screamed at the shark. But he came steadily on. His deliberation was more terrible than his swiftness would have been. I felt that he saw me standing there helpless. He was coming straight toward me now, with no sign of uncertainty in his movements. I saw his fin rise higher out of the water, as if he were summoning all his savage strength for the final rush, and I grew sick at his brutal assurance.

He was only ten feet away now. Whatever fate was in store for me would, I thought, be immediate. Every chance of escape seemed cut off. Yet even in that dark moment an inspiration seized me. Catching the seine violently, I lifted it as high as I could, ducked through the water under it, rose on the other side and dropped the net into place. I had put a defense between me and my pursuer!

But how frail was that defense against the giant strength of the ruthless, cold-blooded creature! Yet for a moment it separated me from his terrible jaws. Now I felt slightly protected, but I could not move from my position, for my feet were still firmly embedded. The shark had already rushed by, and, baffled and perplexed, was circling swiftly. But now again he saw me, and came head on for the seine. I knew that it would not withstand his great weight and dreadful momentum. On he came, literally charging me. But before he struck the net he swerved, so that he did not break through, but turned swiftly along it.

My fascinated eyes followed him. He swam up to the end of the net next to the boat. With the flow of the flood, the boat had swung on her moorings. It now lay up the creek, and thus left a clear gap of ten feet, through which the shark, suddenly accelerating his speed, spurted fiercely. He was on me now; there was nothing between us. One wide circle in the creek would give him his bearings – then he would rush on his prey.

But with the coming of my enemy, my brother Tom also approached. I had forgotten him in my delirious fear. Now I shouted to him at the top of my voice, crying wildly, "Shark! Shark! Help me, or he'll get me!"

I saw him pause; then, catching my words, he broke into a full run. Leaping into the boat, he jerked the painter loose and shoved out rapidly.

Straight as a well-sped arrow the great gray shark raced down upon me. I steeled myself for the sickening shock. But Tom's powerful hands gripped my arms, and he lifted me into the boat. There flashed by the stern the tall knife-fin of the tiger, and the huge creature tore his terrible way through the net as if it had been a cobweb.

Reprinted courtesy of Irvine H. Rutledge, Hagertown, Maryland.

Pheasants

BEYOND AUTUMN

JOHN MADSON

Few contemporary outdoor scribes possess the abilities
of John Madson. His best-known works are in the field of
nature writing, and Madson's books bid fair to entertain
and intrigue readers for generations to come. Here, in a
tight, bright essay on pheasant hunting, he comes about
as close to capturing the elusive essence of what it means
to hunt as is ever likely to be done with words.

There is a dichotomy in pheasant hunting, as in any hunting
that is worth doing. There are sets of paired contrasts: two
pheasant seasons, two kinds of hunters, two types of birds.
Gold and grey, gay and grim, yin and yang.

One pheasant season may last no longer than opening weekend
– a brief, burnished time with Indian summer still on the land,
the afternoons soft and tawny and hunters with their coats open.

231

The other pheasant season is quieter and greyer, reaching far into December. The sky is often stone-colored then, filled with prairie winds that cut with a wire edge, and even on clear days the sunlight is pale and without substance.

In that first pheasant season there were hunters by the hundreds of thousands sweeping the fields in wide lines with deployed blockers, plaguing farmers and each other, shooting at pheasants hopelessly far away, ripping out the crotches of new hunting pants on bobwire fences, and generally having a helluva fine time. They head back to town with or without birds, often making a stop along the way and arriving home late and smelling like hot mince pies. They are not likely to reappear on the landscape for about one year.

The pheasant hunters who do return, and keep returning, have a singular worn quality. Their canvas coats are likely to be weather-stained and shapeless, with the main button missing and a pronounced sag in the region of the game pocket, and their gunmetal is worn to the white. They hunt without haste – dour men in twos and threes, or often alone with an old retriever at heel. Men shaped and colored by circumstance, as fitted to their environment as horseweeds and cockleburs – and just as enduring and tenacious. They must be, to match the birds that they now hunt.

The pheasants of the opening weekend were overwhelmingly birds of the year, callow juveniles that rose clattering into the air within easy gun range. Those birds went home with the opening-day hunters and, like them, will not reappear for another year. The birds that remain are either sagacious old roosters with long spurs, or smart young cocks that won their spurs during the first week of hunting. Such pheasants have much in common with the remaining hunters. Each tempers and hones the other in a process of mutual refinement.

There is some loss of pheasants with the first intense shock of cold weather. There is a marked loss of hunters as well. By then, both pheasant and hunter have evolved beyond their opening-day counterparts – for it needs a tougher breed of hunter to pit himself against the pheasant range of late December, and a tougher breed of pheasant tends to harden and sharpen a bit ahead of the man who hunts him, even the very good man. There comes a point where hunter persistence is outstripped by pheasant resistance – and the roosters always win.

The December pheasant is the real pheasant and to hunt him is to hunt pheasants truly. Which is not to say that opening weekend is unworthy of serious regard. It is a very special time, a season apart, that late October or early November opening. A wedding party and honeymoon in one – green and golden preface to a hardworking marriage between bird and gunner.

Opening day is when a small boy is allowed to tag along for the first time and maybe carry dad's first rooster of the day, and get to keep the tail feathers. The boy will soon be carrying a 20-bore and a rooster of his own.

It is a time when the clans gather, when old hunting pards rendezvous. They come from all compass points, reaffirming the faith. I'll go home to central Iowa again and hook up with Harry Harrison or Skeeter Wheeler. Or Glen Yates – leathery, irascible, ornery, deeply regarded Yates. Sly old cuss Yates, with his bib overalls and tattered coat and Sweet Sixteen, and a profound and abiding knowledge of the ring-necked pheasant. Opening day is playday for us. It's Gooney Bird Day, time to test the young roosters and see how all the folks are doing out there in the fields. As Yates puts it: "Of course Opening Day ain't pheasant hunting. Hell, that ain't new. But it's the start of it – and Kee-rist, Madseen, am I ready!"

It's this Opening Day that largely supports wildlife conservation in much of the Midwest – notably Iowa, Kansas, Nebraska and South Dakota. License sales soar just before the pheasant season, swelling the game and fish coffers while gun and ammunition receipts build the Pittman-Robertson fund. In Iowa, about 300,000 residents buy hunting licenses. About 290,000 of them hunt pheasants – and probably 80 percent are out there on the great Saturday. If there were no pheasant opening in Iowa, as many as 200,000 licenses might go unsold in a given year – and the wildlife conservation program would go down the tube. It is much the same elsewhere. Let us look fondly on Opening Day.

A lot of bird hunting isn't really hunting. For example, you don't hunt waterfowl and wild turkey. You seduce and delude them. Nor do men usually hunt quail. They hunt for the dog that's hunting for the quail.

Early-season pheasant hunting isn't as likely to be hunting so much as just combing through cover. Birds are likely to be almost anywhere in the early November fields and edges, so it's usually a matter of just pointing yourself at the general landscape and grinding out mileage.

But later pheasant hunting may be as pure a form of hunting as there is. The hunter then becomes a classic searcher and stalker, shooting less and hunting much, much more. There are still a few ribbon clerks trying to shoot pheasants from cars – but that's a pallid imitation of sport that doesn't really produce much. While the pheasant season is still young, the birds have begun to shrink away from roadsides. The slow ones are dead, and most of the others are likely to be somewhere back in the fields where things are more peaceful. (With exceptions, of course. We know a man who hunts late-season birds in the thick brome of certain I-80 interchanges. He says he does all right. As near as we can figure it, the only law he's breaking is the one prohibiting pedestrians on interstate highways.)

I don't have much late-season cunning, but one practice that's worked out well is simply getting as far as possible from roads. An obvious reason is that most birds have faded away from roadsides and roadside field edges. Then, too, the very center of a square-mile section of Midwestern cornland may be the untidiest part. It's where a farmer tends to sweep stuff under the rug, back where passersby can't see small farm dumps, weed-patches, messy fencecorners and junk machinery.

I once found a mile-square section whose exact center was low and boggy, and whose owner had never gone to the expense and effort of extending tile lines from there to the nearest road ditch a half-mile away. Since the swale was probably lower than the distant road ditch, drainage wouldn't have been possible, anyway. The result was a little two-acre oasis that was abandoned to wild grasses and forbs. And pheasants, of course. Unless a man stood on the cab of his pickup truck (which I did), this could not be seen from the road.

In contrast is a certain square mile of central Iowa farmland that lies on a terminal moraine. In most of my home country a man can plow all day and not see a stone bigger than a walnut, but this particular township has sprinklings of glacial erratics. Over the

234

years, farmers had removed such debris from their fields to a slight lift of land in the center of my hunting ground, where today a modest boulderfield covers almost an acre – together with several rolls of old fencing and a mantle of goldenrod, lesser ragweed and sumac. This little niche is a magnet for wildlife, although I never hit it hard nor often. Once a season is enough.

Out here in the corn country – and about everywhere else – a man must exploit two extremes in his late-season pheasant hunting. He must hunt close and far, alternating between dense coverts and wide, naked fields.

There are genuine pheasant hunters who think nothing of reducing new canvas pants to shredded rags in the course of a single hunting season. They churn around in terrible places – deep pockets of raspberry canes undergrown with dense grass, rough weedy creekbanks thick with catbriar tangles, and the steep banks of old bullditches with their overgrowth of ragweed and sumac. You know – the kinds of cover that hurt just to look at. But these are the haunts of late-season roosters, and the men who rout them out of such stuff do so with the premise that the only places worth hunting in late season are in cover that no sane man would ever enter.

Such attention to detail, and willingness to suffer for it, applies to open field gunning as well. It may mean hunting in rough plowing, such as plowed pastures where broken sod is left to mellow over the winter. These are the devil's own fields to walk in; the black surfaces of the upturned sods become as slippery as grease during the midday thaw, and a man can break his bones there. Still, roosters may be sheltering in sun-warmed hollows between and under the big clods, and a hunter must go where the birds may be. If there's any comfort in this, it's knowing that pheasants are as reluctant to run in heavy plowing as men are. Well, almost.

This breed of hunter will turn aside from a comfortable fenceline and stumble across a quarter of plowing to hunt a wisp of grassed waterway only a few yards long, or walk hundreds of yards out of his way to investigate a basket-sized tuft of foxtail in a picked cornfield, or a distant hay bale that the farmer failed to pick up. No cover feature in the barren winter landscape is too minor to overlook. It is hunting based on three articles of faith: 1)

235

that much of the pre-season rooster population is still out there, and although 2) there is no cheap late-season pheasant, 3) the longer you hunt without flushing a bird, the closer you are to flushing one.

Pheasants range more widely in winter than at any other time of year. They are constantly adjusting to impending storms, snow-choked roosts, and deep cold and wind. Vagaries of wind and snow-drifting will eliminate certain niches of the birds' range, and bring others into play. Marvelously rugged and adaptable birds, winter pheasants never cease probing and exploring.

Aldo Leopold observed that Wisconsin pheasants were sometimes restless in coverts of less than ten acres. Where small coverts prevailed, pheasants were likely to adopt a winter "circuit-type" movement, traveling from one covert to another in a sequence spreading over a mile of distance and several days' time. Dr. Leopold believed that Wisconsin pheasants in good winter range had an average cruising radius of one-eighth to one-half mile, and two or three miles at the most.

Since today's winter coverts in the primary pheasant range are almost always less than ten acres, such fiddle-footed drifting may be a common trait in many regions. Although a particular covert may not hold birds today, it doesn't mean that they might not be there tomorrow or a couple of days from now. On the contrary, it could mean that they probably will be.

Our most successful wild birds and mammals are those that have not been fixed in rigid frames of specialization, but are generalized in design and function. The pheasant is a pretty good example of this, owing much of his success to a rather generalized form and a knack for ready adjustment. We can't really ascribe much intelligence to the pheasant. After all, the chicken tribe wasn't at the head of the line when the brains were passed out. But the ringneck is certainly "country smart"; he may not know his way to town, but he sure ain't lost. He develops a remarkably shrewd sense of range. Not as well as the red fox or white-tailed deer, perhaps, but infinitely better than the men who hunt him there.

We human hunters are likely to regard countrysides in terms of drainage systems and patterns of cultivation and habitation. Or, at best, in terms of entire brushy creeks, dry sloughs and weedy fields. Wild hunted creatures like the pheasant learn their native

236

heath in terms of minute, intimate crannies – little sections of overhung creekbank, the tree stump covered with vines and weeds, that old roll of fencewire smothered with giant foxtail. Our eyes are always about six feet above the ground; the pheasant's are down there among the details, down in the tangled heart of the covert, and an instant later his eyes may be 40 feet in the air. A pheasant is exposed to the major and minor features of his home range in ways that the hunter can never hope to be, and he is highly capable of exploiting that exposure in stress situations.

While trading from one major winter covert to another, a pheasant is about as likely to walk as fly. In the course of such commuting he continually adds to his experience bank. If the obvious winter hangouts are regularly disturbed by hunters, many ringnecks begin to rely on interim coverts – little pockets of sanctuary that they have happened upon along the way. This occurs too often to be a fluke – occasions when certain birds are not to be found in any conventional shelterbelt or winter slough, but are shut down in the weedy mouth of an old culvert or in a snug form of tented bluegrass in an orchard. The compleat pheasant hunter must learn to think in such terms. This is one of the reasons that I enjoy hunting pheasants on snow. It's all written out there, although I often fail to comprehend what I read.

It's on snow that one can trace daily feeding patterns, some of the winter circuity between far-flung coverts, and the bewildering and often admirable interactions of winter pheasants and their harsh world. Such tracking is more likely to instruct in natural history than to result in shooting. My lifetime success rate for converting pheasant tracks to Sunday dinners can't be much more than two percent. Something usually goes wrong.

But if I've learned one thing about trailing, it's this: never to think in terms of a pheasant resting placidly at the end of a line of tracks. If those tracks are really fresh, the pheasant is almost certainly aware of being trailed and you will rarely get a shot while the bird is on the move. It's his pausing-place that you must find. If the trail appears to lead across rather open ground to a distant pocket of weedy cover, swing far to the side and come in from behind. I think this may be the only way I've ever trailed and killed pheasants – by leaving the trail and flanking the bird at some point ahead. Several times, on fresh snow, I have found that roosters had entered bits of cover and had hooked around in order to watch their backtrails.

Snow lends certain advantages to the pheasant hunter. Birds can be more easily seen in distant feeder fields and coverts in snowtime, crippled birds can be readily trailed, and dead pheasants are easier to find in heavy cover. Yet, snowtime is hardly a situation in which the calloused gunner exploits a vulnerable population and kills pheasants at will. My success rate at tracking and shooting pheasants on snow is about the same as my fox-trailing with a rifle – reinforcing my long-held conviction that the ring-necked pheasant is nothing less than a feathered fox.

There's something I miss in my late-season hunting these days.

For years I have begun pheasant hunts on wheels instead of legs, leaving home in car or truck, driving as many miles as necessary, and returning in comfort. The day that I began to do this marked the end of my boyhood and pushed back the prairie horizons, but it wasn't necessarily progress.

It will never be like just stepping off the back stoop and loading my gun, walking across the garden, and being in hunting grounds almost at once. Pure hunting, that was, from home den out into the coverts and back to den again, like a young fox. It was never diluted, as now, by synthetic beginnings on highways.

Each cover patch would point to one beyond until I had overextended myself as I always did, and night had found me far from home. There is a keen and poignant quality in being a famished boy far afield with night coming on and miles of crusted snow yet to negotiate, the pheasants hanging over your shoulder with their legs tied with binder twine, and the little Monkey Ward double gun beginning to weigh heavy. (I had bought the gun's mismatched 16-gauge shells at Walsh's Hardware, out of a bin where they were all mixed together and served up like rock candy – three cents apiece and you took what came up in the scoop, with no picking over the shells for preferred shot sizes or other such nonsense.)

Night coming on and glory lost, for there would be no daylight in which to parade past neighbor girls' houses, the bright roosters hung from my shoulder. The girls would never know what they had missed, but I would.

Now, for the first time in ten hours, a weakness beginning in the legs, and that exquisite knifelike stab high between the shoulder blades. Ten hours since oatmeal and coffee, with long crossings over plowed ground, and ranging through horseweed thickets laced with wild plum and raspberry canes, through fallow pastures of heavy tented grass, creekside willow slaps, over the high fields and under the bluffs, and into little cattail sloughs whose icy floors were skeined with pheasant tracks. And once, a half-mile dash along a crusted fenceline trying to flush a running rooster and failing to, gasping in the cold air and coughing for an hour afterward.

My lips and nose would be raw and sore from hours of wiping them with the backs of woolen mittens that were quickly frozen. There was a winter twilight when I stopped and leaned against an old wolf cottonwood to rest, and took off my woolen stocking cap to mop my sore nose. It was the first time since morning that I'd taken off the cap; when I ran my fingers through my matted hair it protested at being disturbed, and I remember thinking it was funny that even my hair should hurt, but not funny enough to laugh about.

The wind freshening, swinging into the northwest and freighted with the smell of more snow. By now my corduroy pants are frozen to the knees, as stiff as stovepipes and rattling against each other and against the shoepacs that I had bought with my first fur check the year before. One foot ahead of the other, breaking through snow crust at each step, the slung birds cutting through old sheepskin coat and into thin shoulder, and a sort of homesickness growing at the sight of each lighted kitchen window in farmhouses across the fields. And finally, up ahead in the gathering darkness, a square of yellow reflecting on snow, strangely warm and vivid after the long hours of unrelieved white and grey. There ahead, a circle of light and warmth for a young hunter come home of a winter evening, late in pheasant season.

At last, up the back steps and out of the wild night into the rich kitchen smell of home, where potroast with whole onions and carrots and potatoes is waiting on the back of the stove, and buttercrusted rolls still hot, with much-loved voices laughing and half-scolding and the close comfort of it wrapping a boy like a grandmother's quilt. I would take off coat and mittens before I

239

began eating – but only because mother forced me to. And soon to sleep, out in the back room with its icy linoleum, mounded over with lambs'-wool comforters and fleecy blankets smelling of cedar, the deep guiltless slumber of a hunter who has spent everything that he had of himself, and hunted as well as he knew how.

Just being young was part of this, of course, and coming home was part of it, too. But there was more – a wild purity of hunting that was wholly free and true. It was hunting with all the fat rendered away, and reduced to the clean white bone. It was a closing of the magic circle of man, animal and land, and once a boy glimpses this he remembers it all of his days.

This is the essence for which I will always hunt, for I often misplace it and seem seldom able to find it in the old full measure that I knew. But when it's found, it will likely be on some iron prairie at the knell of the year, with a cunning old ringneck out ahead and showing me the way.

OF BROOKFIELD

BY JOHN TAINTOR FOOTE

John Taintor Foote (1881-1950) was a masterful
storyteller, equally adept at writing about any subject. Yet
it is in his tales about hunting dogs that he really excels.
Perhaps the finest of his many fine efforts in this genre is
"Dumb-Bell of Brookfield." First published in the March,
1927, issue of *Field & Stream*, this engaging tale is about
the runt of a litter who overcame adversity to shine later.
The story also appeared in *Dumb-Bell and Others: The
Great Dog Stories of John Taintor Foote*. Along with Corey
Ford's "The Road to Tinkhamtown," it is one of the two
greatest American hunting dog stories.

The king sat on his throne and blinked at the sunlight
streaming through the French windows. His eyes were
pools of liquid amber filled with a brooding dignity, and
kind beyond expression.

His throne was a big leather chair, worn and slouchy, that stood
in the bay window of the Brookfield living-room. He had slept
there all night, and it was time for a maid to come, open the

241

French window, and let him out into the dew-washed rose garden.

The king was old. He had seized the throne years before. He had been put on the train one day, with nothing but his pedigree and a prayer. He had come home, six months later, champion of champions, greatest field trial setter of his time, lion-hearted defender of the honor of Brookfield.

He never saw the inside of the kennels again. He had been given humbly the freedom of the house. After due sniffings at one place and another, he had taken the leather chair for his own.

From then on, visitors were asked to sit elsewhere, if they didn't mind, because he might want his chair, and he was Champion Brookfield Roderigo.

So now the king sat on his throne, or rather lay curled up in it, with his long, deep muzzle resting on his paws. At the end of that muzzle was a nose. A nose uncanny in its swift certainty. A nose which had allowed him to go down wind, running like fire, stiffen in the middle of one of his effortless bounds, twist himself in the air, and light rigid at a bevy a hundred feet away.

He had done this again and again when only a "derby." He had done it in the National Championship until hard-riding men, galloping behind him, had yelled and shouted like school boys, and Judge Beldon, mad beyond all ethics, had called across to another judge. "The dog never lived that could beat him, Tom!"

This was a flagrant breach of form; it was unpardonable for a field-trial judge to indicate his choice before the official vote. That night Judge Beldon apologized to the owner of the pointer, Rip Rap Messenger, who was running with, or rather far behind, the king at the time.

But the owner of the pointer only said: "Forget it, Judge! Why, I was as crazy as any of you. Man, oh, man, ain't he some dog!"

All this was long ago. It was no longer part of the king's life, and he was not thinking of those triumphant days of his youth. He wondered how soon the maid would come and let him out. Once in the garden, he might find a toad under a rosebush at which to paw tentatively. Perhaps he would dig up the piece of dog cake he had buried in the black earth near the sun-dial.

And there was that mole the terrier had killed; it was certainly worth a sniff or two. No doubt a gardener had removed it by this time, though. . .meddlesome things, gardeners – an unguarded

242

bone was scarcely safe a moment when one of them was about!

Where was that maid? Why didn't she come? Perhaps he had better take a little nap. He closed his eyes. . .He never opened them again. The heart that had pumped so staunch a beat for Brookfield decided to pump no more. A shudder passed over the king's body. . .then it was still.

The maid came presently and called his name. When he didn't stir, she went to the leather chair and looked, her eyes growing wide. She hurried from the room and up the stairs.

"Mister Gregory, sir," she panted at the door, "won't you come down, please? Roderigo – he don't move. He don't move at all, sir!"

She was beside the chair again when the master of Brookfield arrived in his dressing gown.

"He don't move –" she repeated.

The master of Brookfield put his hand on the king's head. He slid his other hand under the king's body between the fore legs and held it there for a moment. Then he stooped, gathered a dangling paw, and rubbed the raspy pad of it against his cheek.

"No. He won't move any more," he said. "Ask Mrs. Gregory to come down."

When the mistress of Brookfield came, she kneeled before the king in a patch of the streaming sunlight at which he had blinked early that morning. She kneeled a long time, twisting one of the king's soft ears between her fingers.

"He liked to have me do that," she said, looking up at Mr. Gregory.

The master of Brookfield nodded.

The mistress of Brookfield bent until her lips were close to the ear she had been stroking.

"Old lover. . .old lover!" she whispered. Then she got up suddenly and went out into the rose garden.

And so there was a chair which no one ever sat in standing in the bay window of the living-room. And it was understood that the chair would remain empty until a dog was born at Brookfield who could lie in it without shame.

Highland Lassie was in disgrace. Her field trial record was forgotten. She had brought three puppies into the world and had smothered two of them before they were six hours old.

"An' to think," wailed Peter, head kennel man at Brookfield,

"the 'ussy's went an' rolled on the only Roderigo puppies this
world'll ever see again! Look what she's got left – one pup, an 'im
the runt!" He poked the pinky-white atom with a stumpy forefinger, and Highland Lassie cuddled the puppy hastily to her side.

Leona, the big blond waitress, removed a straw from Peter's coat
and allowed her hand to linger on his sleeve.

"Are you not to your breakfast coming?" she asked.

But Peter had forgotten for the time that her eyes were blue, that her
bosom was deep, and that she looked like gold and milk and roses.

"Breakfast?" he snorted, "An' what do I care about breakfast?
'Aven't I just told you she's gone an' killed two Roderigo pups, an
'im layin' out there in the orchard?"

Leona gave a gentle tug at his sleeve.

"Always more puppies there will be," she said, and her words
were like the notes of a flute.

Peter straightened up and glared at her.

"Always more puppies there will be!" He repeated her words
slowly, with dreadful scorn. "You go back to the 'ouse!"

Leona departed with a quivering lip to have her statement
swiftly verified. That very day Black-Eyed Susan became the
mother of seven, of whom Dan Gath, winner of the Manitoba All
Age, was the indifferent father.

"A fine litter by a good young sire!" said Peter. "Brookfield ain't
done yet. 'Ow's that for a grand pup – the second one there? 'E'll
be a movin' picture, you 'ear me!"

"Maybe he'll be champion," suggested a kennel boy, hopefully.

"Champion!" said Peter. "So'll your grandmother. 'Ere, put
some fresh straw in that corner an' don't you bother the bitch
whilst you're doin' it, neither."

But when the boy had gone, Peter filled his pipe and stared thoughtfully at Black-Eyed Susan, her eyes still fever bright from birth pangs.

"'E might at that, old gel," said Peter softly. "'E might at that."

Four months later the second puppy in the row of seven had
grown into a thing of beauty that made you gasp when you saw
him. From his proudly chiseled head to the glistening plume of
his tail he was a triumph.

"The grandest pup we've ever bred at Brookfield!" said Peter.
"For looks that is," he added, glancing out toward the orchard.
"Only for looks."

Highland Lassie's puppy grew also. He lived in a land of plenty, unshared by crowding brothers and sisters. He did not dine in frantic haste but deliberately and at his ease, his soft-eyed mother watching.

He was seldom disturbed by callers. Even the abundance he received failed to give him size. He could add nothing, therefore, to the honor of Brookfield. He could only dim, a little, the glory of his sire – and so they let him alone.

Then weaning time came, and his mother neglected him more and more. At last she gave him up altogether, and he was left to his own devices.

He tried hard to make the time pass. A sparrow lighting in his runway was a great event. He would creep toward it, and at the proper distance would halt and stand rigid until the sparrow flew away. Sometimes the sparrow would fly to a wire above the kennel and make a shadow on the ground. When this happened, he pointed the shadow very carefully until it, too, was gone.

Always, he wished to pounce upon the sparrow, or its shadow; but he was a son of Roderigo – the great Roderigo who never flushed a bird – and so he held his point, with no one there to see.

Sparrows were few, however. They seldom came to his yard. In the long hours between their visits he was lonesome. He grew to have a wistful expression, and a grin that went to the heart. He seemed to be grinning at himself. The last son of Roderigo was a runt! It was a joke, a grim joke, and he grinned at it.

When winter withdrew at last and spring marched over the hills to Brookfield, a great washing descended upon the kennels and no one escaped.

Highland Lassie's puppy was smitten with the rest. He was taken by a kennel boy to the washroom and there he suffered in silence. The bath brought out his markings clearly, and after a casual glance at him Peter bent over and examined his left side.

"Now ain't that a curious mark?" he said. "It might 'ave been painted on 'im, it's that perfect. It's like one of them things the strong man 'olds up in the circus – I forget what you call 'em. 'E's the runt, by the old dog out of the Lassie bitch, ain't 'e?"

"Yep," said the kennel boy. 'He's all alone in No. 9 runway."

"You 'aven't growed much 'ave you?" said Peter.

The wee son of Roderigo, his eyes still smarting from carbolic soap, looked up at Peter and grinned.

Peter drew in his breath sharply.

"Bli' me!" he said. "The beggar knows. . .Not much doin' down there in No. 9, is there? 'Ow'd you like to see the world for a while?"

Once more the puppy grinned up at him.

"All right," said Peter. "I'll come an' get you when I'm through."

An hour later Peter opened the gate of runway No. 9.

"Come on out, Runt!" he said cheerfully. And the runt, for that, it seemed, was to be his name, came out. He stood for a moment, dazed by sudden freedom, then sped like an arrow far across the lawn. Peter's eyes lighted.

"'E can move!" he said. Then his face fell. "But what'll that get him?" he muttered. "'E couldn't step over a lead pencil!"

Each morning from then on, the runt was let out to follow Peter about the place. Peter was in a cheerful mood these days. The master and mistress of Brookfield would soon return from Florida, and he was anticipating a triumph.

"Won't the missus squeal when she sees 'im!" he thought, as he brushed the shining coat of the Dan Gath puppy. "Eh, Runt?" he said aloud. And the runt, who had been gravely watching, grinned, "I wish you'd quit that!" Peter told him. "It gives me the creeps!"

When at last the great day came, Peter scorned delay. The mistress of Brookfield was still in her hat and gloves when she heard that he was waiting in the rose garden.

"What does he want?" she asked. "I've hardly caught my breath!"

She was told that he had something to show her.

"Oh!" she said, and went to the terrace that looked down into the garden.

Then Peter had his triumph. He was standing at the foot of the terrace in the sunshine, and by his side was a living marvel, new washed and glistening.

The mistress of Brookfield stared, breathless for a moment.

"Oh, Peter! she gasped. "He's a wonder dog! Bring him inside!"

"Yes, mem," said Peter, beaming.

"Bring him to the living-room, Peter. Mr. Gregory's in there!"

She turned to the door, failing to see that other who had followed Peter uncertainly into the rose garden. She was excited to begin with, and he was very small. Also, he felt that he did not belong in the sunshine beside the wonder dog; so he had hidden himself behind a rosebush and watched her through the leaves.

When they went into the house and left him, he crept up in the steps, crossed the terrace, and halted at the open door. . .Peter had gone in here with the pretty lady, and it was his habit to follow Peter. He put a timid forepaw across the threshold – nothing happened. He tried the other paw – still nothing happened. He caught the scent of Peter now; so slowly and with caution he took up the trail.

Presently he came to a big room, and saw Peter and the pretty lady and a tall man looking at the wonder dog. He wished to keep out of sight until Peter was ready to go. The recess of the bay window seemed an excellent retreat and he slipped into it. A doggy smell came to him as he did so. He advanced and found a huge chair with bulging arms and a well-hollowed seat.

He loved the chair at sight. It seemed so friendly and safe. It seemed to hold out its arms to him in welcome. Why, it actually seemed glad to see him! Perhaps it didn't know that he was a runt. . . He curled down into its soft hollow with a deep sigh of contentment.

The master of Brookfield was still staring at the wonder dog.

"How did you do it, Peter?" he said at last. "He's too good to be true!"

"'E'll be true," said Peter, "if breedin'll do it. 'E's by Dan Gath, out of Black-Eyed Susan. You get one like 'im out of a thousand matin's – maybe."

"He's handsome enough," said the master of Brookfield. "But – what will be do in the field?"

"Listen," said Peter: "I've 'ad 'im on larks a time or two, an' I'm tellin' you now, we never bred a faster, wider, higher-'eaded goin' pup. . .but one." He glanced toward the leather chair, and a look of bewilderment came into his face, which changed to one of horror. "'Eavens above!" he said. "Look there!"

They followed his gaze, conscious for the first time of a strange sound which rose and fell steadily in the bay window.

Curled deep in Roderigo's chair was the runt, and, as Peter told the kennel men afterward, "'E was snorin' that 'eavy you could 'ear 'im all through the room."

"And what the devil is that?" said the master of Brookfield, after a stunned silence.

"The runt of the last litter by the old dog," said Peter. "'E just come along."

247

"Yes – I see he did," said the master of Brookfield. "Come here, you!" he called.

The runt opened one eye, twitched his tail sleepily, and closed the eye again. That was all.

A whip hung in the bay window. The terrier who lived at the house could have told the runt what that whip was for. In a moment the tall man stood above him.

"Get down out of that!" he said, and flicked the whip over the chair.

The runt was frightened. The big chair was his only friend, it seemed. He shrank deeper into it as the whip was raised above him.

"Don't! Please, Jim!" said the mistress of Brookfield. "He's so little. He'll learn soon enough." She came and took the runt by his scruff. "Get down, little mannie," she said, "this place isn't for you."

"I 'ope not!" said Peter.

"Never mind, Peter," she said. "It isn't his fault that he's little and that was his daddy's chair. . . Oh, Jim! See that dumb-bell on his side! Look! It's perfect!"

"That's too bad!" said the master of Brookfield, examining the mark.

"Why too bad?" asked Mrs. Gregory.

The master of Brookfield winked at Peter.

"We'll never be able to lose him," he explained. "Will we?" he said to the runt, and the runt looked up and grinned.

Mrs. Gregory gave a quick little gasp.

"I hate such jokes!" she said. "Is he registered, Peter?"

"No, mem," said Peter.

"Well, register him as Brookfield Dumb-Bell – and give him every chance." Suddenly she stepped close to the runt. "You two may have the *beauty* there," she flashed; "and his missy will look after *him*!"

"Why, Chief!" said the master of Brookfield.

"I don't care!" she said. "He's little – and I think he knows it – and it isn't his fault!" Then she went out of the room.

The master of Brookfield rubbed his chin thoughtfully.

"Now what did *we* do, Peter?" he asked.

It was a hot summer that year. Day after day the sun glared down at Brookfield, and the runt panted as he followed Peter. Often when visitors arrived and Peter was told to bring the wonder dog to the house, the runt came along.

He was always embarrassed during these visits. He felt smaller than ever in the stately rooms of the big house. But he

248

remembered his friend the chair, and while the visitors were exclaiming over the wonder dog he would slip away quietly and crawl into it.

He was whipped for this several times, but he never seemed to learn; so at last he was put back in runway No. 9, where there were no chairs at all, only loneliness and an occasional sparrow.

"One day the master of Brookfield visited the kennels.

"Peter," he said, "ship the Dan Gath puppy to Ramsey, in Tennessee. Ship him tomorrow night. Wire Ramsey. . .Hot, isn't it?"

"What about 'im?" said Peter, jerking his thumb toward a runway.

"What do you mean?" asked the master of Brookfield. Then he saw the occupant of No. 9 staring wistfully out at Peter.

"Oh!" he said, "you break him this fall for a shooting dog. He ought to have a nose on him."

As Peter was going over a dog crate next day he looked up find the mistress of Brookfield watching him.

"Good morning, Peter," she said. "What's that crate for?"

"I'm shippin' the Dan Gath pup away tonight, mem," said Peter. "'E's to 'ave a chance at the trials."

"Why have you brought out only one crate?" asked the mistress of Brookfield.

"I'm only shippin' one dog," said Peter, tapping away with his hammer.

"Ah!" said she. "And when does the runt go?"

"'E don't go," said Peter, "I'm to break 'im myself – for a shootin' dog."

"Peter!" said the mistress of Brookfield.

"Yes, mem," said Peter uneasily.

"Get out another crate, please." And when two crates stood side by side, the mistress of Brookfield touched one of them with her finger tips.

"The little chap," she said, "goes in this crate tonight. Do you understand me, Peter?"

"Yes, mem," said Peter.

"And, Peter – tell Ramsey to send the training bills to *me*."

"Yes, mem," said Peter.

Two weeks later the mails brought a letter to Brookfield. It was address to Peter, and this is how it ran:

Emeryville, Tennessee, R.R. No. 4
Sept. 6, 19 –
Friend Peter:
I take shame in telling you the small pup is lost. He found a bevy the first day I took him out, chased when they flushed, and I ain't seen him since. I've hunted the country over and offered big rewards. Tell Mrs. Gregory, and say a good word for me. The big pup is doing fine. I like every move he makes. I'll keep on looking for the little pup, and that's all at present.

Yours in friendship,
W. Ramsey

Peter sat on a sawhorse and slowly read his letter. He moved to an over-turned grindstone, seeking a better light, and read it again. He looked up toward the house, a black pile against the setting sun, and whistled softly.

"'Ell will be to pay shortly," he muttered, and moved reluctantly to his doom.

The master of Brookfield had been to the cattle barns to watch the milking. When he returned, he found that Peter was something of a prophet. He found his lady bathed in tears, Peter standing miserably before her, and maids running in all directions.

"I'm going to Tennessee tonight!" she gasped. "Read that!"

"But, Chief!" said the master of Brookfield when he had read the letter. "You couldn't possibly do any good down there. If Ramsey, who knows every foot of the country, can't find him, how can you expect to?"

"I'll send down a motor and ride all day," she told him. "You can come too – and Peter – and Felix to drive. . ."

"Is that all?" he said. "We'll be quite a party. It's out of the question, my dear. . .I'll tell Ramsey to double the reward and do everything possible. . . You'll make yourself sick if you don't stop crying!"

"We have lost him, you see! In spite of your horrid joke about it. Now I hope you and Peter are satisfied! I'll write to Ramsey!" she added ominously. "Oh, I'll write to *him*!"

When W. Ramsey, Esq., received a letter a few days later, he whistled over it much as Peter had whistled over his.

"I guess I'd better quit trainin'," he muttered, "an' go to pup

250

huntin' for a perfession!"

And until he went West with his "string," the redoubtable Bill Ramsey, high-priced specialist in the training and handling of field trial setters, turned his field work and yard-breaking over to an assistant, and scoured the country day after day. But no one had seen a "real small setter with a funny mark on his side," and he never found a trace of what he sought.

Brookfield Beau Brummell No. 43721 F.D.S.B., for such was now the wonder dog's official title, was taken to a country where he could go far, and fast, and wide.

In the cramped valleys and thicket-rimmed fields of the East, bobwhite lives close to cover, and field trial dogs are educated in the land of the prairie chicken, where their handlers can keep them in sight for mile after level mile.

The Beau was put down one morning with the veteran Rappahannock as guide, counselor, and friend. The sun was beginning to climb the eastern side of the huge blue void which domed an ocean of grass.

"Hi, yah! Get away!" yelled Ramsey.

Rappahannock, free of the leash, shot over a gentle rise and was gone. He had eaten up a good half-mile of country when the frost-bitten grass began to whisper just behind him. He flattened out in a desperate effort to shake off the whisper, but the whisper grew to the soft pad, pad of flying feet as the Beau, moving like oil, flowed past.

Ramsey lowered his field-glasses and smiled.

"Look out for that one, Mike!" he called to his assistant. "They've bred another bird dog at Brookfield!"

As time went on and the Beau developed into a prodigy of speed, range and nose, Peter went about his work with a far-away look in his eyes. His body was at Brookfield, his spirit in Manitoba. The Beau would make his first start in the great Canadian stake, and – "They can't beat him!" was the word that came from Ramsey.

On the day the stake was run, Peter sat on the grindstone and whittled. He spoke no word to anyone. Late in the evening the telephone bell rang in the kennels, but Peter never stirred. A kennel boy approached him timidly.

"They want you up to the house," said the boy; and Peter

closed his knife and rose.

He found the mistress of Brookfield in the living-room. Her cheeks were flushed, her eyes like stars. She was dancing about the master of Brookfield with a fluttering telegram in her hand.

"Peter!" she said, "Oh, Peter! See what our boy's done!"

Peter read the telegram, then looked at the master of Brookfield through half-shut lids.

"If they don't watch 'im, 'e'll likely take the National," he said.

"It's possible," said the master of Brookfield. "Yes, it's possible."

"Why, of course," said Mrs. Gregory. "Didn't you know that? He's to be champion. . .Outclassed his field!" she sang. "Did you read that, Peter? Read it again."

This was only the beginning. The Beau swept through field trial after field trial, piling victory upon victory. He won again in Canada. He came nearer home, into Illinois, to take the Independent All Age from the best dogs in the field. He went down into Georgia, and left his field gasping behind him in the select Continental. He won "off by himself," as Ramsey said in the Eastern Subscription against twenty-five starters, and "every dog worth a million dollars!"

He was certain to take the National. No other dog could stand his pace in the three-hour running of the Championship. Rival handlers conceded this, and Black-Eyed Susan came into her own.

"Susan is trying not to look down on the rest of us, Peter," explained the mistress of Brookfield.

Peter watched Black-Eyed Susan partake of crackers and cream languidly, and from a silver spoon.

"I can't say as 'ow you're 'elpin' 'er much," he said.

Then suddenly Ramsey was smitten with inflammatory rheumatism, and the Beau was turned over to Scott Benson, who would handle him in his other engagements.

"Don't worry," Peter told the master of Brookfield. "Scott's a good 'andler. It's all over, anyway, but the United States and the Championship. . .Are you goin' down?"

"To the National? Why, yes" said the master of Brookfield. He caught a wistful look in Peter's eyes. "Would *you* care to go?" he asked.

Peter bent over and picked up a willow twig for whittling purposes.

"Why, I expect the boys could look after things here for a day or two," he said.

The United States All Age was the last big stake before the Championship. On the morning after it was run, Peter was whistling as he sprinkled the whelping shed with disinfectant. Footsteps crunched on the gravel outside and he stepped to the door. The master of Brookfield stood there with a newspaper in his hand.

"He was beaten, Peter," he said.

"*No!*" said Peter. And after a silence – "What beat 'im?"

"Little Sam," said the master of Brookfield.

"An' who is Little Sam?" asked Peter.

"I don't know," said the master of Brookfield. "I never heard of him before. Our dog was second. Here! Read it yourself."

The dispatch was short:

Grand Junction, Tenn., Jan. 8.
In the All Age stake of the United States Field Trial Club, Little Sam, lemon and white setter, handled by C.E. Todd, was first. Brookfield Beau Brummel, black, white and ticked setter, handled by Scott Benson, was second. Thirty-two starters.

"C.E. Todd!" said Peter. "Why, that's Old Man Todd – 'e's eighty years old if 'e's a day! What's 'e doin' back in the game?"

"Don't ask me!" said the master of Brookfield. "He's back, it would seem, and he's brought a dog."

"Do you think 'e'll start 'im in the National?" Peter inquired.

"I presume so," said the master of Brookfield. "You're to bring the Beau home, Peter – if he wins."

"An' if 'e don't – win?" asked Peter.

"Why then," said the master of Brookfield, "he can stay in training and try again next year."

Three days later the mistress of Brookfield stood with Black-Eyed Susan in the high stone arch of the front entrance. "You're to bring home the champion, Peter!" she called. "Don't fail us, will you? – Susy and me? There's some light underwear in the black bag, Jim; it may be warm in Tennessee. Good-by. . .Good-by, Peter. . . Your shaving things are in the small bag, Jim! Peter – Peter! Don't forget Susy and me – we'll be waiting!"

"No, mem," said Peter stoutly. But as he watched the landscape slide steadily northward the ties clicked a fearsome refrain: "*Little*

253

Sam!" they said, *"Little Sam!"*

Grand Junction was reached at last. Scott Benson was the first to greet them at the packed and roaring hotel.

"Well," said the master of Brookfield, "how does it look?"

The trainer shook his head.

"Bad, Mr. Gregory," he said. "We've got an awful dog to beat."

"You mean the dog that old Todd's got?" said Peter.

"Yes," said Scott. "That's what I mean – but he ain't a dog."

"What is 'e, then?" asked Peter.

"He's a flyin' machine, with a telescope nose. You got a grand dog, Mr. Gregory, a grand dog. A gamer dog never lived – he'll try all the way; but this here dog that old fool's got a hold of somehow ain't human. In three hours he'll find all the quail in the State!"

"What's 'e look like, an' 'ow's 'e bred?" Peter inquired.

"Get ready to laugh," said Scott. "I forgot to tell you. His breedin's unknown, an' he ain't as big as a stud beagle."

That evening was a trial. Beau Brummell seemed forgotten. The hotel lobby echoed with the name of Little Sam.

"He must be a great dog," smiled the master of Brookfield. "I'll enjoy seeing him run. I think I'll turn in now, Mayor, if you'll excuse me. I'm a little tired from the trip."

Peter sat up longer, half listening to the babble about him. At last he became conscious of a hissing for silence as the secretary climbed to a table top and began to read the drawings for the National.

"Belwin with Dan's Lady!" read the secretary. "Opal Jane with Rappahannock! Bingo with Prince Rodney!" and so the starters in the Championship were paired. At last, at the very end, the secretary paused an instant and smiled grimly. "Brookfield Beau Brummell with Little Sam!" he read, and there was a roar that shook the hotel.

Chuck Sellers leaped upon Peter and took him to his bosom.

"Stick around, Pete!" he yelled. "Stick around for the big show!"

Peter shoved him aside.

"I'm going to bed," he growled. "I 'ope I get a decent 'oss tomorrow."

But fate had a blow in store for Peter. In the scramble for mounts next morning, a big gray mule with a will of his own was "wished on him." as Chuck Sellers put it, and he devoted the next few hours to equestrianship. By the time the second brace was cast off, he had conquered, and he saw good old Rappahannock win on his courage from dashing Opal Jane, who failed to last the three hot hours and was running slower and slower, with a dull nose, when they took her up.

The Championship was run off smoothly. Brace after brace was put down, until at last came Thursday morning and the pair for which they waited.

Peter had been having an argument with his mount, who hated to start in for the day. When it was settled, he looked up to see an old man standing ahead of the judges, with a lemon and white setter who tugged and tugged to be gone. He was small beyond belief, this setter, so small that Peter rubbed his eyes. Then he rode down the line of horsemen until he found Chuck Sellers.

"Don't tell me that's 'im, Chuck?" he said.

"That's him," said Chuck.

"Why a bunch of grass'll stop 'im!" said Peter. "'E ain't big enough to jump it."

"*He* don't jump nothin'," Chuck informed him. "He's got wings."

"'E may lose 'em before three hours," said Peter. "'Im an' 'is breedin' unknown."

"Maybe," said Chuck. "Here's the dog to clip 'em, or it can't be done," and he pointed to Beau Brummell going out to his position.

He was still the wonder dog, a glory every inch of him, and a murmur of admiration rippled down the line of horsemen. . .Peter felt a sudden glow of pride and hope.

But it didn't last.The next moment he was watching a white speck fade away across the stubble. As it grew dimmer and dimmer so did Peter's hopes. The white speck was Little Sam, breeding unknown. When he whirled and came to point, at the far edge of the woods, Brookfield Beau Brummel was a hundred feet behind.

Peter was among the stragglers in the stampede across the field which followed. When he reached the mass of waiting horsemen, Old Man Todd was being helped out of his saddle to shoot over his dog.

With a feeling of numb despair Peter looked for the master of Brookfield. He saw him at last, sitting his horse a little apart from the crowd, his face the color of ashes.

Peter rode to him quickly.

"What's the matter, sir?" he asked. "Are you unwell?"

The master of Brookfield kept his eyes on the pointing dog.

"Look!" he said, "Look!" and Peter looked at Little Sam. Then his heart skipped a beat, fluttered, and sent the blood surging against his eardrums.

Little Sam had his bevy nailed. He stood as though of stone. He looked like white marble against the dark of the woods. And on his side, his left and nearest side, was a perfect lemon dumb-bell. . .

"My Gawd!" said Peter. "My Gawd!"

He swung his eyes along the woods and found another statue. It was Beau Brummell, still as death itself, in honor of his brace mate.

"My Gawd!" said Peter again. "What'll we do?"

"Nothing – now," said the master of Brookfield. "Let the best dog win."

A man should only whisper while the championship is run, but Peter rose in his stirrups, not fifty feet from a brace on point, and disgraced himself forever.

"My money's on the old dog's blood," he howled; *"'an' let the best dog win!"*

"Peter! Peter!" said the master of Brookfield, and took him by the arm.

"I forgot," said Peter sheepishly.

There have been field trials in the past, there will be field trials in the future. But those who saw the whirlwind struggle between the great Beau Brummell and the white ghost with the magic nose will not listen while you tell of them. Eighteen bevies they found that day, and they went at top speed to do it! Not a bird was flushed as they flashed into point after dazzling point, backing each other like gentlemen.

It was perfect bird work, done with marvelous speed, and the Beau had the sympathy of those who watched, for they knew that he was beaten. He had everything that makes a champion, including looks and heart. But the little white dog who skimmed from one covey to the next was more than a champion – he was a miracle. The blazing soul of Roderigo had leaped to life in this, his son, and would not be denied.

An hour or more had passed when Chuck Sellers thought of Peter and sought him out to offer what consolation he could.

"The little dog may quit, Peter," he said, "any time now. It's the last half that tells on the short-bred ones."

Then Peter gave the puzzled Chuck a wide, calm smile.

"Nothing is certain in this 'ere world," he said. "But I'll tell you one thing that is. That little dog won't quit till the pads wear off his feet."

And Peter was right. The announcement of the new champion finished with "breeding unknown."

The crowd swarmed toward the winner, who grinned as they closed about him. They had never seen a National Champion without a pedigree, and they pushed and pulled and laughed and hooted.

A *Field* reporter was yelling at Old Man Todd above the noise.

"The country wants to know this dog's breeding, old man," he said. "And it's got to be traced, if possible."

"He ain't got no breedin', I tell you!" screamed Old Man Todd. "He's a niggah-raised dawg – jes' a niggah-raised dawg!"

The runt was frightened. It must be terrible to be a nigger-raised dog, or all these men wouldn't glare at him and yell! He remembered leaving the place where the big house was, long ago, and riding on a train. He remembered running for miles and miles until he had found that nice shed where he could rest. A black man had come to the shed and given him some milk. He drank it all and went to sleep.

Next he remembered hunting birds with the black man every day. One day an old man had watched him find some birds and had talked with the black man. Then he was taken away by the old man, and had hunted birds with him ever since.

They had had a good hunt today. But now he was tired, and they all yelled at him so – then someone pushed and fought his way through the crowd, and the runt was glad to see him, for it was Peter, whom he had followed long ago.

The runt went to him quickly, and Peter fell on one knee and put an arm about him.

"Runt!" said Peter. "Runt! – You're yer daddy's own son!"

The runt grinned, and Peter put him down and took hold of the leash.

"Let go of this, Old Man," he said.

It is not a good thing to win the championship with a "niggah-raised" dog when that dog has been advertised over an entire State as lost. Old Man Todd looked into Peter's eyes.

"Why – why –" he began, and stopped. Then his fingers

unclosed from the leash and he backed slowly into the crowd.

Peter whirled about and faced the reporter, with the runt close at his side.

"Now, Mr. Reporter," he said. "you can put in your paper that Brookfield Dumb-Bell by Champion Brookfield Roderigo 'as won the National. You can say the new champion is out of Brookfield 'Ighland Lassie. You can tell 'em 'e was bred and whelped at Brookfield – and now 'e's goin' 'ome."

The reporter was dancing up and down. His face was red and he had lost his hat. "How can I verify this?" he yelled. "How can I verify this?"

Suddenly the runt saw the tall man who lived in the big house he dimly remembered. He had always been afraid of the tall man – he was so quiet. He was quiet now. He didn't yell at all, but when he held up his hand everybody kept still.

"I can verify it for you," he said.

"Mr. Gregory!" said the reporter, "Good, very good – excellent! Will you let me have the facts as quickly as possible, please? I've got to catch the evening papers!"

Peter didn't stay to hear what the tall man said, and the runt was glad, for he was tired. But Peter put him on a train and he couldn't sleep it jiggled so, and the baggage man gave him part of his supper. When other men came into the car, the baggage man pointed to him and said something about "National Champion," and "worth ten thousand dollars" and the men came and stared at the runt.

At last they got out of the train, and he and Peter and the tall man rode in an automobile till they went through some gates, and the runt saw the lights of the big house shining through the trees.

"Where shall I take him," asked Peter, "to the kennels?"

The tall man dropped his hand on the runt's head.

"I think not, Peter," he said; and they all got out at the front door.

As they came into the hall someone called from upstairs, and the runt recognized the voice of the pretty lady.

"Oh, Jim!" said the voice. "Why didn't you wire? Did Beau Brummell win?"

"No," said the tall man. "He was runner up."

"Oh!" said the voice, and then nothing more for a while, and the runt could hear the big clock ticking in the hall.

"Is Peter there?" said the voice at last.

"Yes, mem," said Peter.

"You went back on Susy and me, didn't you, Peter?" said the voice.

"Come down here, Chief!" said the tall man. "Unleash him!" he directed in a low voice, and Peter did so.

The runt threw up his head and sniffed. He was so tired by now that his legs were beginning to shake, and he wanted a place to lie down. . .then suddenly he remembered. He walked to the living-room and peered in. . .Yes, there was his friend the chair, holding out its arms to him. . .The runt gave a deep sigh as he curled himself into it.

The tall man who had followed laughed softly.

"And that's all right!" he said.

Just then the pretty lady came in.

"Why – what dog is that?" she asked.

"Don't you know?" said the tall man.

The pretty lady stared at the runt very hard. He became uneasy, and grinned. The pretty lady shrieked and ran to him.

"Little mannie!" she said, hugging him until he could feel her heart beating against his side. "Where did they find you, little mannie?"

"At Grand Junction," said the tall man.

"What was he doing there?" asked the pretty lady.

"A good deal," said the tall man.

The pretty lady gave the runt a last big squeeze, then she straightened up.

"Oh, Runt!" she said. "Darling Runt – you're just as bad as ever!" She put her hand on his collar. "Come!" she said. "This place isn't for you."

But the tall man stepped forward, and took her hand from the collar. His eyes were shining queerly and his voice was husky.

"Let him alone, my dear!" he said. "Let him alone!"

It was nice of the tall man to do this, thought the runt. He must have known how tired, how very tired, he was. He curled himself deep in the chair and began to snore. . . In his dreams he heard the tall man talking, and then the pretty lady bent above him, and a wet drop fell on his nose.

WE SHOT THE
Tamales

BY JACK O'CONNOR

Jack O'Connor (1902-1978) was America's most
popular gun writer. Through his long-running column
as Shooting Editor for *Outdoor Life*, his many books,
and countless feature articles, O'Connor established
himself as a crusty, credible authority on guns. He
could write like a dream. Among his greatest assets
were his feel for place and a rare knack for sharing
adventures in such a way that his reader is carried
immediately to the scene. Here, in a story with a
delightful twist for its conclusion, we join O'Connor
and his wife on a Mexican hunt for Coues whitetails.

he Little Dove was pouting, and when she pouts she is
such a virtuoso that connoisseurs come from miles around
to watch and to admire. Hers is a restrained and ladylike
pout, an I-married-a-madman-but-I'll-bravely-put-up-with-it
pout. It would break your heart to watch her.

She had gone into her act when we pulled up in front of the
group of three adobe houses down there in Sonora and I had

stopped the car in front of the most dilapidated and had said, "Well, here we are. Here's home!" She could look through the doorless entrance and see evidence that cows had used the hut as a refuge during bad weather. She could see the litter of thorny cholla balls, cow dung, sticks and trash that was a pack rat's nest in one corner. Where we sat in the noon-day Mexican sun at over four thousand feet elevation, the thin invigorating high-altitude air was pleasantly warm. The frost of winter nights still hung in that miserable adobe hut, however, and when a gentle breeze stirred we could feel and smell the chill, dank, musty effluvium of the old house. . .bats and manure and pack rats and the faint ghosts of gone and forgotten Mexican meals.

The three houses which formed the village were about a hundred miles south of the American border in Sonora and about twenty-five miles from the good highway that leads from Nogales, Arizona, south to Hermosillo, Sonora. As you shall see, it was and probably still is one of the greatest whitetail countries on earth. I had found the spot the previous year by the simple expedient of turning off the highway and following a miserable excuse for a road that led toward the blue, oak-clad mountains to the east. Now I was sharing my find with my family.

The two boys, Brad and Jerry, then little fellows, were sitting on a pile of bedrolls, food and gear in the back of the car. They looked around with wide-eyed interest.

"Is this where we are going to stay?" Brad asked.

"Yes," I said.

"It stinks, Daddy," he told me.

"Mamma's mad," said Jerry.

"Come on, boys, and help me unload the car and make camp," I ordered.

With the broom which I had brought along I swept out the litter in the hut. The "stove" was a raised platform of adobe (dry mud bricks) under a hole in the roof which served as a chimney. Some of the numerous scrubby chickens that ran around the place dodging skunks, coyotes, foxes, and hawks and somehow making a precarious living from bugs and weed seeds had been roosting on the stove, and it was littered with their feathers and their droppings.

Gradually the boys and I made order in the hut. We put up our four folding cots and laid the bedrolls on them, set up a folding table and stools, stacked the food boxes so they were accessible, built a fire on the *estufa*. Slowly the place warmed up.

Finally I opened a couple of split pints of Hermosillo beer and called my wife: "Come here, my proud beauty, and I'll buy you a beer!" I heard the door of the car slam and presently she came in looking slightly sheepish. She glanced around and grinned.

"I've been acting like a heel," she said, "and I'm sorry. You and the boys have been sweet. I was tired and this place was so horrible I just couldn't face it!"

Some Mexican children had been eyeing the activity in our hut from a distance and now they gathered up enough courage to peer in the door. There were three of them – a little girl about six, a boy of eight or nine, and another of twelve or so. The two youngest children wore only very dirty blue shirts, and the twelve-year-old was clad in what was left of the upper third of what had once been a pair of cotton pants, but which now was little more than a breechclout.

"What are you called?" I said to the children.

The little ones squirmed in horrible embarrassment but the twelve-year-old said, "I am called José."

"Who is your papa?"

"My papa is Manuel Parades, and I know who you are. You are one of the three gringo hunters."

"Where is your papa?"

"He is up the little river to wash for gold."

Eleanor dug around in a grub box and presently came up with a box of chocolate candy someone had given us for Christmas. She extended it to the children. "Like candy?" she asked. With a little coaxing the children each took a piece, sampled cautiously, gobbled enthusiastically, then took another. For a few minutes our boys and the Mexican children stared at each other as if they were from another planet, then they all went out to play.

As the babble of their voices faded away, Eleanor got up off her stool, walked to the corner where her .257 was leaning in its saddle scabbard. She picked it up, withdrew the bolt and looked through the bore, blew some dust from the scope lenses, buckled on a little leather cartridge box. Then she turned to me. "I want to go hunting."

"It's a bit late, old girl, but we'll take a turn and see what we can see," I said.

It was only a little after three when we started out, but the December sun was already headed for the horizon and a faint chill in the thin clean air was replacing the warmth of midday. To the north the mountain range rose like a wall. The lower slopes were thinly clad in picturesque and thorny desert growth—saguaro (giant cactus), palo verde, cholla, different varieties of long-armed feathery ocotillo. High up at the heads of the canyons the thorny stuff was replaced by the evergreen oaks the Mexicans call *encinos*. Still higher on the lofty peaks and ridges grew great yellow pines with red boles and whispering open crowns.

My plan was to hunt south along the foot of the big mountain a mile and a half or so to a cluster of brushy foothills where the year before I had always seen deer. We hadn't gone a quarter of a mile when we ran a young doe out of the brush and up on the mountainside. Deer sign was everywhere. Now and then we'd hear them move off in the brush but for a time we saw no more.

When we got to the little foothills I told the gal to sit down on a hillside overlooking a saddle between the two highest knobs. It was a natural deer pass, and I thought I could run some deer through it by working around the hills. I sat down in the sun and waited for her to climb to the saddle. Once as she toiled up the slope I saw the gray form of a deer slipping through the brush to her right. Finally I saw her come out on the saddle and walk up the hill where she sat down with her rifle over her knees and lit a cigarette. Then I took to the brush.

I hadn't gone fifty yards when I heard a deer move in front of me. Then I heard another. Droppings were everywhere and so were fresh tracks. I was halfway around the hill and was heading back toward the saddle when I heard two shots. When I got to the pass Eleanor was standing over two bucks, one a fine big four-pointer, the other a spike.

"Good going," I said. "How many did you see?"

"Gobs," she told me. "First I saw a whole bunch of does and little cute fawns. I was watching them when a great big buck sneaked by before I could get a shot at him. Then these two came over!"

I laid the old .30/06 up against a boulder, took out my pocketknife and removed the insides from the two bucks. Then I

263

put each across a big boulder, propped open the belly cavities with sticks so the frosty night air would chill them out. "Well," I said finally, "let's wobble back to our little gray home in the West. Night is coming on, my pretty, and if we don't hustle we might get et up by coyotes or mountain lions or something."

"You take the little buck," Eleanor said, "and I'll take both rifles."

"They'll keep. We'll come back with Manuel in the morning with horses."

"If you don't carry that buck in, I'll do it myself. Didn't you notice those kids? They were starving! Did you see those big bellies, those skinny legs, the hollow eyes? I'll bet they haven't had any decent food in months."

In some ways I am a fairly observant character. In others I am not. Since the gal had mentioned it, I remembered that those kids *had* looked pretty gaunt and wide-eyed. It occurred to me that the people along the *rillito* might have been having a tough time. They had a few rocky little *milpas* back in the canyon, where they diverted water from the creek to raise corn and a little chili. When they were feeling industrious they panned gold in the sands, but it was hard, poorly paid work and if they got a few flecks to the pan it was about all they could expect. In addition the storekeepers back in the towns on the highway generally gave them about half what their gold was worth. They had got most of their cash income by acting as cowboys for a rancher who had run cattle in the area, *but* there had been a drought in that country and for a couple of years now there had been no cattle in there. That meant no wages for cartridges, for sugar, for coffee, for lard.

That little spike buck was deliciously fat, though I seriously doubt if he dressed out more than sixty pounds, maybe not over fifty. But as anyone who has ever lugged one in over his shoulder knows, a dead deer is pound for pound probably the heaviest burden in the world. It was almost dark when we got back to our hut. The five kids were playing in front of the shack. José was teaching Bradford how to handle a lariat by roping the little girl. All were smeared ear to ear with chocolate and the box of candy was a shambles.

Manuel, the father of the three, had returned from his placer mining. He came up to greet me with a smile and the characteristic limp handshake of the country Mexican. Manuel was a rough and skinny little hombre, a fine horseman, and a good hunter; but right then he was pale under his tan. When he helped me hang the little buck in the enormous mesquite tree that grew in front of the houses, even lifting his share of that diminutive buck seemed an effort.

"How are things going, Manuel?" I asked.

"So, so," he said.

"I'll take the backstraps of this little buck for breakfast. You take the rest."

"Thanks," he said, his face lighting up.

"Have you had much meat of the deer to eat?" I asked.

"I have no money to buy cartridges!"

"Do you have coffee?"

"We have no money to buy coffee."

The staples of life to the poor Mexican are *frijoles* (beans), coffee, a coarse and unrefined but delicious sugar called *pinoche*, meat, lard, and corn. With no work, no cartridges, little gold dust, the families down there on the creek at the edge of the mountains had been living for months, I found out, on field corn boiled in water with a little salt. Now and then they had devoured one of the scrubby little chickens that had escaped the predators and occasionally they had fed the children an egg

"But we are very poor," he concluded. "Many times the children cry because their bellies hurt. This meat will taste good!" Then his face clouded. "Soon comes the New Year. Now we have meat, but we do not have fat. We cannot make tamales and enchiladas. Alas, we have no coffee. We do not even have an onion! We cannot have a feast!"

Eleanor, whose knowledge of Spanish is far from profound, had nevertheless been catching a word now and then as Manuel and I skinned the buck. When I came in with the backstraps, the glowing gasoline lantern had made the hut bright and cheerful and good smells came from pots on the fire built on the mud platform which was our stove.

"Things are pretty tough with them, aren't they?" she asked.

"They've been living on dried corn boiled in water. They don't even have any fat. Nor do they have coffee. I can't imagine a Mexican house without coffee or tortillas!"

She started rummaging through our supplies.

"We can spare some sugar," she said taking a sack out, "and we can give them a pound of coffee, some lard, and some canned fruit. I'll give them a couple of loaves of this bread we brought from home. I'll make biscuits in the Dutch oven. I can spare some flour, too. With the venison they can have a feed tonight."

"What hurts Manuel," I told her, "is that the New Year is coming up in a few days. They haven't got the makings of tamales and enchiladas. You know how Mexicans are about holidays. Tamales are to them what the New Year's goose is to us!"

"We'll fix that!" she said.

That night there was feasting and merrymaking in the little community. Now that the housewives had lard, they ground up corn into coarse meal in the same sort of stone *metates* their Indian ancestors had used a thousand years before. Then with salt, lard, and water they made the corn cakes called *tortillas* and cooked them on a piece of sheet iron over an open fire. The coffeepot bubbled and from an old lard can on the fire rose the delicious odor of venison and chili bubbling along with an onion Eleanor had furnished. But as the coffee and the tortillas were finished, most could not wait for the stew. Instead they cut strips of meat from the little buck, toasted them over oak and mesquite coals, and devoured them with a little salt. The meat and the coffee made them a little giddy, and later, I fear, someone broke out a jug of home-distilled *sotol*, a drink which tastes, to me anyway, like rubbing alcohol mixed with high-test gasoline.

Before I turned in I sat around the fire for a time and talked to the men about the coming hunt. Manuel promised to be out at the crack of dawn to catch the horses so, as he put it, we "could hunt while the frost still lay on the grass and the big bucks stood stiff and shivering on the ridges." I gave Manuel and his brother Ramon seventy-five pesos in advance for horse and guide hire and in addition twenty-five pesos for *treinta-treinta* (.30/30) cartridges. In those days that was about twenty dollars, but it would buy some cartridges and a lot of simple food. While Manuel hunted with Eleanor and me, Ramon was to ride into town by a short cut with a packhorse and return with frijoles, lard, sugar, coffee and onions. Before I left the fire, the kids had gone to bed in a clammy unheated room in their parents' house. I peeked in to see how they were making out. The three were huddled together on a cowhide which lay hair side up on the dirt floor and over them was a thin cotton blanket!

When I joined my family in our own hut, I was told that a burro had tried to move in on them for the night and they had been forced to throw out a scrubby little rooster they had found perched quietly on the stove. As we dozed off to sleep, the place next door was still jumping.

The next morning I was already awake when the little rooster Eleanor had given the bum's rush the night before greeted the dawn from the big mesquite. I got up, started the fire on the adobe platform, got a bucket of water from the *rillito*, made coffee, fried bacon and backstrap, and browned toast. Presently we were all dressed and organized. But no horses arrived and no sound did we hear from next door.

Presently, though, I heard an axe whacking at the woodpile and went out to see Manuel's wife gathering wood for the fire.

"Where's Manuel?" I asked.

"Sick at the stomach," she told me, shaking her head.

Just then Ramon's *esposa* emerged with a bucket to go to the creek. By a curious coincidence Ramon was also a bit under the weather with an ailing stomach. It was, they told me, a case of too much fresh meat. The *sotol*? Of course the *sotol* could have had nothing to do with it, as it is a fact known all over Mexico that there is nothing like a slug of *sotol* to settle the stomach . . .

I didn't want to let the big buck Eleanor had shot the night before get warm from the sun, so I caught the indignant burro that tried to move in the night before, managed to put an oversize sawbuck pack saddle on him, and while he moaned and protested like a man having his leg cut off I led him into the hills, loaded the buck on him, and managed to get him back.

By that time, so slow had we progressed, it was almost noon. Eleanor told me that not long after I left, Ramon had ridden off to town to buy .30/30 cartridges and grub and that Manuel had gone into the hills to find our horses. In the meantime, Eleanor had taken her shotgun and had hiked with the boys back into one of the *milpas* in the canyon where she shot eight of the gorgeous tropical Benson quail, birds of blue, gray and orange with long orange topknots. So far as I know that little *milpa* is the very northern limit of the range of this, "the elegant quail," as it is sometimes called.

We lived a wonderful, lazy life those ten days we stayed in the village. If we wanted to hunt quail we had our choice of the lovely Benson quail up there in the *milpas* where the little river came out of the mountains through a deep canyon or the Gambel's quail that lived lower down along the arroyos. And that isn't all! One day when we hunted high in the mountains in a region where cattle seldom ranged and the gramma grass was belly high to a horse, Manuel saw some Mearns quail scurrying through the grass. He was carrying the shotgun on his horse for us that day, so Eleanor piled off and went on a quail hunt there at seven thousand feet elevation on the grassy slope of a big peak. The Mearns quail is generally called the fool quail. He is a simple and trusting soul who depends on squatting in the grass for protection against hawks. Often he can be killed with sticks or even picked up in the hand – hence the name. He is, though, one of the most delicious birds in North America. For a quail, he has a very large breast, tender, delicious, faintly flavored with all manner of wild and wonderful things.

And every afternoon not long before sundown hundreds of mourning doves came hurtling down right across our adobe hut from the mountains. They fed up there on weed and grass seeds during the day and then as the afternoon shadows lengthened they came whistling down from the heights to water in the creek and roost in the cottonwoods that grew along its banks. When the flight was on and we wanted a dove stew, all we had to do was to step out of our hut and go into action.

Deer were everywhere – high on the grassy ridges, in the oak thickets of the draws up in the hills, clear down in the cactus and catclaw. Sometimes we'd ride far back into the hills, but often we'd simply walk out from the house. Once Eleanor went on an expedition with the two boys over toward the hills where she had got the bucks the first day. Presently I heard a shot and a little later Brad came running back to tell me that mamma had shot a buck and for me to come and "take its stomach out and throw it away."

I tried to space the shooting of my own limit of three bucks in order to meet the food situation, and I must have seen fifty or sixty mature bucks I never fired a shot at. A couple of times I rode out with Manuel, let him carry and use my rifle to get some meat. I have a suspicion that Manuel and Ramon traded some deer they had killed with the .30/30 ammunition I had bought them for some more food and some clothes because José showed up with a shirt and a pair of pants and the little girl was bouncing around in a calico dress. This was the day after three nice fat bucks disappeared from the big mesquite tree in front of the house.

At any rate, the two families were eating well and were thriving. It was wonderful to see how quickly the gaunt faces filled out and color came into those pale cheeks. The day before the New Year there was a great hustle and bustle in the houses along the creek as the women made tamales for the New Year feast. They ground up corn, mixed it into a white paste with lard, flavored it with salt. They boiled quantities of venison, then diced it up, flavored it with a rich chili sauce. They washed, sorted, and trimmed corn husks. Then the women spread the corn mixture on the husks, put on a dab of the meat and chile mixture and folded it all up into a tamale. That night we could see clouds of mist rising from a big lard tin as they steamed them.

On New Year's Eve, it pains me to admit, the O'Connors were all busy pounding their ears as the old year died and a new one came into being. The boys had insisted that they were going to stay up until midnight, so after we had eaten we tuned in the portable radio on an American station. They had played hard during the day, though, and by nine o'clock they decided it would be nicer to listen from their beds. In a few minutes they were asleep. Earlier that day Ramon had brought us over a bottle of sotol from a still he had back in the hills. Valiantly we tried to drink some of it mixed with grapefruit juice, but it didn't put us into any holiday spirit and by ten o'clock we were in our sleeping bags.

The next morning the sun was well up and the Mexican women were bustling before I awakened. For once my friend the little rooster whom we had run out of the house into the big mesquite had forgotten to greet the dawn. After breakfast Eleanor decided that she'd take the boys and go quail hunting down the creek where there were several coveys of Gambel's. With Ramon I rode down to the southeast to see if I couldn't wind up my limit of three bucks, since about all the meat that was left had gone into tamales.

In a little chain of round, cactus-covered hills, I tied my horse, took my old .30/06 out of the saddle scabbard, and waited on a hillside while Ramon made a wide circle to the mouth of the canyon below me and then rode up it. Long before I could see or

269

hear them, deer started to sneak out the canyon and disappear across the saddle into the head of the next canyon. First came a dainty little blue-gray doe with twin fawns. After her, sneaking along head low came a gaunt old buck. He had a good head but I knew he was too thin to be good meat so I let him pass. Then came a whole flurry of does, fawns, and young bucks.

By now I could hear the sharp click of the feet of Ramon's horse on rocks and I had about decided that we'd have to try another canyon. Then I saw him – a nice, four-pointer in the prime of life, so fat that his grizzled-gray back looked as wide and meaty as that of a feed-lot polled Angus steer. It really wasn't much of a shot. I simply waited for him to go past an opening in the brush and cactus about 125 yards away. Then I led him possibly a foot and squeezed the trigger. I doubt if he even twitched.

Ramon and I brought the deer back and hung him in the tree about the time Eleanor had dinner ready. All in all it was quite a feast – broiled venison chops, mashed potatoes, tomatoes, dove-and-quail stew. She had even made an apple pie in the Dutch oven. We were about to tear into this provender when a delegation of our neighbors showed up. They carried a couple of dozen tamales steaming in their husks and a dozen delicious flat enchiladas, which are corn cakes fried brown and crisp in deep fat, then dunked in chile sauce, and sprinkled with white cheese, chopped up pepper and onion. We were up to our ears in food.

Beaming, the delegation stood by while we sampled the dishes. I devoured a couple of the enchiladas, washed them down with frosty beer. Then I opened up a tamale and took a bite. To my amazement the meat was white.

"This is not venison!" I said to Manuel. "What is it?"

He howled with laughter. "That," he told me, "is the rooster, the noisy one that tried to sleep on the *estufa*, the one that awoke you in the dawn with his shrill cries from the trees!"

I took another bite. That chicken tamale was wonderful. Then I turned to Manuel. "What do you have in the others – the burro?"

And that crack was quoted all through the area. It established me not only as the husband of *La Cazadora* (the lady hunter) but as a wit and quite a guy in my own right!

Reprinted by permission of Bradford O'Connor, Seattle, Washington.